The Fish-Lovers' Cookbook

The Fish-Lovers' Cookbook

More Than 300 Kitchen-Tested Recipes

by Sheryl and Mel London

Editor: Charles Gerras

Interior Design: John Landis
Illustration: Lutz Schmidt
Photography: Carl Doney
Photographic Food Styling: Laura Hendry Reifsnyder

 Rodale Press, Emmaus, Pa.

Printed in the United States of America on recycled paper, containing a
high percentage of de-inked fiber.

Library of Congress Cataloging in Publication Data

London, Sheryl.

    The fish-lovers' cookbook.

    Includes index.
    1. Cookery (Fish) 2. Cookery (Sea food)
I. London, Mel, joint author. II. Gerras, Charles.
III. Title.
TX747.L66   641.3'92   80-13846
ISBN 0-87857-299-6 hardcover
2 4 6 8 10 9 7 5 3 1 hardcover

OTHER BOOKS BY SHERYL AND MEL LONDON

SHERYL LONDON

Eggplant & Squash: A Versatile Feast
(Atheneum, 1976)

Making the Most of Your Freezer
(Rodale Press, 1978)

MEL LONDON

Getting into Film
(Ballantine, 1977)

Bread Winners
(Rodale Press, 1979)

Contents

PART 3: Sauces   64

PART 4: Soups, Stews, Bisques, and Chowders   124

PART 5: Stuffings for Fish   140

TO THE LATE JOHN VIGLIONE . . .
Who taught us the basics of fishing

TO RUDY DE HARAK . . .
Who taught us the craft of fishing

TO LARRY NICHOLSON . . .
Who taught us the joy of fishing

Acknowledgments

We have learned through the writing of our other books to keep a record of the calls, the letters, the names of those who help, of those who so graciously answer our questions, give information freely and, in general, join in the enthusiasm of a new publication. This book is no exception, and the list is long, and to each of them we give our thanks for their unstinting help:

To Joseph Slavin, Deputy Director, Office of Utilization and Development, National Marine Fisheries Service, U.S. Department of Commerce, for his especially valuable guidance in the areas of the underutilized species. To Carol Everingham, for her research, devotion, long travel days, and enthusiasm in her second endeavor with us.

To the people of Rodale's Test Kitchens, particularly Linda Gilbert, who supervised the testing, improved on some of our recipes, and asked the necessary questions, and to Faye Martin and Susan Hercek who assisted her.

To Tom Ney, Director of Food Services and Test Kitchens for Rodale Press, who brought his expert knowledge of fish anatomy to bear just when we needed it most, and who gave so generously of his experience in the seafood restaurant business.

To our devoted fishmongers, Mike and Louie DeMartino, who gave of their time and their expertise, as well as of their "fish stories."

To Dolores Plikaitis, who made herself indispensable as the proofreader on *Bread Winners,* and who has proven her ability and intelligence anew on this project. Further appreciation to Ann Snyder, Copy Manager at Rodale, who is always willing to "check it once more, just to be sure." And to Carol Hopkins for editorial assistance—taking the time it takes to make details just right.

An appreciative salute to Barbara Herman for keeping this book on track through the perils of production.

Our thanks, too, to the people, the organizations, universities, and Sea Grant Programs across the United States and Canada, with hopes that we have not left out anyone in the long list below:

John Nightengale, the curator of the Seattle Aquarium

Cooperative Extension Program, University of California

Minnesota Marine Advisory Service at the University of Minnesota

The Sea Grant Programs at Texas A. & M., University of Wisconsin, and University of North Carolina

U.S. Fish and Wildlife Service, U.S. Department of Interior

U.S. Department of Agriculture

Cooperative Extension Program, University of Michigan

N.Y. State Department of Environmental Conservation

Division of Nutritional Science, Cornell University

Extension Marine Advisory Program, Oregon State University

Fishery Council of New York

Massachusetts Seafood Council

Cooperative Extension Service, University of Maine

Gulf and South Atlantic Fisheries Development Foundation

The Fisheries Association of British Columbia

Maine Department of Marine Resources

Florida Division of Marine Resources

Seafood Marketing Authority, Maryland Department of Economic and Community Development

South Carolina Marine Resources Program

College of Marine Studies, University of Delaware

The photography department at Rodale has been outstanding in its enthusiasm and support during this project, so we want to thank Carl Doney, Laura Hendry Reifsnyder, and the others involved in producing the exciting photographs contained in this book.

It is not our intention to deliberately make our editor the perpetual "last but not least"—but we feel that he is deserving of his own niche of gratitude in our work for his incredible joy, his encouragement, and his good sense. Thus, we say "last but not least"—our deepest thanks and love to Charles Gerras, and may we share many future books together.

Everyone should believe in something. I believe I'll go fishing.

Thoreau

It might have been predicted that our lives would change when we built the house on our island—two "city kids" who knew only the corner supermarket, polluted air, and the hot sidewalks of summer. The garden was first to open our eyes and, as the bounds of the spindly fencing grew, an overabundance of eggplant and squash spawned Sheryl's first book showing dozens of ways to cook these bounteous delicacies. The inundation of fresh vegetables, berries, and gifts from the sea literally forced her into her next book—about making the most of your freezer.

It was bound to happen that Mel, a filmmaker by profession, would discover new talents and interests as a result of being transplanted to the country. His first book for Rodale evolved from his bread-baking hobby, an enthusiasm to which he was introduced by an island neighbor.

It was soon clear to both of us that a book about catching and cooking fish could not be far behind.

Our Great South Bay and the nearby Atlantic Ocean teem with fish—*fluke* and *flounder, weakfish* and *bluefish, blackfish, striped bass,* and *porgy*—not to mention the *blue crabs* that come swimming into the bay during the months of early autumn. Mel had not been fishing since he was 13—but, before long, the new rods and the lures began to take up more and more space in the weekend house. Soon the freezer began to bulge with the season's catch. There just never can be too many fish!

But, all of North America is also blessed. We have coastlines that stretch from Alaska to Mexico and Nova Scotia to Florida; we have gulfs, bays, inlets, rivers, streams, lakes—all with a range of climate and temperature that harbors such a vast variety of fish that this book would be too heavy to lift if we discussed all the kinds they contain.

In addition, fishing seasons vary from coast to coast and the names of fish change from region to region—for example, the fish known as *weakfish* around our island is called *sea trout* almost everywhere else. The people who fish for *drum* could be landing *croaker* or *corbina*—all the same fish. Because this happens often, we give interchangeable recipes, whenever we can, for fish with the same basic characteristics.

And—we try to add to the fisherman's relaxation and pleasure by giving some hints on how to keep the catch fresh until he or she gets it home, along with some easy methods for preparation. The frozen, anonymous fillets, the commercially breaded, precooked fish sticks sold in supermarkets are a far cry from the fresh, natural, incomparable bounty from our lakes, oceans, bays, streams, and rivers—*if* they're taken care of properly, from water to kitchen to pot or freezer.

Of course, some of us don't fish, can't fish, don't want to fish. This book takes the mystique out of how to shop for fish in the market and what to buy when the names and the identities confuse you. We give advice on how to keep the fish in good condition once you've bought it and, most important, how to prepare it for variety and nutrition.

This book is a valuable aid indeed, for all of us who are trying to ease the food budget in these days of high prices. While it is true that fish have generally skyrocketed in price (just as meat has), there are varieties of fish as well as methods of preparation that can provide a family dinner at amazingly reasonable costs.

On our trips through the United States, we have discovered that, most times, fish is simply fried—and nothing else. It tastes marvelous that way—both of us agree that nothing surpasses freshly fried catfish, for example—but when bounty overflows the kitchen, the search for new recipes must begin! Over the years, in the course of our travels, we have collected and culled recipes from friends around the world. We are still collecting—probably always will, for the horizons are endless.

And, as we've traveled, we've met so many "fish-lovers"—lobstermen and crabbers, fish farmers and cooks. We've been to fish markets, fish fries, fish dinners, and fish festivals. We've listened to fish stories and we've swapped fish recipes and fishing tips. Throughout the book we share some of this excitement with you through stories and photographs.

Every recipe we give uses only natural and healthful ingredients. We don't use salt in cooking fish, for example, because, when fish is really fresh, the contrast between the sauce and the fish is more delicate if no salt is used. The natural flavor the sea imparts is briny enough so that added salt is not necessary, and we all know that excess salt in the diet can be unhealthy. We suggest the use of citrus juices, vinegar, fresh and dried herbs, fruit and vegetables, and whole grains to enhance the delicate flavor of the fish. Every recipe in the book follows these principles and has been tested either by the authors or by the marvelous cooks in the Rodale Test Kitchens.

We must admit that there has been one distressing part to the writing of this book. During the entire time that we were planning, discussing, testing, and writing *The Fish-Lovers' Cookbook,* we had no time to go fishing! But it has been worth it. This book is our tribute to the sea. We are both people who have had a love affair with the sea since, as the saying goes, we were "tadpoles."

We hope our stories and recipes will convey this love to you.

Mel and Sheryl London
Fire Island, New York

Part 1: Getting Fish Ready to Cook

How to Keep Your Catch

Most people who like to fish will wince at the suggestion that the fish you buy at the market is sometimes "fresher" than the fish you just brought home from the lake, stream, or ocean. When the professional fisherman hauls in the nets, the fish are immediately flash frozen or, at the very least, dropped into a hold heaped with a bed of ice. From fishing boat to market, the fish are kept chilled and, when you find them displayed in front of you, they are *still* on ice. The chances are that they are fresh (in the sense that they do not smell, have clear eyes, and are ready for the dinner table). Too often (and the authors have been guilty at times) people do not take the time to keep their freshly caught prizes properly.

Sometimes we are just too lazy or too busy. (It's hard to stop fishing when the birds are working over the nearby water and the *bluefish* are biting in a frenzy.) Of course it's very simple for the fisherman to toss the catch into an ice chest rather than onto the bottom of the boat. But how many of us do it?

Fish deteriorates rapidly—whether caught or bought. The longer a fish is out of water without proper icing, the sooner the bacteria and enzymes begin their work, and the sooner we begin to smell what is accurately described as a "fishy" odor. Fresh fish simply do not smell!

In the Boat

The easiest way to keep your catch as fresh as possible is to take along an ordinary ice cooler with a layer of crushed ice on the bottom. As soon as you catch a fish, drop it into the cooler and go back to fishing. Another thing that helps maintain freshness is to gut, gill, and bleed the fish as soon as possible—even before dropping it into the cooler. There are times, of course, that you don't want to waste even a moment before the line goes back in. We understand. Do the next best thing: gut and clean the fish as soon as possible, perhaps back at the shoreline or at the marina.

Here are some simple tips that will make the difference between a truly fresh fish and a fish that is beginning to smell fishy:

Tip: *Do* take along an ice chest, tub, or other container with some crushed ice or, at the very least, those marvelous ice packs that you freeze in your refrigerator freezer compartment. They last for several hours. If you use ice, add some sea water or lake water to make slush.

Tip: *Don't* let the fish jump around on the bottom of the boat or on the dock after you catch it. The jumping merely bruises the delicate flesh and speeds up the degeneration process.

Tip: *Don't* keep your fish on a string or line trailing along behind the boat or tied to a post on the dock unless the water is very cold.

Tip: *Do* cut out gills with a sharp knife or heavy kitchen shears and then gut and clean the belly cavity of the fish as soon as possible. Merely cut along the belly from near the gills to the anal opening and clean it out. Make sure

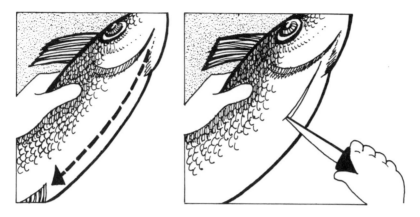

you clean out the intestines, the dark red mass along the spine (the kidneys), and then wash the fish out right in the lake or stream or salt water. This will also retard spoilage.

Tip: *Do* keep the fish in a shady spot after you've gutted it, if ice is not available. Wrapping it in a damp cloth or damp newspaper will also help.

At Home

For the best possible taste and nutrition, freshly caught fish should be cooked within 24 hours. The same holds for fish bought at the market. Refrigerate it immediately, and keep it refrigerated until you are ready to cook it. In a pinch, you can keep it for an extra day or two, but only if it is freshly caught.

How to Prepare Fish for the Freezer

Freezing the fish you have caught should be done at once. (Do not freeze the fish you buy from your market. Much of the "fresh" fish offered for sale has already been frozen—perhaps on the boat, or by the wholesaler. Once it is cooked, of course, it can be frozen safely.) After it has been thoroughly cleaned and cut into recipe-size portions, set your freezer at −10°F. until the fish has frozen solid; then you may return your freezer setting to 0°F. This temperature preserves the best taste, quality, and highest nutrition. If the fish is fatty (see chart on page 10), it should be treated to allow for longer freezer storage by dipping it into an ascorbic acid-and-water bath for one minute. Mix one-and-a-half tablespoons of ascorbic acid crystals (vitamin C which you can buy at your local drugstore) with one quart of very cold water. Then wrap the fish tightly in moisture-proof freezer paper, or heavy-duty aluminum foil *while still wet*. (We find the wetter the fish while freezing, the longer it lasts.) Squeeze all the air out of the package, tape securely, and label with this information:

1. The date frozen

2. The name of the fish and whether lean or fatty (see chart, page 10)

3. The amount and how it is cut (fillets, steaks, and the like)

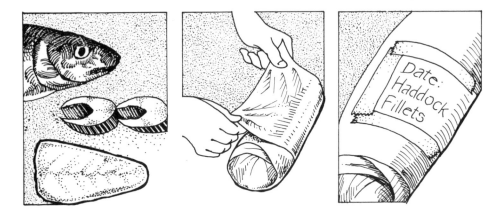

It is a good idea to wrap for individual portions and then put the portions into a plastic bag, allowing enough for one meal. It is faster and easier to defrost such packages than to pry apart one lump of congealed fish fillets.

If the fish is lean, the most common method is to immerse the fish for 30 seconds in a saltwater solution (one-half cup salt to one quart water) and freeze as wet as possible. But for those of us who limit salt intake, we suggest "ice-glazing," or freezing in a block of ice which prevents dehydration and increases the freezer storage life.

For ice-glazing, dip the fish in icy cold water. Wrap it while wet and freeze it so an ice crust forms. Unwrap and repeat, dipping in very cold water to make the glaze heavier.

To freeze fish in an ice block, we find milk cartons filled with icy cold water work just fine. Fill each carton half-full of water, put the fish into it, and fill to within one inch of the top of the carton. Staple the top and put the carton in the freezer. When frozen solid, cartons may be stacked flat and the paper covering torn off for defrosting. This ice-glazing, or ice-block freezing, prevents contact of dry freezer air with the surface of the fish. The moisture and storage life improves considerably. When fish, lean or fatty, is treated in this manner before freezing, the storage life increases. Instead of the three months the experts predict, our frozen fish is in perfect shape as long as eight months later.

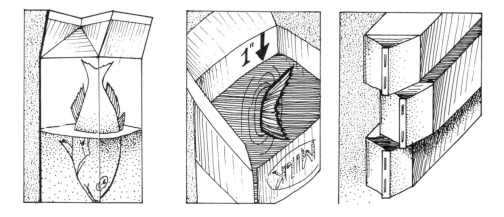

The Blessing of the Fleet

It began when St. Peter, the patron saint of all fishermen, blessed fishermen James and John, who were later to become the disciples of Christ. Through the centuries, a commemorative blessing has remained a part of the heritage and the lore wherever fishing fleets set out to sea—in Portugal, in Spain, in Greece, and here in North America. It is a ceremony for the sponge fishermen of the Florida Gulf as well as for the fishing fleets of New England—in Stonington, Connecticut, in New Bedford and Gloucester, Massachusetts, and in Cape Cod's Provincetown where we took these pictures during the month of June. It was a special day because, for the first time in three years, the blessing took place without the sadness of looking back on a hard winter marked with the loss of a ship and its crew.

Before the first boat was blessed, the bugler played *Taps* in memory of all the men from Provincetown who had been lost at sea during the 350-year history of the town. The day was also marked by parades, local bands, and a high mass at St. Peter the Apostle Church. Portuguese flags flew in the breeze, for Portugal is Provincetown's heritage and most of its fishermen trace their origins to that country. The music was supplied by Scottish bagpipers and marching bands. Down at the waterfront, the boats assembled for the blessing—fishing boats, motorboats, sailboats, and armada that included boats of every size and every description. And, as they passed, each boat was blessed and sprinkled with holy water—with one motorboat returning three times just to insure a lasting blessing.

The Blessing of the Fleet 7

Tip: Before freezing, prepare fish so it is ready for cooking when defrosted to save freezer space and preparation time.

Tip: Keep a large freezer container with a plastic liner inside it (so it can be lightly tied to exclude air) and fill it with accumulated bones, scraps, heads, and skin (they preserve the briny natural tang of the sea) to make Fish Stock (see Index) which is the base of all good soups and sauces. Fish Stock, incidentally, is one product you cannot buy commercially. It must be made at home.

Tip: If you have a small freezer, as we do, fish frozen in cartons can take up a lot of your precious room. We compromise by wetting the fish thoroughly for 20 to 30 seconds and then wrapping it dripping wet in heavy-duty aluminum foil.

Tip: Some fish like *weakfish (sea trout)* actually *improves* after freezing. The flesh seems to firm up and the fish has a better texture when cooked.

How to Thaw Frozen Fish

Place fish, still in original freezer wrap, in the refrigerator. Allow it to thaw overnight. For faster thawing, our own preference is to place the frozen fish in its original freezer wrap in a deep bowl under *gently running* cold water. Allow one hour for a one-pound package.

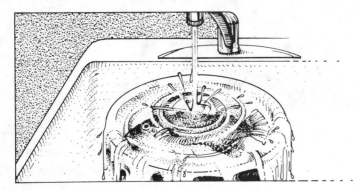

Tip: *Never* thaw fish at room temperature.

Tip: *Never* refreeze fish once it has been thawed.

Tip: If you must cook frozen fish, generally the length of cooking time should be doubled. Better to play safe and thaw the fish completely, so that there will be no question as to the length of time to cook it.

Handling Lean Fish and Fatty Fish

The range of lean to fat, white flesh to dark flesh—delicate taste to more intensity of flavor—dry or moist—and delicate texture to coarse texture—allows an infinite variety of recipes when cooking. It may also be somewhat confusing.

Basically, there are two groups of fish—*saltwater* and *freshwater*. Both these groups include *lean, moderately fatty,* and *fatty* fish. Most fish recipes, whether given for saltwater or freshwater fish, are interchangeable if you know the particular properties of fish. You can usually substitute any saltwater or freshwater fish in a recipe by just remembering these points:

1. Fish is lean, moderately fatty, or fatty. If it is *lean,* it will take nicely to buttery sauces or other liquids. It may be cooked using any method of cooking, but when broiling or baking, it must be basted with extra butter or oil to prevent it from drying out.

2. *Moderately fatty* fish is particularly well suited for broiling or baking since it requires very little extra lubricating butter or oil to keep it moist. It takes nicely to Mayonnaise-Based Sauces (see Index) and vegetables.

3. If you prefer a milder taste when cooking the *fatty* fish, use citrus juices or vinegar.

The Fat Content of Various Fish

For years we've been hearing of "fatty" fish and "lean" fish and we've been told that once we knew the composition of any fish, we would then know how to cook it properly. Well, to a degree, that's true. However, the fat content given for some fish can never be exact.

Comprehensive studies made by the U.S. Department of Agriculture in recent years show that the fat content of individual fish varies widely during different seasons of the year, in various stages of maturity, and in different locales as well. Therefore, the following chart is just a general guide for use in cooking. The lean fish takes well to sauces and different methods of preparation that retain, or add to, whatever moisture the fish has. The fattier fish may simply be broiled without drying out and needs few, if any, additions to keep it moist.

Key

Lean fish	less than 2 percent fat
Moderately fatty fish	2 to 6 percent fat
Fatty fish	over 6 percent fat

Freshwater Fish

Bass	Lean
Burbot (or Freshwater Cod)	Lean
Carp	Moderately fatty
Catfish	Moderately fatty
Crappie	Lean
Pike Family:	
Buffalo Fish	Moderately fatty
Muskellunge	Moderately fatty
Pickerel	Lean
Pike	Lean
Smelts	Fatty
Trout	Fatty
Whitefish (or Cisco)	Moderately fatty
Yellow Perch	Lean

Saltwater Fish

Bass, Black Sea	Lean
Blackfish (or Tautog)	Lean
Black Drum	Lean
Blowfish Tails	Lean
Bluefish	Fatty
Butterfish	Fatty
Cod Family:	
Cod	Lean
Cusk	Lean
Haddock	Lean
Hake or Whiting	Moderately fatty
Pollack	Lean
Scrod	Lean
Crab	Lean
Crevalle (or Common Jack)	Moderately fatty
Croaker	Lean
Eel	Fatty
Flatfish Family:	
Dabs	Lean
Fluke	Lean
Gray Sole	Lean
Lemon Sole	Lean
Winter Flounder	Lean

Frogs' Legs	Lean
Grouper	Lean
Grunt	Moderately fatty
Halibut	Lean
Kingfish	Moderately fatty
Lingcod	Lean
Lobster	Lean
Mackerel	Fatty
Monkfish	Lean
Mullet	Fatty
Ocean Perch	Lean
Pompano	Fatty
Porgy (or Scup)	Moderately fatty
Red Snapper (or Yellow Tail Snapper)	Lean
Rockfish	Lean
Roe	Moderately fatty or fatty, depending upon the fish
Salmon, Atlantic and Pacific	Fatty

(continued on following page)

Sardines (or Sea Herring)	Fatty		Striped Bass	Moderately fatty
Shad	Fatty		Swordfish	Moderately fatty
Shark	Lean		Tilefish	Lean
Shrimp	Lean		Tuna	Fatty
Skate	Lean		Weakfish (or Sea Trout)	Moderately fatty
Smelts	Moderately fatty		Whitebait	Moderately fatty
Squid	Lean			

SOURCE: *Composition of Foods*, Agriculture Handbook No. 8, Washington, D.C.: Agricultural Research Service, U.S. Department of Agriculture.

How to Buy Fish

When a high-toned friend accused us recently of being "ichthyophagists," we ran to *Webster's Dictionary* to find out if it was an insult or a compliment. It means that we "practice the eating of fish." Boy, do we!

Fresh fish is such a glorious food that we say catch it or buy it, or plead with your fishermen friends for their extras—we don't care how you get it, just so you do get it! Of course, we are prejudiced in favor of the freshly caught product, but we realize that geography and seasonal availability can limit your options. Frozen fish is better than no fish. Don't let anything keep you from joining the ranks of the "ichthyophagists."

Buying Frozen Fish

Choose packages that feel solid, and keep them that way by getting them into your freezer at once. If, by some chance, your frozen fish must be stored in a freezer compartment where the temperature is likely to be 10°F. or more, do not keep it for more than one week. Never hold thawed fish for more than 24 hours.

Never buy fish that has batter or breading on it. Make your own; then you know what it covers. Also, you can increase the food value of the breading with batters made with whole grain flours, plus herbs and seasonings to your own taste.

Buying Fresh Fish

Your local fish dealer will know what is in season, therefore plentiful and less costly. Talk to him before you make your decision. Then examine the fish carefully for signs of freshness before you make your selection.

Whole Fish

Flesh: It should be elastic and firm to the touch. If you poke it, the flesh should spring back leaving no indentation. It should not separate from the bone easily.

Odor: Fresh fish does not have a strong, fishy odor. It has the mild, characteristically briny smell of the sea.

Eyes: Look for bright, clear, full eyes. As fish becomes stale, the eyes cloud over and become sunken.

Gills: The color of the gills should be bright reddish. With age, they fade first to pink, then gray, then to brownish green.

Skin: Shiny and bright skin with tight scales is what to look for.

The Fabulous Fulton Fish Market

To get to New York's Fulton Fish Market in time for the most activity, you either stay up all night or you get up very, very early. Probably the most famous fish market in the world, it begins to hum at 3 A.M. and by the time the Wall Street workers and the tradespeople of lower Manhattan come in to work, the market is shut tight. The fish comes into the market by truck and the activity flows up and down the aisles as restaurateurs and middlemen bid for the vast array of seafood, most of which will be shipped to distribution points ranging from Boston to the Chesapeake Bay. There are no set prices—the fish is bargained for just like at any auction. The pace gets frantic and during the bidding for hundreds of varieties of seafood, no money changes hands—everything is settled up late in the morning.

If the names of the fish are varied—*halibut, yellowtail, mako, cod, squid, bass, soft-shell crabs*—the nicknames of the fish-market merchants are even more unusual. No one is called by his given name it seems—Butch, Pinkie, Bloomers, Moishe, Doctor, Chickens, Cabbage, General, The Pro, Storyteller were the names we heard shouted. Even the city inspector who smells for freshness and who knows "a million kinds of fish by sight" has his nickname. He's "The Nose."

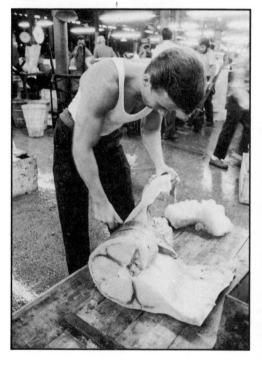

Our grandmothers never bought a fish they couldn't look straight in the eye. It is still best to see the whole fish before buying it, and then have it dismantled to suit your recipe. But if you can only buy fillets or steaks that are already cut—or perhaps whole fish where the head has been cut off—here is some guidance.

Precut Fish

The texture should be firm without any browning or dryness around the edges. The odor should be fresh and mild. The fish should be kept on, and sold from, a bed of crushed ice.

What Are They Selling?

The Forms Fish Take in the Marketplace

Whole Dressed: This is fish looking pretty much as it comes from the water, except that it has been scaled, gutted, and the fins have been removed. Allow about three-quarters of a pound per person, depending upon the kind of fish. (Some fish have smaller bodies and larger heads, which affect the proportion of edible meat.)

Pan Dressed: Generally a small fish is presented this way, scaled and gutted, with the head, tail, and fins removed (three-quarters of a pound to one and one-half pounds). For very small fish, such as *whitebait* or *smelts,* the head and tail are left on. Allow about one-half pound per person.

Fillets: The sides of the fish are cut lengthwise to get fillets. They may be skinned or not skinned, but they have no bones.

Ask to have the fish boned into fillets in front of you to insure maximum freshness. When you have a fish filleted to your order, you may also ask for the head, the skeleton, and the scraps to take home and make into a Fish Stock (see Index). However, many fishing boats fillet their catch just after leaving their boats, putting the fillets into large buckets and feeding the "waste" to the hovering sea gulls. Why feed the sea gulls when Fish Stock can be made easily and economically and can be kept frozen for a long time? The stock can then be used as a base for poaching and for sauces.

Butterfly Fillets: These are fillets cut away from the backbone and held together by the belly skin of the fish.

Steaks: A fish is cut across the *width* to get these. They are generally from large firm-fleshed fish, such as *halibut, salmon, cod,* or *swordfish.* Allow one pound for serving two or three people, depending upon their appetite and their capacity.

Chunks: Chunks are cross sections of the fish after it has been dressed. Portions of the backbone are left in.

Readying Your Fish for the Fire

If the fish was caught (rather than bought), we assume that you treated it properly while it was still in the boat, at the lake, shore, or on the beach. (See page 1.) Some of our local fisherfolk once built a cleaning stand that overhung the water, with a large hole in the center so that the entrails could drop through into the bay to feed the sea gulls. However, after a time, it was covered over with scales and residue and we never got the feeling that the fish was truly clean after preparing it there. Now we finish the cleaning at home and we find it much easier and more comfortable. The running water from the tap also makes life simpler. Once you learn how to prepare the fish or fillet the catch properly, the mess is quite minimal and the fish is easier to handle.

Our Friends the Fishmongers

When our own fish is not caught, it is, of course—bought. For years we have shopped at a small, but superb fish store called DeMartino's. There brothers Louie and Mike hold forth as purveyors of fresh seafood, neighborhood friends, and raconteurs of fish lore extraordinary. In fact, many of the fish used in our testing—especially the underutilized species—were acquired for us by the two brothers. On one of our last visits, when the book was nearly complete, Louie told us a most unusual "fish story."

Behind the eyes of some fish such as halibut and sea bass is a small, curved bone, about the size of a fingernail, that forms a pocket in the head. For centuries, the fishermen of the Mediterranean have held that the bone brings luck, for if you hold it up to the light, it looks like a shrine or grotto, and inside you can make out what could be the figure of the Virgin Mary.

The Tools You'll Need

A *fish scaler* is essential in preparing a fish to serve whole. There are several simple ones on the market. We carry one in our fishing boxes so that this first part of the cleaning process can occasionally be done while we're still down at the boat or on the dock. However, if you plan to scale the fish at home, be sure you have plenty of newspaper under your catch.

A *very sharp knife* is, of course, indispensable. We have several that are made especially for filleting fish, and we keep a sheathed knife in our fishing box for the first cleaning while in the boat.

A *knife sharpener* will preserve your knife and make your work easier. Unfortunately, the electric sharpeners will wear away the edge of the knife. You can use a whetstone or you can use any one of the specially made Carborundum sticks that are on the market. (We use one that's called a "Zip Zap"—about four inches long—and better than anything else we've found.) The most important thing is that the knife must be kept sharp! After every few strokes, sharpen it again.

Preparing the Whole Fish

Of course, if we discuss the "whole" fish, we include the head. For us, and for many of our friends, there is nothing quite so elegant as a whole fish, steamed or broiled, presented at the table and covered with the ambrosia of a tempting sauce. The Chinese discovered this method of presentation centuries ago, but some of our friends would disagree. Many times we have delivered a gift of fish, only to be asked to please fillet or pan dress it because some members of the family would turn green if they saw the head.

Certainly the head can be removed during the process of cleaning, but remember that keeping it on does serve a function—the fish will stay moist longer during cooking because the head keeps the body fluids inside the fish. However, this is a personal choice. The directions that follow do include the head.

1. Using plenty of newspapers under the fish to catch the scales, hold it firmly by the tail and scrape the scales, using a brushing motion that goes from tail back to head. If the fish is too small or tends to slip out of your grasp, merely hold the tail down firmly with a two-pronged carving fork. Remove the top layers of the newspaper after scaling one side of the fish and repeat with the other side.

2. Assuming you have cleaned part of the fish while still at the water, complete the job more thoroughly. If, however, the fish has not been cleaned at all, cut the belly from between the gills down to the anal opening. Look for the roe—you'll see them in two long sacs, the color depending upon the type of fish. Cut them away carefully,

being sure that the sacs are not damaged. Wash them and reserve for another meal. (See Index for chapter on Roe.)

3. Cut away the innards, then cut out the gills by holding them firmly in your hand, cutting around the membrane and finally removing them where they join the body with the cut of a strong pair of scissors.

4. The fins are next and there are two methods you can use to remove them. The simplest way is to cut them off with a large pair of scissors. Another way is to insert a sharp knife along the fin, making a cut that forms the first part of a V, then repeat on the other side and lift the fin out. We prefer the first method; it's easier and just as effective.

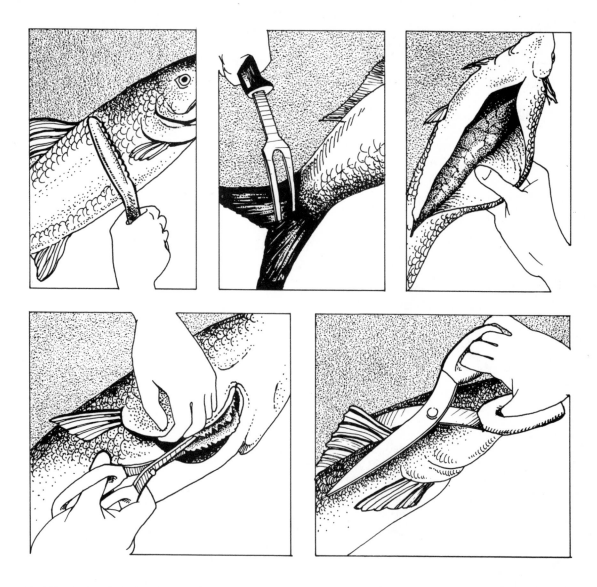

5. Wash the fish thoroughly under running water. Make sure all the blood spots are removed and that none of the entrails are still attached to the cavity.

6. Wipe the fish dry with a paper towel, cover with foil or plastic wrap, and refrigerate immediately. If you intend to freeze the fish, for directions see the Index under "Freezing."

Note: Skinning and preparing fish without scales are covered in the chapter on Catfish (see Index).

How to Make Fish Steaks

Again we assume that you have not bought your fish—that on one lucky day, a huge one *didn't* get away. It's too large to fillet and it wouldn't fit in the oven if you tried to broil it. The only way to serve it is in steaks or chunks. The method for preparing these is fairly easy, but you'll need one additional tool in your kitchen—either a large, strong cleaver or a saw—to get through the spine.

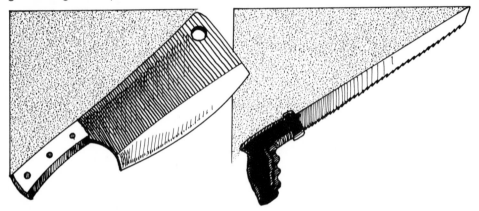

1. First, remove the head right behind the gills. Slice through the flesh with your sharp knife, and then complete the job with the cleaver or the saw. With smaller fish, the knife will do the job all the way and, occasionally, you'll find that if you snap the spine with your hand, you can then cut through it completely. Don't discard the head—save it for making fine fish stews, chowders, or stock (see Index).

2. Slice the steaks in exactly the same way that the head was removed. Cut them to just the width you want the steaks to be.

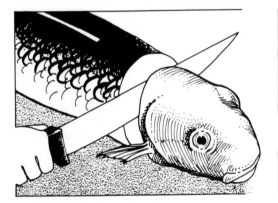

Note: Some people suggest using the standard Chinese cleaver for the job of cutting through the spine. We strongly recommend against it and we believe that you should use either a heavy-duty butcher's cleaver or a large, sturdy knife. The Chinese cleavers seem to be made of softer metal and Mel ruined several of his cleavers in coming to realize that they just won't do the job.

How to Fillet

This takes a bit of practice, but once you've mastered the technique, you'll be amazed at just how easy it is—and the family will marvel at your dexterity. The secret, as we've told you before, is a sharp knife, plus a little knowledge of fish anatomy. *There is no need to scale the fish before beginning the filleting process.*

1. Place the fish on newspaper or on a cutting board. Make a cut right behind the gills, going from the top of the fish diagonally down to the belly. Don't cut too deeply or you will puncture the belly cavity, making the job just a bit messier. Ideally, filleting a fish should be surgically clean and neat.

2. Turn the fish with its backbone toward you and make a cut just about an inch deep along the fish from head down to tail, feeling the bones with the knife. This is another of the secrets of good filleting. When you continue to cut, make sure you feel the bones touching the knife blade.

3. Hold the knife at a slight angle and begin to cut down along the center bone, using a slicing and sliding motion of the knife. With your other hand, pull back the flesh so you can see what you're doing. When done, the entire side of the fish should lift off, though the fillet will still be attached at the tail. *Do not separate them.*

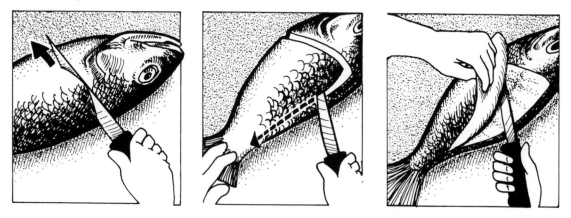

4. With the first fillet still attached, turn the fish over onto the other side and repeat the process. The reason you do not remove the first fillet until the second is cut is that we find that the fish presents a firmer base on which to work when left whole. If the first fillet is removed, the fish has a tendency to collapse toward the board, making the second fillet more difficult to cut.

5. Cut the fillets away at the tail. You should have two lovely looking pieces of fish, the skin still attached and, if done properly, with little or no meat still clinging to the skeleton. Discard the carcass. (Or, if it's large enough, reserve for fish soups or stock (see Index).

6. Clean the board or remove a layer of paper. We find that this next step is best done on the board itself, since the fish should lie very flat for the skinning. Turn the skin down toward the board, hold the tail firmly with your fingernail or with a fork, and begin to cut from tail end by holding knife firmly between skin and flesh at a flat angle. Using a slight sawing motion, separate the skin from the flesh—and, as you progress, grasp the skin firmly while the knife slices between skin and flesh. This will keep the knife from cutting through the skin itself. If the fish is properly skinned, the fillet should be clean looking and the skin should be clean with no meat clinging to it.

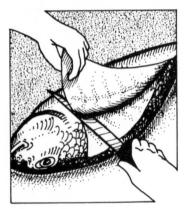 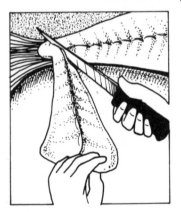 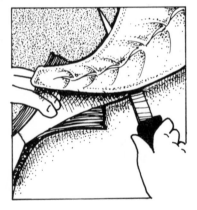

Filleting a Tiny Fish

There are times that you want to fillet even the smallest of fish, such as we do with the *bluefish snappers* early in the autumn. We merely scrape the scales with a knife and then make one single cut to remove the flesh from the skeleton. Most people who pass us on the dock usually exclaim, "How can you fillet a fish that tiny?" Well, we can and we do—and they're delicious pan fried for only a few seconds on each side.

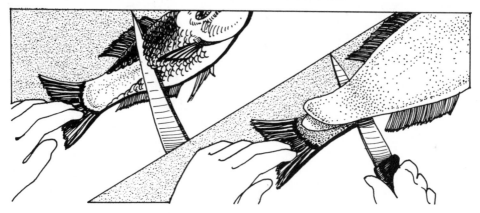

A Word about the Cheeks

The cheeks have been called the "filet mignon" of the fish, among other complimentary names. Since we prefer fish to meat, we generally feel that the cheeks of the catch are the prize delicacy for which no name suffices. If the fish is large enough, feel the head right behind the mouth and you'll find the flesh of the cheek. Scoop it out with a knife and peel the skin, or if the fish has been prepared whole, make sure you savor it at the table. The Chinese serve the cheeks to the honored guest.

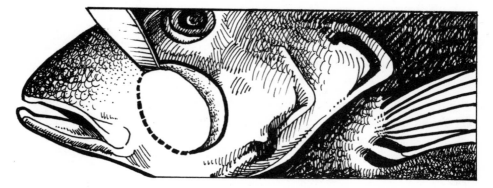

Refrigerating Your Fish

Whether we buy our fish, as we do in the city, or catch it as we sometimes do at our Fire Island home, we try to eat it as soon as possible. That generally means within a few hours or, at most, a day. If we can't prepare it that quickly, we freeze it. There is no doubt in our minds that the fresher a fish is, the better it tastes.

After the fish is dressed, place it on a plate or platter and cover it tightly with plastic wrap, aluminum foil, or freezer paper. Place in the refrigerator at once and try to cook it within a day or two.

Actually, a fish *will* keep at a low refrigerator temperature for two to three days, but it deteriorates rapidly. The lower your refrigerator temperature, the longer your fish will remain fresh. At 32°F., the fish will keep almost twice as long as it will in a refrigerator set at 37°F.; the absolute limit is 40°F.

Figuring Individual Servings of Fish

Basic Guide

1. Individual appetites dictate the size of the servings, and the amount of bone in the fish must be taken into account.
2. If the fish is to be served with a rich sauce, reduce the portions.
3. Keep in mind what other foods are to be served before and after the fish, for this also influences the portion size.

Keeping these three things in mind, use the following guide when deciding on how much to serve.

Tip: Remember, the thickness of the fish, *after* it is dressed, dictates the method of cooking.

Fish	Amt. per Person	Amt. for 6 People
Whole	1 pound	5 to 6 pounds
Whole (dressed or drawn)	½ pound	3 pounds
Fillets	⅓ to ½ pound edible flesh per person	2 to 3 pounds
Steaks (allowing for bones)	½ to ¾ pound	3 to 4½ pounds

Good Eating– Good Health

We vividly remember the years of growing up when the word "nutrition" was still new to the dictionary. Somehow our mothers knew, even then, what learned scientists of a later age would prove in their laboratories and sophisticated marine research centers: "Eating fish can help you stay healthy and be smart!"

The weekly fish dinner was not a favorite among us kids, but our mothers urged us to consume it with the all-encompassing command, "Eat—it's good for you!! It's brain food!" We never dreamed, at that time, that one day we'd come to love the flavor, smell, taste, and myriad other pleasures offered by all fish. Our mothers were right again (and how many years they spent reminding us of that!)—but why did it take us so long to appreciate the glories of a fine kettle of fish?

Part of the answer appeared in a recent government publication. It turns out that we were not alone. The Fisheries Advisory Committee (U.S. Bureau of Fisheries) even conducted a survey to discover why people ate less fish than meat. The fascinating results suggest that the study might well have been called "Fish Fears and Delusions":

26 percent disliked or objected to the bones

20 percent just weren't in the habit of buying fish

19 percent did buy fish—but only on Fridays

13 percent claimed they could not find good quality fish

11.5 percent disliked preparing fish for cooking

6.5 percent thought fish too expensive

2.6 percent just thought they were terrible cooks and did not know how to prepare fish

Happily, we find that all this is changing, and more and more people now consider fish a vital part of their diets. For some reason—possibly our revitalized interest in health, and particularly nutrition—fish is being rediscovered as a valuable source of nourishment and is rising fast on the list of America's favored foods. Here are a few of its attractions:

Fish is relatively low in calories.

Fish is made up of complete, highly digestible protein.

Fish contains no saturated fats and is rich in the desirable polyunsaturated fats.

Fish contains large deposits of essential vitamins and minerals.

Calories

For years now, doctors have been pounding out a message that affects most of us: keep your weight down! Mel's mother used to tell him that the kid next door (his name was Harold) was healthy *because he was fat.* But all of us (including our mothers) know now that controlling body weight is central to our general health. So we jog; we play tennis; we swim; we even do exercises while sitting in a plane. But nothing helps as much as proper diet and a lower caloric intake. All the exercise in the world won't take weight off if we couple it with a "junk food" diet. It all boils down to what we eat—and how much—no matter how we try to avoid the issue.

There's no doubt that eating more fish will reduce your caloric intake, and still provide plenty of protein to meet daily requirements. Fish has virtually no carbohydrates and, pound for pound, fish has only one-half to two-thirds as many calories as beef or pork. For example, a low-fat fish contains less than 100 calories in a three-and-one-half ounce serving, while meat often goes as high as 300 calories for a similar portion:

Calories in a 3½-Ounce Serving

Beef	303	Shrimp	158
Pork Chops	298	Fin Fish	101
Eggs	163	Crab	81

Courtesy of the National Fishery Education Center, National Marine Fisheries Service, National Oceanic & Atmospheric Administration, U.S. Department of Commerce.

Protein

Protein is the major material our bodies use to form muscles, blood, skin, hair, nails, and internal organs. Of the 22 acids that make up the complex protein structure, our bodies manufacture all but 8 of them, the essential amino acids. We must obtain these from food, and fish has them all in generous proportions.

Four ounces of fish will provide about one-half the protein required by the body each day, and fish protein is 85 to 90 percent digestible. That makes it a perfect food for children or older people.

Of course, the amounts of protein vary, depending upon the kind of fish you choose, but protein content is always high—generally higher than pork or beef—and always of excellent quality. *Tuna* has 24.7 percent protein, and fish such as *rainbow trout* or *snapper* ranges between 19 and 20 percent protein. Beef and pork average a bit over 17 percent protein.

Fats

No one disputes the fact that fats are quite necessary for proper body functioning. However, bit by bit, we are learning that the various types of fat we eat affect our health in different ways.

Although no certain link has been established between saturated fats, cholesterol, and heart disease, one thing is certain: the polyunsaturated fats in seafood definitely encourage an optimal cholesterol level in the body. These polyunsaturates are relatively low in calories and they also contribute to the body's production of healthy skin and shiny hair.

Vitamins

Read the charts on seafood nutrition and you'll be amazed, as we were, at the treasure trove you find. The principal scientist of the Fisheries Research Board of Canada, Dr. Hugh Tarr, maintains that man could obtain all his normal vitamin requirements from marine animals.

Fish liver oils are the most abundant of all natural sources of vitamins A and D, and they also supply substantial amounts of Vitamin E. Small amounts of vitamin C turn up in fish liver oils and fish roe. The flesh and skin of most fish contain, among many other vitamins, large amounts of the various elements of the B complex. Lean fish offers as much vitamin B as an equal portion of meat.

Minerals

The ocean, the natural habitat of most fish, is the world's richest storehouse of minerals. No wonder these marine creatures are such good sources of the elements our bodies require.

Fish is loaded with phosphorus which, in proper combination with other constituents, absolutely works to make our bodies (and minds) more vigorous. Without phosphorus, B vitamins are indigestible, and calcium (also plentiful in fish) is useless.

The old wives' tale that red meat makes good blood is true enough, but the iron contained in fish will also keep the red-cell blood count high and maintain hemoglobin levels just as effectively as meat does, and the iodine we get from sea fish protects the thyroid.

Ironically, sodium is one major mineral that is barely present either in fresh-water or saltwater fish. For this reason fish is especially appealing to health-conscious people, particularly heart patients whose bodies require high-quality protein in low-sodium foods.

Fish is short on fiber, but that can easily be added by including vegetables and whole grains in fish meals—a perfect combination. Many of the recipes in the book reflect this plan.

A Nutritional Bargain

And finally, we come to the cost of this nutritional gold mine. There is no waste if you choose to buy fillets and, if you buy whole fish, the price goes down to compensate for head and bones (which you can use anyway for stock). You have many kinds of fish from which to choose—over 250 varieties of edible fish swim in the oceans, the rivers, the lakes, and the streams. If the price of one variety is up at the moment, there is always another type you can choose, equally flavorful, equally nutritious. There is absolutely no doubt in our minds that dollar for dollar, ounce for ounce, fish offers a nutritional bargain that is very hard to beat.

If you need further convincing, we offer the following chart taken from the U.S. Department of Agriculture. It will amaze you!

Nutritional Values in Selected Fish
(Based on 100 Grams Edible Portion)

Food and Description	Food Energy (cal.)	Protein (g.)	Fat (g.)	Carbohydrates Total (g.)	Fiber (g.)	Calcium (mg.)	Phosphorus (mg.)	Iron (mg.)	Sodium (mg.)	Potassium (mg.)	Vitamin A Value (I.U.)	Thiamine (mg.)	Riboflavin (mg.)	Niacin (mg.)	Ascorbic Acid (mg.)
Bluefish: Baked, broiled	159	26.2	5.2	0	0	29	287	0.7	104	—	50	0.11	0.10	1.9	—
Cod: Cooked, broiled	170	28.5	5.3	0	0	31	274	1.0	110	407	180	0.08	0.11	3.0	—
Crab: Cooked, steamed	93	17.3	1.9	0.5	—	43	175	0.8	—	—	2,170	0.16	0.08	2.8	2
Croaker, Atlantic: Cooked, baked	133	24.3	3.2	0	0	—	—	—	120	323	70	0.13	0.10	6.5	—
Cusk: Cooked, steamed	106	23.4	0.7	0	0	27	283	1.0	74	386	—	0.03	0.10	2.7	—
Haddock: Cooked, fried	165	19.6	6.4	5.8	0	40	247	1.2	177	348	—	0.04	0.07	3.2	2
Halibut: Cooked, broiled	171	25.2	7.0	0	0	16	248	0.8	134	525	680	0.05	0.07	8.3	—
Lobster, Northern: Canned or cooked	95	18.7	1.5	0.3	—	65	192	0.8	210	180	—	0.10	0.07	—	—
Mackerel, Atlantic: Cooked, broiled with butter	236	21.8	15.8	0	0	6	280	1.2	—	—	530	0.15	0.27	7.6	—
Ocean Perch, Atlantic: Cooked, fried	227	19.0	13.3	6.0	0	33	226	1.3	153	284	—	0.10	0.11	1.8	—

(continued on following page)

Nutritional Values in Selected Fish
(Based on 100 Grams Edible Portion)

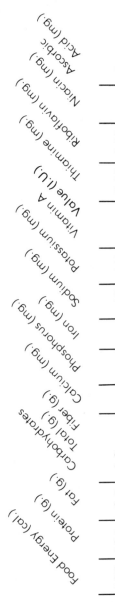

Food and Description	Food Energy (cal.)	Protein (g.)	Fat (g.)	Carbohydrates Total (g.)	Fiber (g.)	Calcium (mg.)	Phosphorus (mg.)	Iron (mg.)	Sodium (mg.)	Potassium (mg.)	Vitamin A Value (I.U.)	Thiamine (mg.)	Riboflavin (mg.)	Niacin (mg.)	Ascorbic Acid (mg.)
Rockfish: Cooked, oven-steamed	107	18.1	2.5	1.9	—	—	—	—	68	446	—	0.05	0.12	—	1
Roe: Cooked, baked, broiled	126	22.0	2.8	1.9	—	13	402	2.3	73	132	—	—	—	—	—
Salmon: Cooked, baked, broiled	182	27.0	7.4	0	0	—	414	1.2	116	443	160	0.16	0.06	9.8	—
Shad: Baked	201	23.2	11.3	0	0	24	313	0.6	79	377	30	0.13	0.26	8.6	—
Shrimp: Cooked	225	20.3	10.8	10.0	—	72	191	2.0	186	229	—	0.04	0.08	2.7	—
Swordfish: Cooked, broiled	174	28.0	6.0	0	0	27	275	1.3	—	—	2,050	0.04	0.05	10.9	—
Weakfish: Cooked, broiled	208	24.6	11.4	0	0	—	—	—	560	465	—	0.10	0.08	3.5	—

Source: Composition of Foods, Agriculture Handbook No. 8, Washington, D.C.: Agricultural Research Service, U.S. Department of Agriculture.

A Word about Shellfish

He is a bold man who first swallowed an oyster.
King James I of England
seventeenth century

Unfortunately, in many parts of the world, the quote attributed to King James would still hold true—but for an entirely different reason. As countries become more industrialized and the factories and cities pollute the waters that surround us, the *oyster*—along with the *clam,* the *mussel,* and the *scallop*—is fast becoming a potential villain. Many of our bivalves are taken in waters that are near the centers of pollution. Even near our home on Fire Island, we watch as clam beds are closed, then opened, then closed again by federal authorities. It is a shame. Once we devoured these superb sea creatures with gusto—and suddenly they are implicated in outbreaks of hepatitis and paralytic shellfish poisoning.

We have discussed this problem at Rodale Press and, with great reluctance, have decided against including recipes for the bivalves. At some future date—in another edition, perhaps—when the waters around us will have been cleansed and the oysters, the clams, the mussels, and the scallops will once more be safe enough to grace our dining tables, we can feel free to break out our exciting recipes for them.

We should add, however, that we *have* included recipes in this book for crustacea, such as *lobsters, crabs,* and *shrimp,* for they are taken in deeper waters which are less likely to be polluted.

Part 2: How to Cook Fish

Basic Advice for Cooking Fish

1. Fish does not need a great deal of cooking to tenderize it. It already *is* tender. On the contrary, it should be cooked only the minimal amount of time. Overcooking toughens fish, makes it dry, and ruins its delicate flavor. The biggest error made in cooking fish is overcooking it.

2. Raw fish is translucent. It turns milky-white in color, or opaque, when cooked. To test for doneness, stick a metal skewer into the thickest part of the fish. (A skewer is preferred since it makes only one puncture rather than the four punctures that the tines of a fork would make.) When the fish is cooked, the flesh will flake easily and separate from the bones, and the flesh will no longer be translucent.

3. Remember, the things to control in cooking fish are *time* and *temperature* according to the thickness of the fish.

Tip: Use a ruler to measure the thickness of the fish by standing the ruler straight up against the thickest part.

Tip: Allow about ten minutes per one inch thickness of fish.

Tip: If fish fillets are baked with or covered with sauces, allow an additional four to five minutes more per inch at the thickest part.

Tip: If you cook frozen fish without defrosting it first, double the cooking time per inch of thickness, or 20 minutes per one inch thickness of fish.

Tip: Cook all fish at the proper temperatures and as quickly as possible, to keep it succulent and delicious—but watch carefully and test often.

Seven Basic Cooking Methods, with Special Tips

Method I—Pan Fry or Saute

A small, whole fish or a fish fillet is best suited to this method. A large fish is too thick to cook through if this very rapid cooking procedure is used, and the outside crust will probably burn in the process. Be sure the fish is completely dry before you put it into the fat or oil when pan frying to prevent spattering.

1. First dip fish in liquid or sauce. It can be milk, yogurt, buttermilk, salad dressing, or beaten egg mixed with either water or milk. This allows the dry ingredients to adhere properly. If you marinate the fish in citrus juice first, for 30 minutes, it flavors and seasons the fish beautifully, so that no salt is needed.

2. Then, coat the fish with dry ingredients to seal in the juices—use stone-ground cornmeal, finely pulverized crackers, finely crushed, dried bread crumbs, whole grain flours, whole grain, crushed breakfast cereal or wheat germ, or any combination of these things. Add black pepper or other dried herbs or seasonings to taste.

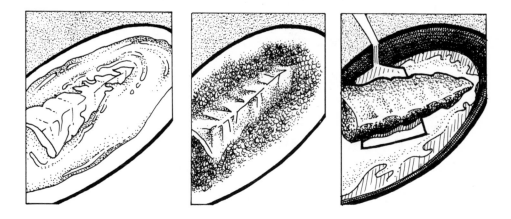

Tip: Spread the coated fish on wax paper, in a single layer, to dry for five minutes. If egg is used in the coating, the coating will not get soggy if the fish is placed in the refrigerator to dry—even if left there for several hours before frying. However, if egg is not included in the coating, allow no more than five minutes for drying or the coating *will* become soggy.

3. Use only enough oil or clarified butter (see Index), which does not burn as easily as regular butter, to cover the bottom of the pan about one-quarter inch—only enough to prevent sticking. Heat the fat or oil to 350° to 370°F. before adding fish.

4. Cook the fish over moderate heat until it is golden brown on one side. Turn once with a wide spatula so fish will not break apart, and brown the other side. Start testing with a skewer after the fish has been cooking about three minutes on the second side. Turn the fish again and allow three minutes more—then test again.

Tip: Keep one pan for cooking fish *only*. When the pan cools after cooking, simply wipe it well with paper towels and coarse salt, which is used as an abrasive, to keep the pan well seasoned. Do not use soap and water. For each batch of fish, wipe out the pan, add fresh butter or oil, and bring it to the correct temperature before adding fish.

Tip: For those who don't like the smell of fish cooking, burn one-half cup of vinegar in a pan after cooking fish.

Tip: Use lemon or salt water to remove the fish smell from your hands.

Method II—Oven Fry

1. Prepare fish for cooking, as in Method I.

2. Preheat the oven to 500°F.

3. Place the fish in the *oven*, not the broiler.

4. Use a well-buttered, oven-to-table baking dish. The fish cooks quickly and does not have to be turned over, and the less handling the better.

5. Dot fish with butter or brush with oil, and cook for about eight to ten minutes according to the thickness of the fish. Test early with a skewer.

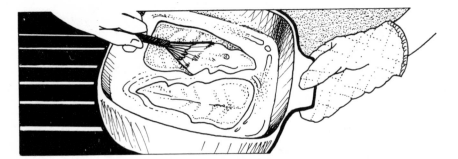

Tip: Oven frying and pan frying (as compared with deep frying) are good for people whose diets call for a lower fat intake. To get the delicious flavor of butter and still keep your cholesterol level down, mix a small amount of melted butter with polyunsaturated oil.

Method III—Deep Fry

When fish is deep fried properly, it is *not* greasy. The batter seals the moisture in and the coating keeps the outside brown, dry, and crisp.

1. Prepare the fish for cooking, as in Method I. These are *dry* batters. With deep-fat frying, *moist* batters may be used as well. (See Index for specific batter recipes.)

2. If using a *dry* batter coating with egg as the liquid, chill the fish on wax paper for 30 minutes so it will dry before cooking. With *moist* batters, dip the fish in the batter, then put it right into the fat.

3. Use only clean, fresh vegetable oil when deep frying.

Tip: Corn oil or peanut oil can reach higher temperatures than safflower oil without smoking or burning.

4. Heat oil to 370°F. Use a thermometer for accuracy and use a deep, heavy pot to prevent spattering. Lower fish gently, a few pieces at a time, into the hot fat; do not overcrowd the pieces of fish. Cook until crisp and golden brown. It may take only a few minutes, depending on the size of the fish. If not using a basket, lift out fish with a slotted spoon or tongs. Drain fish on paper towels and keep it warm.

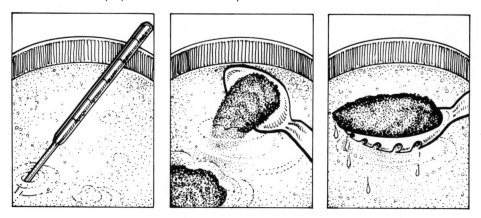

Tip: Most fats and oils smoke and burn at 400°F., so keep the temperature of the oil under that—we suggest 370°F.

5. When frying large amounts of batter-coated fish at one time, it may be necessary to recrisp the fish right before serving. Raise the fat temperature to 380°F. in this case and immerse the basket of fish for a few seconds just before serving. Drain well on paper towels and serve very hot.

Moist Batters

Moist batters seal in juices and seal out penetrating oil to allow enough batter for one pound of cubed fish or two pounds of fillets cut into serving pieces; try this basic recipe and vary it according to your own taste and whims:

BASIC MOIST BATTER

1½ cups whole grain flour
    black pepper to taste and any dried herb or combination of herbs
2 teaspoons baking powder (optional)
1½ cups liquid—made up of 1 large egg plus the juice of a lemon and water or milk to fill

Mix just long enough to blend all the ingredients.

Yield: about 2½ cups

Tip: For a puffier batter, use baking powder—avoid the kinds that contain aluminum salts.

Tip: To make a lighter batter, use 1 tablespoon of oil as part of liquid.

(continued on page 47)

Simple Batter-Fried Fillets with Fresh Herbs and Citrus Fruit   For this recipe, see page 266

Baked Tilefish with Mushrooms, Scallions, and Dill   For this recipe, see page 199

Tip: If you want a crisper batter, use water instead of milk.

Tip: Marinate fish in citrus juice before coating, for better flavor.

Tip: Mix batter only until combined, before dipping fish into it.

Tip: A thick batter requires thorough browning to insure that the batter is cooked through.

Tip: Make sure fish is completely dry before coating with the batter. The following are moist batter recipes that yield enough to coat two pounds of fish fillets:

Lemon Batter
Celery and Garlic Batter
Herbed Batter

LEMON BATTER

1½ cups whole wheat pastry flour
1½ teaspoons baking powder
 4 eggs, lightly beaten
 ½ cup cold water
 2 tablespoons lemon juice

Mix flour and baking powder together. In a separate bowl, mix eggs, water, and lemon juice. Gradually stir into flour mixture until completely blended.

Yield: 2 cups

Tip: If there is any batter left over, add 1 tablespoon of additional flour to ½ cup batter and dip pieces of fruit or vegetables into it to fry and serve with the fish.

CELERY AND GARLIC BATTER

1½ cups whole grain flour
⅛ teaspoon nutmeg
¼ teaspoon black pepper
2 teaspoons baking powder
1½ teaspoons grated celery
1 teaspoon butter, melted
1½ cups milk
1 clove garlic, finely minced, or 2
    tablespoons grated onion
2 eggs, beaten

Mix first 4 ingredients together.

In a separate bowl, mix celery, butter, milk, garlic or onion, and eggs together. Let flavors blend for about 10 minutes. Then add the liquid to the dry ingredients and blend.

Yield: 2 cups

HERBED BATTER

1½ cups whole grain flour
¼ teaspoon black pepper
2 teaspoons baking powder
2 teaspoons finely minced, fresh parsley
½ teaspoon dried basil
1 teaspoon grated lemon rind
4 eggs, beaten
¼ cup cold water

Mix dry ingredients together.

In another bowl, combine remaining ingredients. Add the liquid ingredients to the dry and beat until fairly smooth.

Yield: 2 cups

Method IV—Poach

Poaching means immersing a fish in an aromatic broth and simmering the fish for the required time, according to its size and thickness.

In poaching a fish, the liquid must almost cover the fish. The poaching technique is always the same for any recipe; only the ingredients for the liquid vary.

Actively boiling water will cause a delicate-textured fish to break apart, so keep the heat at low simmer.

1. Measure the fish at its thickest part with a ruler to determine cooking time. Allow about nine minutes per inch of thickness, or six to eight minutes per pound.

2. Before poaching any large fish, wrap entire fish in a double layer of moistened cheesecloth before placing on a rack in the pot, or in a fish poacher. Moisten cheesecloth by dipping it in the poaching liquid and then wrap it around the fish loosely.

Allow ten inches of extra cheesecloth on each end. Twist the ends and make knots to use as handles when removing the fish.

3. Immerse fish in boiling broth, bring to a boil again, and lower heat to simmer immediately. The cooking takes place with very low heat. Never allow the liquid to boil and never stop the simmer. Remove fish at once to prevent further cooking.

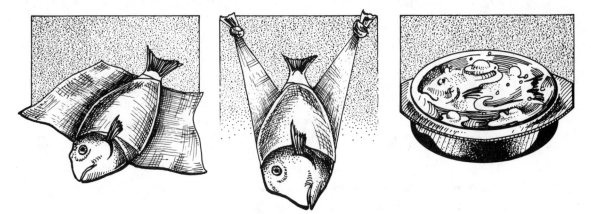

Tip: It is most important, when removing a large fish from the poaching rack, to have a second person assist you by supporting the midsection of the fish from underneath with a very broad spatula. Otherwise, the weight of the unsupported center will cause the fish to break apart.

4. After removing the fish from the broth, let it cool a bit on the rack, still wrapped in the wet cheesecloth to keep moist. As a rest for the rack, place two pieces of wood crosswise over the top of the poacher. (We use chopsticks.) Allow the liquid to drain back into the pan. Resting it this way also helps firm up the flesh. When the fish is cool to the touch, unwrap the cheesecloth carefully.

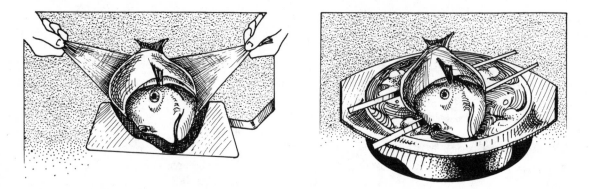

Tip: Whole fish or fish steaks are excellent when poached, particularly when you plan to serve fish for more than one meal. Left-over, cooked fish can then be broken into flakes and easily prepared for soups, salads, mousses, souffles, croquettes, and the like.

Fish poachers come in several sizes, so consider your needs when making a purchase: a 20-inch poacher (17½ inches inside) will hold fish under four pounds; a 24-inch fish poacher will hold a whole four-pound fish with the head intact; a 36-inch poacher, an eight-to ten-pound fish.

Tip: Remember the poacher you buy will have to fit on the top of your stove, so take its length into account when shopping.

Tip: If the fish you are going to cook is too big to fit into your poacher, use a little ingenuity. You can cut the fish in half crosswise to fit your poacher, and cook each half separately. Then put it together on the serving platter and hide the cut with a decorative garnish.

Tip: In a pinch, your covered roaster with a bottom rack can double as a poacher. Fish poachers are costly but a good investment.

Poaching Liquids

These aromatic liquids can be strained then frozen, and reused again for soups and sauces, or for poaching or steaming another batch of fish. Since the fish, when poached, is placed directly into the liquid, the flavors of both the fish and the liquid are intensified—the natural fish flavor is enhanced, not disguised, and the liquid is delicately flavored by the fish.

There are three basic groups of poaching liquids: (1) *COURT BOUILLON*— any blend of water, aromatic herbs, and vegetables. When fish scraps are added, it becomes (2) *FISH STOCK*—used for soups and for poaching as well. When the fish stock is boiled down to a concentrated form, it becomes (3) *FISH FUMET*—used mostly as a base for sauces. Any Court Bouillon that does not contain vinegar can be concentrated by boiling it down for a fumet.

Try the following recipes for poaching liquids to add variety to this most subtle of preparations for fish:

Aromatic Broth
Aromatic Milk Broth
Fish Stock (and Fish Fumet)

Court Bouillon
Spiced Broth
Oriental Citrus Broth

AROMATIC BROTH

8   cups water
½   cup tarragon vinegar
2   carrots, sliced
2   onions, sliced
3   stalks celery with leaves, chopped
2   sprigs parsley
1   bay leaf
8   peppercorns
¼   teaspoon whole cloves
1   pound fish scraps including bones, head, and the like (optional)

Put water and all other ingredients in a large pot. Bring to a boil, then lower heat, cover pot, and simmer for 30 minutes. Strain before using.

Yield: about 7 cups

Note: Substitute lemon juice for vinegar if you wish to prepare a Fish Fumet (see page 53) from the left-over broth.

AROMATIC MILK BROTH

Use to poach delicate, white-fleshed fish.

6   cups water
2   slices lemon
2   carrots, cut into quarters
1   large onion, cut into quarters
3   sprigs each thyme and parsley (or ½ teaspoon dried thyme and 3 sprigs parsley), tied with string
8   peppercorns
1½ cups milk

Bring all ingredients, except milk, to a boil. Lower heat and simmer for 15 minutes, then add milk and cook 10 minutes more. Remove bouquet of thyme and parsley.

Yield: about 6 cups

Note: Save the flavored milk left after poaching to use as a base for sauces.

FISH STOCK
(AND FISH FUMET)

2½ to 3 pounds fish bones, including
      head, with gills, skin, and eyes
      removed
12 cups water
 4 stalks celery with leaves, chopped
 2 large onions, chopped
 2 whole leeks, chopped
 1 clove garlic, split
 4 sprigs thyme or ½ teaspoon dried
 1 bay leaf
 3 sprigs parsley
 ½ teaspoon peppercorns
    juice of 3 lemons

Tie the fish head, scraps, and bones loosely in cheesecloth for easy removal. Put all other ingredients, except lemon juice, into a large kettle and lower cheesecloth containing fish scraps and bones into liquid. The French would add 1½ cups dry white wine at this point. Bring to boiling point, lower heat, and simmer for 25 minutes; then add lemon juice.

Put the pot in the sink. Lift out the cheesecloth and tie it around the water spigot, allowing the juices to drip back into the pot. When the cheesecloth is cool to the touch, gently squeeze remaining liquid from it into the stock. Strain the liquid.

Aside from its value as a poaching liquid, this stock can serve as the base for all soups, sauces, and aspics (with addition of gelatin). It is always good to have several batches of Fish Stock on hand, since it is so versatile. Freeze some in 1-quart containers and freeze some in ice cube trays. (The cubes, when kept frozen in plastic bags for easy removal, are best to use for sauces.)

Yield: about 9 cups

Tip: Do not be wasteful. Most times a large fish head and skeleton contain enough cooked fish to make a cold salad. Open the cheesecloth and pick off the fish. You may also pour some stock over the fish bits and freeze them to use another time in other recipes.

If you wish to make Fish Fumet for sauces, strain the Fish Stock and bring it to a boil rapidly, with the cover off the pot. Reduce heat to moderate and cook uncovered until it is reduced by one-half. Use this concentrated liquid to add great flavor to any sauce.

COURT BOUILLON

8 cups water
2 carrots, cut into quarters
1 large onion or 4 shallots, chopped
4 scallions or 2 small leeks, chopped
2 sprigs tarragon or ½ teaspoon dried
2 sprigs thyme or ¼ teaspoon dried
2 bay leaves
4 sprigs parsley
10 peppercorns
   juice of 2 lemons

Combine all ingredients, except lemon juice, and bring to a boil. Lower heat to simmer. Cover pot and cook for 30 minutes. Strain and add lemon juice.

Yield: about 8 cups

Note: Traditionally, the French use 1½ cups dry, white wine in this recipe for the poaching liquid.

SPICED BROTH

Use only to poach fatty fish or as a boil for crustaceans.

8 cups water
1 tablespoon allspice
1 to 2 dried, hot chili peppers, or
        according to taste
2 teaspoons whole cloves
2 whole bay leaves
1 large onion, sliced
4 cloves garlic, peeled and left whole
2 whole lemons, thinly sliced

Put water in large pot. Tie the 4 dry spices in cheesecloth and add to the water. Add the onion, garlic, and lemon slices. Bring to a boil, then lower heat to simmer. Cover pot and cook for 30 minutes. Strain.

Yield: about 6 cups

Tip: There are certain commercially prepared mixed spices called Crawfish, Shrimp, or Crab-Boil which can be used, if you are pressed for time. One excellent brand, "Zatarain's," is packed in New Orleans and contains mustard seed, coriander seed, allspice, clove, bay leaf, cayenne pepper, and dill seed.

ORIENTAL CITRUS BROTH

5 cups water
½ cup Japanese rice wine vinegar*
½ cup orange juice (2 whole oranges)
½ cup lime juice (2 to 3 whole limes)
½ teaspoon peppercorns
2 whole allspice
1 tablespoon tamari soy sauce

Mix all ingredients except soy sauce. Bring to a boil. Lower heat and simmer for 30 minutes. Strain and add soy sauce.

Yield: about 6 cups

*Japanese rice wine vinegar has only 4 percent acidity making a milder-flavored broth. All other vinegars have a 5 percent acidity.

Method V—Steam

1. Place fish to be steamed on a rack *above*, not immersed *in*, a simmering liquid, such as wine, water, or a combination of both, or above a flavored broth of onion, carrot, and celery. A fish poacher with the lid on is preferred for this procedure, though any covered steamer will do.

2. Cooking time varies with fish size (small fish or pieces of fish fillets are best for steaming). For three pounds of fillets—enough to serve six people—figure on 10 to 12 minutes. Test early to avoid overcooking.

Tip: Steamed fish takes nicely to sauces, since steaming seems to preserve the delicacy of the natural taste. Steamed fish, like poached, is excellent for fat-free diets.

Method VI—Broil

In broiling, fish is cooked quickly three to four inches below the source of heat. Broiling is best for fatty fish, since the high heat (550°F.) can dry out fish that is not lubricated and basted.

It is possible, however, to broil lean fish with excellent results. Large fish cut into chunks (or skewered), small fish left whole after dressing, and fillets, steaks, and whole fish that are split open and laid flat (butterflied) can all be broiled if you will keep these procedures in mind:

1. Oil or butter a perforated rack. One that fits over another pan is best. A wire rack does *not* support the fish properly and the fish tends to break and fall through or stick to the wires.

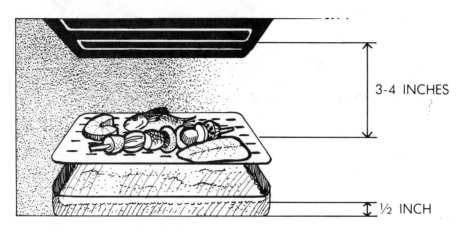

3-4 INCHES

½ INCH

Tip: Add one-half inch boiling water to the pan under the perforated rack—this creates steam and helps to keep the fish moist.

Tip: If fish seems to be drying as it broils, brush with a bit more melted butter or oil.

2. Measure the thickness of the fish, allowing about nine to ten minutes broiling time per inch.

Tip: Make sure that the fish to be broiled is only one-half inch to one and one-half inches thick, no matter how it is cut, or it will dry up before it is cooked through.

3. Set oven at "Broil."

4. Broil three to four inches below the source of heat.

Tip: If top of fish seems to be getting brown too quickly, move the pan to the shelf below.

5. Start testing it with a skewer after half the total time has elapsed. Continue to broil and test until the fish flakes and color changes from translucent to opaque. Do not overcook!

Tip: Fish that is at least three-fourths of an inch thick can be set closer to the source of the heat and can also be turned over more easily than a thinner piece of fish.

Tip: If fish is less than one-half inch thick, it will probably break when turned over—so don't turn it, just cook on one side and keep testing it with the skewer for doneness. The same holds for fish with skin on it. Cook it on one side only. Whole, split fish should be turned over carefully and broiled on the other side as well. Use a very wide spatula.

6. It is also possible to steam or poach a fish first, and then butter or oil the top and slip it under a hot broiler very close to the source of heat for one to two minutes, only to brown the top. Because the activity in a restaurant kitchen sometimes does not allow for the precise timing needed for broiling fish, many fine chefs use this method with success. The fish keeps moist from the poaching or steaming process and the top can be buttered and browned very quickly and watched as carefully as it should be, to avoid its getting overcooked and dry.

Method VII—Bake

Any kind of fish, whatever its size, shape, or form, can be baked. Any sauce can be added to it, or it can bake on a bed of vegetables or it can be stuffed if left whole. Fillets can also be rolled around a stuffing and baked, and fish steaks can be baked too.

1. Preheat oven to 350° to 375°F.

2. Oil or butter a baking dish. An oven-to-table one is best, so the fish can be served without transferring it.

3. Remember to bake fish about nine to ten minutes per one inch of thickness—so measure the thickest part with a ruler to calculate the amount of time necessary. Allow more time if fish is stuffed or sauced. Start testing for doneness after half the total cooking time has elapsed.

Tip: Baking a whole fish with the head on, not only yields extra delicious pickings but it seals in the juices as well. Some people are offended by seeing the head of a fish attached to the body when it is being served but, personally, we feel that *without* the head, the fish looks incomplete. We once picked one-and-one-half pounds of cooked fish from the head of a large, striped bass. That was enough fish to feed six more people!

How to Bone and Serve a Cooked Fish

1. With the fish on its platter, the backbone should be opposite you. You'll need a fork and a fish-serving knife, very much like a cake server, with a cutting edge on one side and a flat surface with which to lift the fish as you detach it from the skeleton.

2. Hold the fork on the fish to steady it and then begin to peel the skin carefully, working from the backbone down the fish toward you. When you get to the fin, remove it with the skin that surrounds it.

3. Starting at the head and working toward the tail, slide the knife under the flesh, working it carefully along the backbone. This is very much like filleting a freshly caught fish, except that the flesh is more delicate and, as a result, the process must be done more carefully. As you cut toward the tail, if any bones come up with the flesh, push them away with the knife. When complete, the entire side of the fish should be separated from the bone.

4. If the fish is small, divide the fillet into portions and serve. However, if the fish is quite large, cut slices beginning at the tail, then divide the upper part of the fish into portions for your guests by cutting into the fish up the center line. Remove the section closest to you by pulling toward you with the knife. Discard this portion of the fish. Then divide the remaining section either by cutting into slices or dividing it into portions just large enough to serve.

5. Turn fish over and repeat the steps on the other side.

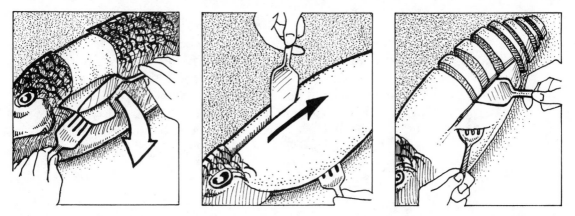

A Touch of the Old South

While on a trip through North Carolina, a friend of ours highly recommended dining at River Forrest Manor at Belhaven. If it was fish and fresh vegetables that we were after, then Mrs. Axson Smith was the person to see!

River Forrest Manor is in the style of the antebellum mansions throughout the South, charming and elegant. It was completed in 1904, with the ceilings carved by Italian craftsmen, sparkling, cut-glass-leaded windows, hand-carved oak mantels for each of the 11 fireplaces, and pure crystal chandeliers. The manor only has 12 guest rooms, but its main attraction for us was the incredible smorgasbord that Mrs. Smith puts out each and every day, with everything fresh and dishes selected according to availability and season. The *shrimp* are bought fresh each morning at the docks where Mrs. Smith's friend, Mr. Jones, runs a huge shrimp processing center.

The buffet is enormous—nearly a hundred different dishes from which to choose: shrimp creole and crab meat casserole, freshly broiled *bluefish*, garden fresh escarole, radishes, spring onions, yellow carrots, pascal celery, tomatoes right from the vine, and homemade applesauce. The array is quite overwhelming and, as we began our adventure down the aisles, the bottom line of Mrs. Smith's menu caught our eye: "Eat, Drink and Be Merry, for Tomorrow You May Diet!"

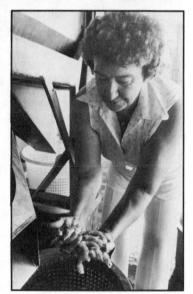

Suggested Equipment for Cooking Fish

Metal skewers

Ball of string or twine

Pastry brush

Baster

Cheesecloth

Fish poacher—available in sizes ranging from 20 to 36 inches. We suggest one about 28 inches long.

Heavy iron skillet

Two sizes oval, oven-proof, open casseroles which can also be used to serve right at the table

Perforated racks to fit over pans for broiling or steaming

Two wide, perforated spatulas for lifting fish

Tongs

Strong pair of scissors

Fish scaler

Flexible filleting knife, 6½- to 7-inch blade

Wooden mallets for cracking shells of crabs or lobsters

Lobster picks and claw crackers

Oval steel frying pan

Fat thermometer

Parchment paper

Six- to seven-quart heavy stockpot for soups, stews, and the like

Strainer

Ladle

Wooden spoons

Wire whisk

And though you don't really need them, it sometimes helps considerably to have an electric blender and a food processor.

Sources for Equipment

Most good department stores and specialty food shops carry just about everything you'll ever need for cooking seafood. However, from time to time, you'll want a specialized item like a large fish poacher or a particular frying pan. If there's a commercial kitchen and hotel supply store in your neighborhood, that's generally a good source. In addition, we've noticed that gourmet kitchen shops are springing up from coast to coast in the United States and Canada. However, in case you want a special item, we've listed a few of our favorite suppliers below. They provide a mail-order resource for cooks all over the country:

Bazaar de la Cuisine, 1003 Second Avenue, New York, NY 10022. Telephone: (212) 421-8028. They specialize in cookware and kitchen gadgets. A catalog is available.

Lekvar-by-the-Barrel (H. Roth & Son), 1577 First Avenue, New York, NY 10028. Telephone: (212) 734-1111. They specialize in gourmet foods, spices, household items, kitchen supplies, and cookware. A catalog is available.

Williams-Sonoma, (Mail-Order Dept.), P.O. Box 3792, San Francisco, CA 94119. Telephone: (415) 658-7845. They specialize in cookware and gourmet foods. A catalog is available.

Zabar's, 2245 Broadway, New York, NY 10024. Telephone: (212) 787-2000. They specialize in gourmet foods and cookware. A catalog is available.

Part 3: Sauces

100 Sauces to Enhance Your Fish Cookery

You don't have to be one of the great chefs of France to create the classic sauces that will enhance and enlarge your fish repertoire. You don't have to speak French or even know how to pronounce the names of the sauces. Most are derived from simple foundations with several basic variations.

Emulsified sauces, both cold and hot, are made with oil and vinegar or lemon juice—mayonnaise is one of these.

Bechamel is based on butter, flour, and milk or cream—really what we know as a white cream sauce.

Veloutes include any of the white sauces enhanced with fish stock.

There are the *tomato-based sauces* and *sauces enriched with heavy cream or sour cream*—and *yogurt-based sauces. Butter-based sauces,* both *cold* and *hot,* can be varied endlessly by the addition of any citrus juice and rind (lemon, lime, orange) or any fresh or dried herbs such as parsley, chives, shallots, tarragon, oregano, sage, and chervil.

Fish can be transformed from ordinary to sublime with imaginative use of the proper sauces. The sauces can be used with any simply cooked fish in this book, whether you decide to poach, broil, bake, or saute. (See Index for Seven Basic Cooking Methods.)

The colors of sauces also add eye appeal to fish. Sometimes two sauces of contrasting colors can be poured over a simple, cold poached fish in a striped design, lending an attractive, decorative touch.

Follow the few general rules given below for using sauces, and you can create an entirely new and different repertoire by experimenting with them:

Rule One: Bland, delicate fish, such as *flounder, sole, red snapper,* and *halibut,* should have a delicate or rich sauce that does not overpower it.

Rule Two: Fish that declares its own natural flavor, such as *mackerel, bluefish,* or *mullet,* can take an assertive sauce based upon lemon juice or vinegar, or strong, tomato-based sauces.

Rule Three: Poached fish is complimented by herb-based sauces.

Rule Four: Cold seafood can take piquant or mayonnaise-based sauces nicely.

Bechamel Cream Sauces

Basic Bechamel Sauce (White Cream Sauce)
VARIATIONS
Egg and Parsley Sauce
Fresh Grape Sauce (Sauce *Veronique*)
Mustard-Cheese Sauce
Tomato Sauce

BASIC BECHAMEL SAUCE
(WHITE CREAM SAUCE)

4 tablespoons butter
3 tablespoons whole wheat pastry flour
1½ cups milk, or 1 cup milk plus ½ cup Fish Stock (see Index)
¼ teaspoon white pepper
⅛ teaspoon nutmeg
1 teaspoon grated onion (optional)

Melt butter, add flour, and cook together, stirring constantly. Add the liquid slowly and continue to cook over low heat, stirring with a whisk until thickened—about 10 minutes. Add pepper, nutmeg, and onion.

Yield: 1¼ cups

VARIATIONS

EGG AND PARSLEY SAUCE

---

2 hard-cooked eggs, coarsely chopped
1 teaspoon grated onion
1 tablespoon lemon juice
⅓ cup finely minced, fresh parsley
1 cup Basic Bechamel Sauce (see page 66)

Stir eggs, onion, lemon juice, and parsley into hot Basic Bechamel Sauce. Cook until heated through.

Yield: 1½ cups

FRESH GRAPE SAUCE
(SAUCE VERONIQUE)

---

1 cup Basic Bechamel Sauce (see page 66)
½ cup light cream
1 cup seedless fresh, green grapes

Dilute Basic Bechamel Sauce with cream. Add grapes and heat. Do not boil.

Yield: 2 cups

MUSTARD-CHEESE SAUCE

---

1 cup grated, sharp cheddar cheese
1½ teaspoons dry mustard
1 cup Basic Bechamel Sauce (see page 66)

Mix all together. Dilute with as much milk as necessary to maintain creamy consistency.

Yield: 1⅓ cups

TOMATO SAUCE

3 tablespoons Basic Tomato Sauce (see page 100)
1 cup Basic Bechamel Sauce (see page 66)

Mix ingredients, stir, and heat through.

Yield: 1 cup

Butter Sauces (Cold)

Anise Butter
VARIATION
Green Peppercorn Butter
Basil and Parmesan Butter
Bercy Butter
Chivry Butter
Hungarian Paprika Butter
Lobster Butter
Shallot and Garlic Butter (Also Called "Escargot Butter")
Tomato and Oregano Butter
Walnut Sauce
VARIATIONS
Almond Sauce
Pistachio Nut Butter

ANISE BUTTER

1 teaspoon anise seed, finely crushed
1 teaspoon lemon juice
½ cup softened butter

Add anise seed and lemon juice to softened butter. Beat well and chill.

Yield: about ½ cup

VARIATION

GREEN PEPPERCORN BUTTER

Substitute 2 teaspoons green peppercorns (mashed) for anise seed. (Green peppercorns come in dry packs or packed in water; the latter must be drained before use.)

Yield: about ½ cup

Tip: This variation can be frozen into a bar and used later, mixed with heavy cream and a cube of frozen Fish Stock (see Index), that has been melted, for a sensational sauce.

BASIL AND PARMESAN BUTTER

½ cup fresh basil
1 tablespoon lemon juice
2 tablespoons finely minced, fresh parsley
¼ pound butter, cut in half and softened
¼ cup grated Parmesan cheese
¼ teaspoon black pepper

In a blender, chop the basil leaves with the lemon juice. Add parsley, butter, cheese, and pepper. Blend until smooth. Chill. Spread on fish before or after broiling.

Yield: about ¾ cup

BERCY BUTTER

---

2 shallots, minced (young spring onions may be used)
1 tablespoon lemon juice
1 tablespoon vinegar
¼ teaspoon black pepper
½ cup softened butter

Put shallots in heavy pan with lemon juice and vinegar. Cook slowly until shallots are soft, and liquid has nearly evaporated. Add pepper. Cool and mix with softened butter.

Yield: about ⅔ cup

CHIVRY BUTTER

4 shallots, finely minced (young spring onions may be used)
2 tablespoons finely minced, fresh parsley
1 teaspoon finely minced, fresh tarragon or ¼ teaspoon dried
1 tablespoon finely minced, fresh chervil or 1½ teaspoons dried
½ cup boiling water
½ cup softened butter

In a bowl, mix shallots and herbs together. Pour boiling water over all and let steep for 5 minutes. Drain in a strainer and then dry on paper towels.

Place dried herbs in a blender and blend until fine. Add the softened butter and blend again. Put mixture in a cup and refrigerate for ½ hour or so to develop the flavors before using. Can be frozen as a bar and sliced to melt over hot fish as a sauce.

Yield: about ¾ cup

HUNGARIAN PAPRIKA BUTTER

½ cup softened butter
1 small onion, grated
2 teaspoons paprika (hot or sweet depending on your own preference)
¼ teaspoon black pepper

Melt 1 tablespoon butter over low heat and add onion. Cook until softened. Add paprika and pepper. Cool mixture and beat into remaining softened butter. Serve at room temperature.

Yield: about ¾ cup

LOBSTER BUTTER

shells only from 1 lobster
½ cup butter

Chop shells in a food processor. Put the shells and the butter into the top of a double boiler. Melt slowly over hot water. Line a strainer with a man's large linen handkerchief or a piece of cheesecloth and strain the lobster butter. Cool and keep in refrigerator or freezer to use for adding flavor to other sauces, or melt the Lobster Butter and pour it over poached fish.

Yield: ½ cup

Note: You can also use this procedure with washed, uncooked shrimp shells to make Shrimp Butter.

SHALLOT AND GARLIC BUTTER
(ALSO CALLED "ESCARGOT BUTTER")

½ cup softened butter
2 tablespoons finely minced shallots
(young spring onions may be used)
2 cloves garlic, finely minced
¼ teaspoon white pepper
1 teaspoon lemon juice
3 tablespoons finely minced, fresh
parsley

In a bowl, cream butter until smooth. Add shallots, garlic, pepper, and lemon juice and mix them well. Then add parsley and mix again. Remove butter and form into log shape. Wrap in plastic wrap and freeze. Slice as needed and use to spread on fish *before* broiling or baking.

Yield: about ⅔ cup

TOMATO AND OREGANO BUTTER

½ cup softened butter
2 tablespoons Basic Tomato Sauce (see Index)
1 tablespoon finely minced, fresh oregano or 1½ teaspoons dried
1 teaspoon grated onion
¼ teaspoon black pepper

Mix all ingredients together until smooth. Chill for 1 hour and then cut into slices to use when cooking. Can also be frozen.

Yield: about ½ cup

WALNUT SAUCE

¼ cup walnuts
1 teaspoon lemon juice
¼ pound butter, cut in thirds and softened
¼ teaspoon black pepper

In a blender, process nuts with lemon juice. Add pieces of softened butter, one at a time, and blend well each time. Remove mixture from blender and stir in pepper. Chill. Use to spread on broiled fish.

Yield: about ¾ cup

VARIATIONS

ALMOND SAUCE

Substitute almonds for walnuts.

PISTACHIO NUT BUTTER

Use 3 tablespoons chopped pistachio nuts (shelled and inner skins removed) in place of walnuts. Add 1 tablespoon finely minced, fresh parsley to other ingredients and add with pepper.

Butter Sauces (Hot)

BASIC CLARIFIED BUTTER

1 pound sweet butter

Melt butter in saucepan over low heat. Let stand for 15 minutes. Skim off foamy top. Let milky solids remain on bottom. Spoon out clear yellow liquid. Serve hot.

Yield: 2 cups

Note: This butter can be refrigerated and kept for several weeks. It is excellent for sauteing since it does not spatter or burn as easily as fresh butter.

BLACK BUTTER SAUCE

2 cups sweet butter
1 tablespoon vinegar

In a small, heavy skillet heat butter slowly and cook until very dark, but not burned. Skim foam from surface and remove from heat. Let cool. Add the vinegar, stir and cook for a few more minutes. Serve hot.

Yield: 1 cup

VARIATION

MAITRE D'HOTEL BUTTER

1 tablespoon lemon juice

Replace vinegar with lemon juice and follow procedure for Black Butter Sauce.

FENNEL BUTTER SAUCE

Use this for fatty fish.

1 small bulb fennel (or 4 stalks), finely chopped
boiling water to cover
2 tablespoons olive oil
½ cup butter, melted
¼ teaspoon black pepper
pinch nutmeg

In a saucepan, cover chopped fennel with boiling water. Continue to boil for 1 minute, then pour into strainer and run cold water over. Dry fennel on paper towels.

Over a low heat, mix olive oil, butter, pepper, and nutmeg together. Add fennel. Serve warm.

Yield: about ¾ cup

HERBED
BUTTER SAUCE
(BEURRE NANTAIS)

¼ cup finely chopped shallots (young
     spring onions may be used)
3 tablespoons vinegar
¼ teaspoon white pepper
4 tablespoons cold water
¾ pound cold butter
2 teaspoons chopped, fresh tarragon or ½
     teaspoon dried
2 teaspoons chopped, fresh chervil or 1
     teaspoon dried (optional)
2 teaspoons chopped, fresh parsley
1 tablespoon lime juice

Combine the shallots, vinegar, pepper, and water in a saucepan. Bring to a boil, turn down heat to very low, and cook until the liquid is reduced by half. Cut the butter into cubes and add ⅓ to the sauce, beating vigorously with a whisk over very low heat. Do not allow the mixture to boil, or it will curdle.

Continue adding butter and beating until butter is just heated through and melted. Remove from heat and stir in tarragon, chervil, and parsley. Add the lime juice and beat again. Serve immediately.

Yield: about 2 cups

MUSTARD
BUTTER SAUCE

1 tablespoon dry mustard
1 tablespoon cold water
½ cup butter
2 tablespoons lemon juice
1 tablespoon minced, fresh dill

Mix dry mustard with cold water and let stand for 10 minutes to develop flavor. Melt butter, add mustard and water mixture, and lemon juice. Stir and heat. Add dill. Serve hot.

Yield: ⅔ cup

ORANGE BUTTER AND CHIVE SAUCE

½ cup butter
2 tablespoons orange juice
1 teaspoon grated orange rind
1 tablespoon minced, fresh chives
¼ teaspoon white pepper

Melt butter and add all ingredients together until smoothly blended. Serve warm.

Yield: about ¾ cup

SOY SAUCE BUTTER

¼ cup softened butter
2 tablespoons tamari soy sauce
1 tablespoon lemon juice
¼ teaspoon black pepper
1 teaspoon minced, fresh chives

Melt butter and add soy sauce, lemon juice, and pepper. Stir in chives. Serve hot.

Yield: about ¾ cup

TARRAGON-LEMON BUTTER SAUCE

½ cup butter
2 tablespoons lemon juice
1 teaspoon grated lemon rind
¼ teaspoon white pepper
2 tablespoons finely minced, fresh tarragon or 2 teaspoons dried, crushed tarragon

Melt butter and add all other ingredients. Serve warm.

Yield: about ⅔ cup

VARIATIONS
LEMON
BUTTER SAUCE

Use ⅛ teaspoon cayenne pepper and 1
  tablespoon minced, fresh parsley in
  place of white pepper and tarragon.

MINT
BUTTER SAUCE

Use 2 tablespoons chopped, fresh mint in
  place of tarragon.

WHITE
BUTTER SAUCE
WITH VINEGAR
(BEURRE BLANC)

 2 tablespoons finely minced shallots
       (young spring onions may be used)
 7 tablespoons white vinegar
½ teaspoon white pepper
10 ounces (2½ quarter-pound sticks)
       slightly soft butter, cut into small
       pieces
 1 tablespoon lemon juice
 2 tablespoons finely minced, fresh
       parsley (optional)

Put shallots in heavy saucepan with
vinegar. Add pepper and simmer over very
low heat, stirring frequently until shallots
have wilted and vinegar is completely
cooked away. (Tip the pan to test. There
should be no liquid at all, but shallots
should be very moist.)

Transfer to top of double boiler over very
hot water. Do not put heat on. Add ⅓ of
the pieces of butter and, with a wire whisk,
beat until smooth and creamy but do not
allow butter to melt. When smooth, add
the lemon juice and beat again. Add the
next ⅓ of the butter and beat vigorously
again. When that is smooth and creamy,
add the last ⅓ and beat well.

Fold in parsley and keep warm over low
heat, but no warmer than body
temperature or about 98°F. Serve warm.

Yield: about 1⅓ cups

Heavy Cream (or Creme Fraiche) Sauces

Basic *Creme Fraiche*
Creamy Egg and Garlic Sauce
Duglere Sauce (Cream and Tomato Sauce with Anise)
Green Herb Cream Sauce
Horseradish Cream Sauce
Mushroom Cream Sauce
Shrimp and Scallion Sauce
VARIATION
Crab Meat and Shallot Sauce
Sorrel and Egg Sauce

BASIC CREME FRAICHE

2 cups heavy cream
3 tablespoons buttermilk

Mix together, cover, and let stand in glass jar at room temperature for 10 to 12 hours. Stir and then refrigerate.

Yield: 2½ cups

Note: This will keep for 2 weeks in the refrigerator. It is a slightly tart, thick cream that will not curdle in sauces. It cannot be whipped.

Herb Batter Crepes Stuffed with Lobster and Duglere Sauce　　For this recipe, see page 298

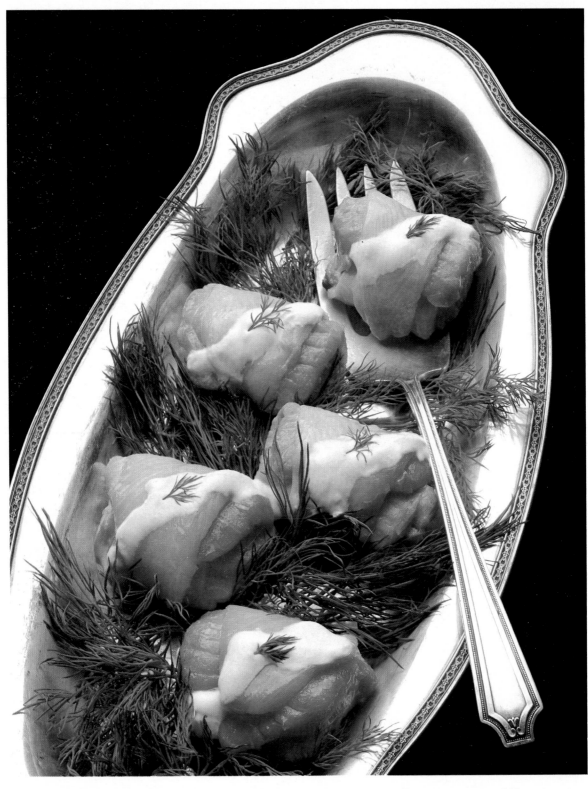

Lemon Sole Stuffed with Salmon in a Lemon Dill Sauce   For this recipe, see page 263

CREAMY EGG AND GARLIC SAUCE

4 egg yolks, well beaten
1 cup sweet butter, melted and kept warm
1 large clove garlic, finely minced
¼ teaspoon cayenne pepper
¼ teaspoon white pepper
2 tablespoons lemon juice
2 tablespoons whipped cream

Using a wire whisk, beat the egg yolks in the top of a double boiler, over simmering hot water, until they just begin to thicken. Remove pot from heat at once, and slowly begin to dribble the warm melted butter into the yolks, beating hard with the whisk. Whisk in the garlic, cayenne and white pepper, and the lemon juice. Fold the whipped cream into the sauce. Serve hot.

Yield: 1½ cups

DUGLERE SAUCE
(CREAM AND TOMATO SAUCE WITH ANISE)

1 tablespoon butter
3 tablespoons grated onion
1 tablespoon finely chopped shallots (young spring onions may be used)
2 tablespoons lemon juice
2 cups peeled and coarsely chopped, fresh tomatoes
¼ teaspoon black pepper
1 teaspoon anise seed, crushed
1 cup Basic *Creme Fraiche* (see page 78)

Melt butter, and add onion and shallots. Cook until wilted, stirring constantly so they don't brown. Add the lemon juice, tomatoes, and pepper, and simmer for 15 minutes.

Remove from heat and whirl in a blender.

Return pureed tomato mixture to saucepan and add anise seed and Basic *Creme Fraiche*. Cook for 10 minutes more over moderate heat, stirring occasionally. Serve hot.

Yield: 1½ cups

GREEN HERB
CREAM SAUCE

3 tablespoons butter
1 cup Fish Stock (see page 53)
½ teaspoon black pepper
½ cup Basic *Creme Fraiche* (see page 78)
2 egg yolks
2 tablespoons finely minced, fresh
    parsley
2 tablespoons finely minced, fresh chives
1 tablespoon finely minced, fresh dill
1 tablespoon finely minced, fresh chervil
    or 1½ teaspoons dried
10 leaves fresh sorrel, finely shredded
1 teaspoon lemon juice

Melt butter in saucepan. Add Fish Stock and pepper. Bring to a boil, lower heat, and add the Basic *Creme Fraiche*. Let simmer for 5 minutes.

Beat egg yolks with a wire whisk. Add some of the hot sauce to the egg yolks, continuing to beat with the whisk. Then return to saucepan. Continue to beat until sauce is thickened. Keep heat low so sauce will not curdle. Cook for 5 minutes more until thickened. Then add all the herbs and lemon juice. Remove from heat and serve hot.

Yield: 1½ cups

HORSERADISH
CREAM SAUCE

1 cup heavy cream, whipped
4 ounces horseradish root, grated (or
    drained, if bottled)
2 tablespoons lemon juice
⅛ teaspoon white pepper

Mix and chill. Serve cold.

Yield: 1⅓ cups

MUSHROOM CREAM SAUCE

3 tablespoons butter
2 tablespoons finely minced shallots
    (young spring onions may be used)
½ pound mushrooms, finely minced
1 teaspoon Tomato Paste (see page 123)
1 cup Fish Stock (see page 53)
4 tablespoons Basic *Creme Fraiche* (see
    page 78)
¼ teaspoon ground cumin

In a saucepan, melt butter and add shallots. Stir 1 minute. Add mushrooms and cook over medium heat, stirring for 5 minutes.

Mix the Tomato Paste into the Fish Stock and add to the mushroom-shallot mixture. Cook over medium heat for 10 minutes. Add the Basic *Creme Fraiche* and cook until entire mixture is slightly thickened. Add cumin. Serve hot.

Yield: 2 cups

SHRIMP AND SCALLION SAUCE

4 tablespoons butter
6 green scallions, green part only,
    minced
½ cup water
1 cup Basic *Creme Fraiche* (see page 78)
¼ pound raw shrimp, shelled, deveined,
    and coarsely chopped
1 tablespoon lemon juice
¼ teaspoon white pepper
2 tablespoons minced, fresh parsley

In a heavy skillet, heat butter and then add scallions and water. Cook over medium heat until water has boiled away and scallions are soft. Add Basic *Creme Fraiche* and bring to a boil and cook for a few minutes, until slightly thickened. Add the shrimp and cook 1 minute or until shrimp are cooked.

Remove from heat and stir in lemon juice, pepper, and parsley. Serve hot at once.

Yield: 1 cup

VARIATION

CRAB MEAT AND SHALLOT SAUCE

6 shallots
½ cup crab meat
2 tablespoons chervil instead of parsley

Substitute shallots for scallions, crab meat for shrimp, and chervil for parsley. Then follow procedure for Shrimp and Scallion Sauce (see page 83).

SORREL AND EGG SAUCE

¼ cup finely chopped shallots (young spring onions may be used)
3 cups Fish Stock (see Index)
1½ cups heavy cream
¼ teaspoon white pepper
¼ pound fresh sorrel, stems removed and shredded*
3 egg yolks
1 tablespoon butter
1 tablespoon lemon juice

In a deep skillet, combine shallots and Fish Stock and cook uncovered for about 40 minutes over high heat to reduce liquid to 1 cup. Add 1 cup of cream, pepper, and sorrel and bring to boiling point. Lower heat to medium and cook 2 minutes.

Beat the egg yolks with remaining ½ cup of cream.

Remove the sauce from the heat and slowly stir in the egg yolk mixture. Cook 1 minute. Stir well and swirl in the butter. Season with the lemon juice.

Yield: 2½ cups

*If it is difficult to get fresh sorrel, you may use fresh spinach and about 2 tablespoons additional lemon juice.

Hollandaise-Based Sauces

Basic Hollandaise Sauce
VARIATIONS
Mousseline Horseradish Sauce
Sauce Hollandaise Aurora
Sauce *Maltaise* (Orange Hollandaise)
Sauce *Mousseline*
Greek Egg and Lemon Sauce *(Avgolemono)*
Sauce Bearnaise
VARIATION
Sauce *Choron*

BASIC HOLLANDAISE SAUCE

3 egg yolks
2 teaspoons water
¼ pound softened butter, cut into 3 or 4 pieces
¼ teaspoon cayenne pepper
2 tablespoons lemon juice

In top of double boiler, over 2 inches of hot (but not boiling) water, beat egg yolks and water together with a wire whisk, until slightly thickened. Add butter, piece by piece, beating constantly after each addition, until blended and smooth and thickened. Add cayenne pepper and lemon juice. Sauce is served warm.

Yield: ¾ cup

Tip: If sauce becomes too thick, dilute with a bit of cool water. If sauce curdles or separates, don't panic. Restore it by adding a few teaspoons of *cool* water, one at a time, and beating after each addition until smooth.

VARIATIONS

MOUSSELINE HORSERADISH SAUCE

Add:
¼ cup horseradish, drained
½ cup whipped cream
To:
1½ cups warm Basic Hollandaise Sauce
(see page 85)

Yield: about 2 cups

SAUCE HOLLANDAISE AURORA

Add:
2 tablespoons Tomato Paste
(see page 123)
To:
¾ cup warm Basic Hollandaise Sauce
(see page 85)

Yield: about ¾ cup

SAUCE MALTAISE (ORANGE HOLLANDAISE)

Add:
2 tablespoons orange juice
1 teaspoon grated orange rind
To:
1½ cups warm Basic Hollandaise Sauce
(see page 85)

Yield: about 1½ cups

SAUCE MOUSSELINE

Add:
¼ cup whipped cream
¼ cup beaten egg white
To:
¾ cup warm Basic Hollandaise Sauce
(see page 85)

Yield: 1⅓ cups

GREEK
EGG AND LEMON
SAUCE
(AVGOLEMONO)

3 eggs
  juice of 1 large lemon
1 tablespoon cornstarch
½ cup cold water
1 cup boiling Fish Stock (see Index)
¼ teaspoon white pepper

Beat the eggs with a wire whisk until foamy and slowly add the lemon juice. Mix the cornstarch in the cold water, add to the boiling Fish Stock, and add the pepper. With the whisk, beat the broth very slowly into the egg-lemon mixture.

Cook over medium heat, beating constantly until it thickens. Serve hot or cold.

Yield: 1 cup

Note: If you are on a low-fat diet, this sauce is excellent to use instead of mayonnaise since it has no butter or oil.

SAUCE
BEARNAISE

2 tablespoons water
2 teaspoons finely minced, fresh tarragon
    or ½ teaspoon dried
2 tablespoons finely minced, green onion
    (or scallions)
1 tablespoon minced, fresh parsley
6 tablespoons wine vinegar
4 egg yolks
1 tablespoon lemon juice
¼ teaspoon cayenne pepper
¾ cup butter, melted and kept hot

In a small saucepan, mix water, tarragon, onion, parsley, and vinegar. Cook slowly until it is almost a glaze. Reserve.

In a blender, place egg yolks, lemon juice, and cayenne pepper. Blend and gradually add hot butter slowly but steadily until thickened. Add herb mixture and beat well. Serve warm.

Yield: 1 cup

VARIATION

SAUCE CHORON

Add:
2 tablespoons Tomato Paste (see page 123) to warm Sauce Bernaise (see page 87)

Serve warm.

Yield: 1⅛ cups

Marinades for Fish

Caribbean Marinade
Chinese Fish Marinade
Garlic and Rosemary Marinade
Honey and Lemon Marinade
Onion Marinade
Orange Marinade
Oriental Vegetable Marinade
Turkish Marinade

CARIBBEAN MARINADE

½ cup lime juice
1 teaspoon tamari soy sauce
2 tablespoons safflower oil
1 small, hot pepper, seeded and chopped

Mix all the ingredients together and let stand for 10 minutes to develop flavor. Then marinate any kind of fish and use marinade as basting sauce when baking.

Yield: ½ cup

CHINESE FISH MARINADE

6 tablespoons tamari soy sauce
1 tablespoon peanut oil
1 tablespoon finely minced scallions
1 teaspoon finely minced, peeled, fresh ginger root or 1 teaspoon ground ginger
½ clove garlic (or more to taste), finely minced
½ teaspoon honey
1 teaspoon vinegar
2 tablespoons water

In a glass bowl, mix all ingredients together. Marinate any kind of fish for 15 minutes. Use marinade as a basting sauce when baking.

Yield: ½ cup

GARLIC AND ROSEMARY MARINADE

¾ cup olive oil
¼ cup red wine vinegar
3 cloves garlic, slivered
1 teaspoon fresh rosemary or ½ teaspoon dried

Mix all the ingredients and let stand for 30 minutes to develop flavor before using as a marinade.

Marinate any fatty fish in this marinade for ¾ hour. Lift fish out and broil. Heat marinade to boiling point. Spoon a few tablespoonfuls over the fish after it is cooked, as a sauce, but use sparingly, as garlic and rosemary are imposing flavors.

Yield: 1 cup

Tip: This marinade is particularly good with shrimp. Make the marinade. Devein and wash the shrimp. Split each shrimp down the curve, almost through. Lay the shrimp flat in the marinade. Cover and let stand at room temperature for at least 1 hour. Broil.

HONEY AND LEMON MARINADE

¾ cup fresh lemon juice
1 tablespoon mild honey
½ teaspoon paprika
¼ teaspoon cayenne pepper
1 clove garlic, crushed

Mix all ingredients together and use as a marinade. Marinate any kind of fish for ½ hour. Lift out the fish and allow the marinade to cling to the fish. Do not dry. Broil.

Yield: ½ cup

ONION MARINADE

1 small onion, grated
1 tablespoon lemon juice
1 teaspoon paprika
½ cup olive oil
½ bay leaf, crushed
⅛ teaspoon ground cloves
1 tablespoon minced, fresh parsley

Mix ingredients together and use as a marinade. Marinate any kind of fish for ½ hour, then pour around fish in baking dish and use as a basting sauce.

Yield: ⅔ cup

ORANGE MARINADE

½ cup cider vinegar
1 bay leaf, crushed
1 teaspoon finely minced, fresh thyme or
    ½ teaspoon dried
4 tablespoons orange juice
1 tablespoon grated orange rind

Mix all ingredients. Heat to boiling. Then simmer for 1 minute. Cool and use as a marinade. Marinate any fatty fish for ¾ hour. Use the marinade as a basting sauce when the fish is either baked or broiled.

Yield: ½ cup

ORIENTAL VEGETABLE MARINADE

1 cucumber, cut into thin matchsticks
1 carrot, cut in very thin strips, 2 inches long
1 teaspoon peeled and finely minced, fresh ginger root or ½ teaspoon ground ginger
¼ cup finely minced scallions
½ cup honey
2 tablespoons peanut oil
2 cloves garlic, finely minced
½ cup tamari soy sauce
1 cup Fish Stock (see Index)

Mix all the ingredients together and simmer for 5 minutes. Cool and use as a marinade. Pour over any kind of fish and let marinate for 15 minutes. Lift out fish and dry. Cook fish by frying or sauteing. Rewarm marinade and pour over fish and use as a sauce.

Yield: 3 cups

TURKISH MARINADE

6 tablespoons olive oil
7 tablespoons lemon juice
2 tablespoons grated onion
¼ teaspoon paprika
1 bay leaf
1 tablespoon minced, fresh parsley
1 tablespoon tamari soy sauce

Mix all the ingredients together and let stand for 10 minutes before using as a marinade. Marinate any kind of fish for ½ hour. Use marinade as a basting sauce when baking fish.

Yield: 1 cup

Mayonnaise-Based Sauces

Aioli Sauce (Garlic Mayonnaise)
VARIATION
Quick Aioli
Cold Green Sauce with Sage
Cold Walnut and Garlic Mayonnaise
(Turkish Tarator Sauce)
Cresson Mayonnaise (Watercress
Mayonnaise)
Cucumber Mayonnaise Sauce with Dill
Hard-Cooked Egg Yolk and Herb Sauce
Homemade Mayonnaise
Mustard Cucumber Sauce
Remoulade Sauce (Pungent
Mayonnaise Sauce)
Sorrel Mayonnaise
Tomato Tarragon Mayonnaise
Spinach and Chive Sauce

AIOLI SAUCE
(GARLIC MAYONNAISE)

3 large cloves garlic, finely chopped
6 tablespoons lemon juice
2 eggs
½ teaspoon white pepper
1½ cups olive oil
1 whole, peeled garlic clove

In a blender, process garlic and lemon juice. Add eggs and pepper and process again at high speed. Pour oil into blender, a few drops at a time at first, while blender is going. Then gradually add oil in a steady stream.

When mixture has thickened, spoon into a bowl and refrigerate. Stir before serving and top with a whole, peeled garlic clove to identify the sauce, since it looks like plain mayonnaise, but it definitely is not.

Yield: about 2 cups

VARIATION

QUICK AIOLI

1 tablespoon finely minced, fresh garlic
1 cup Homemade Mayonnaise (see
    page 95)

Stir together until thoroughly mixed. Let sit for at least ½ hour before serving to let flavors marry.

Yield: 1 cup

COLD GREEN
SAUCE
WITH SAGE

½ cup fresh spinach, stems removed and
    finely chopped
½ cup watercress, stems removed and
    finely chopped
¼ cup finely chopped, fresh parsley
1 teaspoon crushed, dried sage
¼ teaspoon black pepper
1 tablespoon lemon juice
1 cup Homemade Mayonnaise (see
    page 95)

Mix all ingredients into the Homemade
Mayonnaise and refrigerate overnight to
develop flavor. If you have a food
processor, it can be used to mince the
greens well, and then add to the
Homemade Mayonnaise.

Yield: about 2 cups

COLD
WALNUT AND GARLIC
MAYONNAISE
(TURKISH TARATOR SAUCE)

2 cloves garlic
½ cup walnuts (pine nuts may be used)
2 slices stale, whole grain bread
3 tablespoons Homemade Mayonnaise
    (see page 95)
1 teaspoon dry mustard
¼ teaspoon black pepper
¼ cup cold water
1 tablespoon chopped, fresh parsley

In a blender or food processor, grind garlic
and nuts until very fine.

Soak bread in water and squeeze dry.

Mix mayonnaise with mustard and add the
bread and pepper.

Process all ingredients together until thick
and smooth, diluting it with the water as
necessary. Sprinkle with parsley.

Yield: 1 cup

CRESSON MAYONNAISE
(WATERCRESS MAYONNAISE)

1 cup Homemade Mayonnaise (see
    page 95)
½ cup finely minced watercress leaves
1 teaspoon lemon juice
1 teaspoon finely minced, fresh chives
⅛ teaspoon black pepper

Mix all together and chill. Serve cold.

Yield: 1 cup

CUCUMBER MAYONNAISE SAUCE WITH DILL

1 medium cucumber, peeled, seeded,
    and finely chopped
    grated rind of 1 lemon
2 scallions, green part only, finely
    minced
1 cup Homemade Mayonnaise (see
    page 95)
1 tablespoon minced, fresh dill

Mix all ingredients together and chill until
ready to use. Serve cold.

Yield: 1½ cups

HARD-COOKED EGG YOLK AND HERB SAUCE

3 hard-cooked eggs, with yolks and
    whites separated after cooking
1 teaspoon dry mustard
½ teaspoon black pepper
1 cup olive oil
1 tablespoon wine vinegar
3 tablespoons finely minced, assorted,
    mixed fresh herbs (chives, parsley,
    tarragon and chervil are the usual
    combination; if dried herbs are
    used, half the amount will do)

Mash the egg yolks with a fork, adding the
mustard and pepper until well blended.
Gradually beat in the oil with a wire
whisk. When the oil is completely
absorbed, add the vinegar and egg whites
(finely chopped) and then the rest of the
ingredients.

Blend well and let stand for 1 hour to
marry the flavors. Serve cold.

Yield: 1½ cups

HOMEMADE MAYONNAISE

2 egg yolks at room temperature
1 cup oil (¼ cup olive oil and ¾ cup
    soybean oil)
1 tablespoon lemon juice
1 teaspoon dry mustard
¼ teaspoon white pepper

Rinse a glass bowl with warm water. Beat the egg yolks well in the bowl with a wire whisk. Very slowly, a drop at a time, add ½ cup of the oil to the egg yolks beating constantly. When the mixture starts to thicken, stop to check the thickness. Add 1 teaspoon of the lemon juice to dilute. Continue beating and add the rest of the oil slowly in a steady stream.

Mix the rest of the lemon juice, the mustard, and the white pepper together and let stand for a few minutes while you remove the mayonnaise to a bowl. Stir this into the mayonnaise with a wooden spoon. Refrigerated, it will keep for at least 2 weeks in a tightly covered container.

Yield: about 1 cup

Note: 1 teaspoon of hot water added to the finished mayonnaise will help prevent it from separating.

MUSTARD CUCUMBER SAUCE

1 tablespoon dry mustard
1 tablespoon cold water
1 cup Homemade Mayonnaise (see
    above)
1 medium cucumber, peeled, seeded,
    and finely chopped
¼ teaspoon white pepper
1 tablespoon lemon juice

Mix dry mustard with cold water and let stand for 10 minutes. Add to mayonnaise and mix. Stir in cucumber, pepper, and lemon juice. Chill for 20 minutes for flavors to blend. Serve cold.

Yield: about 2 cups

REMOULADE SAUCE
(PUNGENT MAYONNAISE SAUCE)

1 cup Homemade Mayonnaise (see
    page 95)
1 tablespoon finely chopped scallions
2 teaspoons dry mustard
1 hard-cooked egg, finely chopped
2 teaspoons finely minced, fresh tarragon
    or ½ teaspoon dried
1 teaspoon lemon juice

Blend all ingredients together and chill for
1 hour or more to develop flavor.

Yield: 1 cup

SORREL MAYONNAISE

½ pound fresh sorrel, stems removed and
    leaves shredded
1 teaspoon butter
2 tablespoons finely minced, fresh chervil
    or 1 teaspoon dried
2 tablespoons finely minced, fresh
    parsley
1 hard-cooked egg, finely chopped
1 cup Homemade Mayonnaise (see
    page 95)
¼ teaspoon black pepper

Prepare sorrel and wilt in a skillet with the
butter. Stir just for a few seconds until color
changes from bright to dull green. Add the
chervil, parsley, egg, and mayonnaise and
whirl in a blender. Add the pepper and
blend all ingredients until mixed well.
Serve chilled.

Yield: 1½ cups

TOMATO TARRAGON MAYONNAISE

½ cup Basic Tomato Sauce (see page 100)
2 cups Homemade Mayonnaise (see page
    95)
1 finely minced green or red pepper
1 teaspoon minced, fresh chives
½ teaspoon minced, fresh tarragon or ⅛
    teaspoon dried

Cook the tomato sauce over moderate heat,
stirring until it is very thick and most of the
liquid has evaporated. Chill until cold.

When cold, fold into the mayonnaise and
add the pepper and herbs. Serve cold.

Yield: 2¾ cups

SPINACH AND CHIVE SAUCE

1 cup Homemade Mayonnaise (see page 95)
2 tablespoons finely chopped, fresh chives
2 tablespoons finely minced, fresh parsley
3 tablespoons chopped, cooked spinach, drained and squeezed dry
¼ teaspoon black pepper
1 teaspoon lemon juice

Combine all ingredients and mix well. Chill for 1 hour in refrigerator for flavor to develop.

Yield: 1¼ cups

Sour Cream Sauces

Dill, Cucumber Sour Cream Sauce
Mustard, Sour Cream, and Shallot Sauce

DILL, CUCUMBER SOUR CREAM SAUCE

1 cup sour cream
2 tablespoons milk
1 tablespoon finely minced, fresh dill
1 small cucumber, peeled and finely chopped
1 teaspoon grated onion
1 tablespoon finely minced, fresh chives
¼ teaspoon white pepper

Mix all ingredients together. Chill for ½ hour for flavor to develop. Serve cold, or spread on fish 5 minutes before it is finished cooking.

Yield: about 1 cup

MUSTARD, SOUR CREAM, AND SHALLOT SAUCE

2 tablespoons water
2 tablespoons dry, English mustard
1 tablespoon lemon juice
1 tablespoon finely minced shallots
    (young spring onions may be used)
¼ teaspoon white pepper
1 teaspoon finely minced, fresh tarragon
    or ¼ teaspoon dried
1 cup sour cream

Mix water and mustard and let stand for 10 minutes. Then mix all ingredients together. Chill for several hours to develop full flavor. Serve cold.

Yield: 1⅓ cups

Sour Cream-and-Mayonnaise-Based Sauces

Almond Ginger Sauce
Dill Sauce
Mustard-Horseradish Sauce
Tarragon Sauce

ALMOND GINGER SAUCE

½ cup Homemade Mayonnaise (see page 95)
½ cup sour cream
1-inch piece peeled and grated, fresh ginger root
1 tablespoon lime juice
1 teaspoon mild honey
¼ cup slivered almonds, toasted

Combine all ingredients, except almonds. Chill sauce for 1 hour in refrigerator. Stir in almonds just before serving. Serve cold.

Yield: 1 cup

DILL
SAUCE

1 cup sour cream
½ cup Homemade Mayonnaise (see page 95)
3 tablespoons minced, fresh dill
½ clove garlic, minced
1 teaspoon lemon juice
½ teaspoon white pepper

Mix all ingredients together and refrigerate for 1 hour to blend flavors. Serve cold.

Yield: 1½ cups

MUSTARD-
HORSERADISH
SAUCE

1 tablespoon dry mustard
1 tablespoon cold water
1 tablespoon horseradish, drained
1 cup sour cream
½ cup Homemade Mayonnaise (see page 95)

Mix the mustard with cold water and let stand for 10 minutes. Add mustard to horseradish.

Mix the sour cream with the mayonnaise.

Blend all ingredients. Chill for 15 minutes or more to let flavors blend.

Yield: 1½ cups

TARRAGON
SAUCE

1 cup Homemade Mayonnaise (see page 95)
½ cup sour cream
2 teaspoons dried, crushed tarragon
2 tablespoons lemon juice
1 tablespoon grated onion
¼ teaspoon white pepper

Combine all ingredients and chill for 10 minutes to develop flavor. Serve cold.

Yield: about 1⅔ cups

Tomato Sauces

Basic Tomato Sauce
Basil, Eggplant, and Tomato Sauce
Ecuadorian *Aji* Sauce (a Potent Hot Sauce)
Gazpacho Sauce (a Tomato and Raw Vegetable Sauce)
Indian Tomato Onion Sauce
***Salsa Cruda* (a Mexican Hot, Fresh, Tomato Sauce)**
Sauce *Provencale* (a Tomato-Garlic Sauce)

BASIC TOMATO SAUCE

2 tablespoons olive oil
1 small onion, finely chopped
4 green onions (scallions), finely chopped
1 clove garlic, minced
5 tomatoes, peeled and coarsely chopped
2 tablespoons Tomato Paste (see Index)
½ teaspoon finely minced, fresh oregano
 or ¼ teaspoon dried
¼ teaspoon finely minced, fresh thyme or
 ⅛ teaspoon dried
¼ teaspoon black pepper
3 tablespoons minced, fresh parsley

In a saucepan, heat olive oil and add onions. Cook until wilted, add garlic, and stir. Add tomatoes, tomato paste, and all seasoning except parsley. Cook over low heat for 30 minutes. Add parsley and stir and cook 2 minutes more.

Puree mixture in blender or food processor.

Serve hot or cold, or as a base for other sauces.

Yield: 2 cups

BASIL, EGGPLANT, AND TOMATO SAUCE

2 medium onions, coarsely chopped
3 tablespoons olive oil
2 medium eggplants, peeled and cut in ¾-inch cubes
½ cup water
1½ cups Basic Tomato Sauce (see page 100)
¼ teaspoon black pepper
1 tablespoon minced, fresh basil or 2 teaspoons dried

In a skillet, saute onion in 1 tablespoon olive oil until wilted. Remove and set aside. Add the remaining olive oil to the same skillet and heat. Add the eggplant and toss. Add the water, lower heat, and cook 10 minutes or until eggplant is soft. Remove ¼ of the eggplant cubes and reserve. Add the Basic Tomato Sauce and the reserved onion to the eggplant and simmer for 10 minutes until sauce is slightly thickened. Puree in a blender and then add the pepper, basil, and reserved eggplant cubes. Heat through and serve hot.

Yield: about 3½ cups

ECUADORIAN AJI SAUCE
(A POTENT HOT SAUCE)

1 fresh, red chili pepper—the thin, 6-inch long tapered ones
  juice of 1 lime
1 tablespoon olive oil
  water
3 sprigs parsley (or coriander), finely minced
2 scallions, white part only, finely minced

Wear rubber gloves to split and seed the hot pepper. Place in a blender and puree until very fine, with the lime juice, oil, and enough water to make the sauce thin. Remove and stir in the parsley and scallions.

Yield: ½ cup

Note: To nonnatives, this sauce may seem lethal! Use it sparingly. The Ecuadorians use it on everything and it is always on the table as a condiment. If you love hot, spicy food, this one is for you.

GAZPACHO SAUCE
(A TOMATO AND RAW VEGETABLE SAUCE)

1 cup Basic Tomato Sauce (see page 100)
2 cloves garlic, finely minced
1 onion, finely minced
1½ small, green peppers, seeded and chopped
1½ small cucumbers, peeled, seeded, and chopped
3 drops Dried Hot Pepper Sauce (see page 120)
2 tablespoons vinegar
3 tablespoons olive oil
¼ teaspoon ground cumin
¼ teaspoon finely minced, fresh oregano or ⅛ teaspoon dried
1 tomato, peeled and chopped

Combine the Basic Tomato Sauce with the garlic and onion. Reserve ¼ cup each of the green pepper and cucumber for garnish. Add the rest with the Dried Hot Pepper Sauce, vinegar, olive oil, and herbs to the sauce mixture. Mix in blender and refrigerate for several hours.

Serve cold with chopped tomato and the reserved green pepper and cucumber as a garnish.

Yield: 3 cups

INDIAN TOMATO ONION SAUCE

1 small onion
1 large tomato, peeled
1 clove garlic, minced
⅛ teaspoon ground ginger
1 teaspoon curry powder
¼ cup tomato juice
1 tablespoon vinegar

Use a blender. Blend onion, tomato, garlic, ginger, and curry powder. Mix tomato juice and vinegar and add gradually to onion mixture while blender is on.

Yield: 2 cups

SALSA CRUDA
(A MEXICAN HOT, FRESH, TOMATO SAUCE)

2 cups peeled and coarsely chopped tomatoes
2 tablespoons vinegar
½ cup finely minced onion
1 or 2 hot peppers—usually *jalapeno* type—depending on size and preference, chopped*
1 ice cube
1 tablespoon finely chopped, fresh coriander leaves

Combine all ingredients and stir until the ice cube melts. Let flavors ripen in the refrigerator for 10 minutes.

Yield: 2½ cups

*Put hot peppers on a fork and char the skin over flame (or put peppers under a broiler). Then place in a brown paper bag, close tightly, and leave until skin loosens and can be easily peeled (about 10 to 15 minutes). Remove seeds. Use rubber gloves while handling. Hot peppers' volatile oils may burn your hands.

SAUCE PROVENCALE
(A TOMATO-GARLIC SAUCE)

2 tablespoons olive oil
4 cloves garlic, minced
8 medium-size tomatoes, peeled and finely chopped
2 fresh basil leaves or ½ teaspoon dried
2 tablespoons chopped, fresh parsley
1 teaspoon fresh rosemary or ½ teaspoon dried
1 teaspoon fresh oregano or ½ teaspoon dried

Heat oil and add the garlic. Cook until soft, then add tomatoes and basil. Cover and simmer for 30 minutes. Remove basil leaves and add parsley and rest of herbs.

Yield: 3½ to 4 cups

Veloute Sauces (Thickened Fish Stock)

Basic *Veloute* Sauce
VARIATIONS
Enriched *Veloute* Sauce
Aurore Sauce (a Tomato Sauce)
Crab Meat Sauce
Shrimp Sauce
Lobster Sauce (Sauce Cardinal)
Duxelles *Veloute* (a Mushroom Sauce)
Basic Duxelles (Chopped Mushroom Sauce Base)
Seafood Shell Sauce
Mornay Sauce (with Gruyere Cheese)
Mushroom, Shrimp, and Dill Sauce
Soubise Sauce (an Onion Sauce)
Spanish Saffron *Veloute* Sauce

BASIC VELOUTE SAUCE

2 tablespoons butter
2 tablespoons whole wheat pastry flour
1 cup Fish Stock (see Index)
¼ teaspoon white pepper

Melt butter and blend in flour, stirring with a whisk. Gradually add Fish Stock and cook, stirring constantly, until it thickens, about 10 to 15 minutes. Add pepper. Serve hot.

Yield: 1 cup

VARIATIONS

ENRICHED VELOUTE SAUCE

Add:
1 cup heavy cream
3 egg yolks
To:
1 cup Basic *Veloute* Sauce (see above)

Beat cream and egg yolks together and gradually add to Basic *Veloute* Sauce. Cook, stirring over low heat until thickened. *Do not allow to boil.*

Yield: about 2 cups

AURORE SAUCE
(A TOMATO SAUCE)

Add:
½ cup Basic Tomato Sauce (see page 100)
To:
1 cup Enriched *Veloute* Sauce (see page 104)

Cook over low heat, stirring constantly. *Do not allow to boil.*

Yield: about 1½ cups

CRAB MEAT SAUCE

Add:
½ cup crab meat
⅛ teaspoon nutmeg
To:
1 cup Enriched *Veloute* Sauce (see page 104)

Mix over low heat, stirring constantly. *Do not allow to boil.*

Yield: about 1¼ cups

SHRIMP SAUCE

Add:
½ cup finely chopped, raw shrimp
1 teaspoon minced, fresh chives
To:
1 cup Basic *Veloute* Sauce (see page 104)

Put shrimp in Basic *Veloute* Sauce while cooking over low heat, stirring constantly until shrimp turn pink. *Do not allow to boil.* Remove from heat. Add chives.

Yield: about 1¼ cups

LOBSTER SAUCE
(SAUCE CARDINAL)

Add:
½ cup coarsely chopped lobster
⅛ teaspoon cayenne pepper
⅛ teaspoon paprika
To:
1 cup Enriched *Veloute* Sauce (see page 104)

Mix all ingredients over low heat, stirring constantly until lobster is heated. *Do not allow to boil.*

Yield: about 1¼ cups

DUXELLES VELOUTE
(A MUSHROOM SAUCE)

¾ cup Basic *Veloute* Sauce (see page
     104)
3 tablespoons Basic Duxelles (see below)
¼ cup Tomato Paste (see page 123)
1 teaspoon lemon juice

Heat Basic *Veloute* Sauce in top of double boiler. Add all other ingredients and cook until hot. Serve hot.

Yield: about 1 cup

BASIC DUXELLES
(CHOPPED MUSHROOM SAUCE BASE)

1 cup sliced mushrooms
2 tablespoons butter
1 small onion, finely minced
⅛ teaspoon nutmeg
¼ teaspoon black pepper

Use a food processor or blender to chop mushrooms very fine. Remove and put in a piece of cheesecloth or a man's large, linen handkerchief, twist and squeeze out the moisture.

Melt the butter and add the onion. Cook over low heat until translucent. Add the mushrooms, nutmeg, and pepper. Raise the heat, stir and cook until the moisture cooks off. Cool and store in refrigerator to add to the other sauces.

Yield: ½ cup

SEAFOOD
SHELL
SAUCE

The shells of crustaceans are full of flavor. When they are cooked with herbs and vegetables, they become the base of a beautiful coral-colored sauce that enhances the delicate flavors of white, lean fish such as flounder, sole, and other flatfish. The sauce can also be used with cooked shrimp or lobster and served over rice as a luncheon dish.

  1 left-over shell from a large lobster
    left-over shells from 1 pound of shrimp
        (uncooked and rinsed)
  2 cups water
  ¼ cup lemon juice
  1 small carrot, shredded
  1 small onion, cut in half
  2 sprigs parsley
  2 small stalks celery with leaves on, cut
        into chunks
  ½ bay leaf
  4 peppercorns
  1 whole clove
  4 tablespoons butter
  2 tablespoons whole wheat flour
  2 cups heavy cream
  1 egg yolk, beaten
  ⅛ teaspoon nutmeg
  ⅛ teaspoon paprika
  ½ teaspoon cayenne pepper

Break up the lobster shell into pieces and put into a large saucepan with the shrimp shells; add water and lemon juice. Add the carrot, onion, parsley, celery, bay leaf, peppercorns, and the clove. Bring to a boil and boil rapidly for 15 minutes.

Strain the liquid and measure it. You should have about 1 cup. If there is less than a cup, add more water. If there is more than a cup, boil it down until it measures the proper amount.

Using the top of a double boiler, melt the butter, then add the flour and stir with a wooden spoon until smooth. Gradually stir the reduced stock into the butter and flour mixture. Cook over very low heat until thick and smooth, stirring constantly with a wire whisk. This should take about 10 minutes.

Mix the cream with the egg yolk, nutmeg, paprika, and cayenne pepper and gradually add to the mixture in the top of the double boiler. Continue to cook over low heat until smooth and hot. Taste and adjust the seasoning.

Yield: 3 cups

Note: If there is any red roe or the green liver left over from the cooked lobster, add it to the sauce after the egg yolk and cream mixture have been added to the stock.

MORNAY SAUCE
(WITH GRUYERE CHEESE)

½ cup grated Gruyere cheese
1 cup Enriched *Veloute* Sauce (see page 104)
2 tablespoons milk or light cream to dilute, if necessary
⅛ teaspoon cayenne pepper

Add grated cheese to Enriched *Veloute* Sauce and cook over low heat until cheese is melted. Dilute with milk or cream, if necessary, and add the cayenne pepper.

Yield: 1 cup

Note: When a fish with this sauce is put under a broiler for a few seconds, a bubbly, browned, top crust forms—fish au gratin.

MUSHROOM, SHRIMP, AND DILL SAUCE

¼ pound small mushrooms, quartered
1 tablespoon lemon juice
2 tablespoons butter
2 tablespoons rye flour
1 cup milk
1 tablespoon finely minced, fresh dill
¼ teaspoon white pepper
½ pound shrimp, cooked, shelled, and finely chopped
½ cup heavy cream

In a small skillet, mix mushrooms with lemon juice. Cover and steam over low heat until mushrooms are wilted. Set aside.

In a saucepan, melt the butter and add the flour, stirring several minutes. Gradually add the milk and stir with a whisk until smooth and thickened over low heat. Add the mushrooms and any liquid that has accumulated. Add the dill and pepper.

Just before serving, stir in shrimp and heavy cream and heat. Serve hot.

Yield: 2 cups

SOUBISE SAUCE
(AN ONION SAUCE)

1 tablespoon butter
1 large onion, finely chopped
2 tablespoons water
1 cup Basic *Veloute* Sauce (see page 104)
½ teaspoon lemon juice

Melt butter and add onions and water. Lower heat and cover pan. Cook until onion is soft and transparent. Add to Basic *Veloute* Sauce. Heat and add lemon juice. Serve hot.

Yield: 1¼ cups

SPANISH SAFFRON VELOUTE SAUCE

1 cup Basic *Veloute* Sauce (see page 104)
½ teaspoon crushed saffron strands
1 tablespoon heavy cream
1 large tomato, peeled and finely chopped
1 teaspoon lemon juice
1 teaspoon grated onion

Heat Basic *Veloute* Sauce in top of double boiler. Mix saffron strands with cream and let stand for 5 minutes. Add to sauce with tomato, lemon juice, and onion. Simmer for 5 minutes more.

Yield: 1½ cups

Vinegar- or Lemon Juice- Based Sauces

Aioli Sauce II
Sauce *Rouille* II (a Sweet Pepper and Garlic Sauce)
Chinese Sweet and Sour Sauce
Green Sauce with Blue Cheese
Mustard-Dill Sauce
Sweet and Sour Pineapple and Vegetable Sauce
Piquant Sauce

AIOLI SAUCE II

6 cloves garlic
½ cup stale, whole grain bread, torn apart into small pieces
2 tablespoons cider vinegar
3 egg yolks
1½ cups olive oil

Put garlic through press. Moisten bread with vinegar. Process garlic and bread together in a blender until smooth—the consistency of a damp paste. Remove and reserve. Clean blade well. Add egg yolks and blend well. Slowly add oil, drop by drop, while the blender is on, until the sauce is very thick and dense. Add bread paste and mix well. Serve at room temperature.

Yield: 1 cup

SAUCE ROUILLE II
(A SWEET PEPPER AND GARLIC SAUCE)

2 thick slices stale, whole grain bread
4 tablespoons Fish Stock (see Index)
2 large, sweet red peppers, seeded
1 fresh hot pepper, peeled and seeded
2 large cloves garlic
4 tablespoons olive oil
1 teaspoon lemon juice

Soak the bread in the Fish Stock. Squeeze out excess moisture and reserve. The bread should be mushy and not too dry.

Using a food processor or blender, place the red peppers, the hot pepper, bread, and garlic in the bowl and process for 2 minutes. With the machine still running, trickle oil slowly into the mixture and then add 2 tablespoons of the reserved Fish Stock and the lemon juice.

Let stand for 1 hour to develop flavor.

Yield: 1½ cups

CHINESE SWEET AND SOUR SAUCE

¾ cup pineapple juice
¼ cup vinegar
1 tablespoon tamari soy sauce
2 tablespoons honey
1 small, sweet red pepper, seeded and cut into shreds
½ cup Fish Stock (see Index)
2 teaspoons peeled and finely minced, fresh ginger root or 2 teaspoons ground ginger
2 tablespoons cornstarch
⅓ cup water

Mix pineapple juice with vinegar, soy sauce, and honey. Add the pepper, Fish Stock, and ginger and heat to a boil in a saucepan. Mix the cornstarch and water together and add to the boiling sauce, stirring constantly with a wooden spoon. Cook for 1 minute until sauce is thick and clear.

Yield: 2 cups

GREEN SAUCE WITH BLUE CHEESE

12 fresh spinach leaves, finely chopped
    (about 2 cups)
 2 tablespoons finely minced, fresh chives
 2 tablespoons finely minced, fresh
    parsley
 1 ounce crumbled blue or Roquefort
    cheese
 4 tablespoons safflower oil
 2 tablespoons lemon juice
¼ teaspoon black pepper

Add all ingredients in a blender, and blend until smooth. Serve at room temperature.

Yield: 1 cup

MUSTARD-DILL SAUCE

3 tablespoons dry mustard
3 tablespoons water
2 tablespoons cider vinegar
1 teaspoon mild honey
6 tablespoons safflower oil
¼ teaspoon black pepper
4 tablespoons finely minced, fresh dill

Mix dry mustard with water and let stand for 20 minutes.

In a blender, put vinegar, honey, mustard, safflower oil, and pepper. Blend at high speed until well mixed, or beat well with a wire whisk.

Stir in dill and chill for 20 minutes to develop flavor.

Yield: ⅔ cup

SWEET AND SOUR PINEAPPLE AND VEGETABLE SAUCE

1 small clove garlic, minced
2 tablespoons peanut oil
½ cup mild honey
1 cup water
¾ cup vinegar
¼ cup tamari soy sauce
½ teaspoon black pepper
½-inch piece peeled and finely chopped, fresh ginger root
3 tablespoons cornstarch
2 tablespoons water
2 small, white onions, peeled and cut into quarters
2 small tomatoes, peeled and cut into quarters
1 small, green pepper, seeded and cut into strips
½ cup fresh pineapple, peeled and cut into cubes

Saute garlic in hot peanut oil until slightly tan. Mix honey with water, vinegar, and soy sauce, and add to pan. Add the black pepper and ginger and cook for 1 minute over medium heat. Mix the cornstarch with the water and add, stirring constantly until the mixture has thickened. Add the onions, tomatoes, green pepper, and pineapple. Cook for 5 minutes more until vegetables are tender, but still crisp. Serve hot.

Yield: 4 cups

PIQUANT SAUCE

½ cup peanut oil
¼ cup tarragon vinegar
1 tablespoon dry mustard
2 teaspoons horseradish root, grated (or drained, if bottled)
1 tablespoon Tomato Paste (see Index)
¼ teaspoon cayenne pepper
1 hard-cooked egg, chopped
¼ cup finely minced scallions
¼ cup finely minced celery

Using a wire whisk, beat the oil and vinegar with the mustard, horseradish, and Tomato Paste. Then add the pepper and egg. Blend until smooth.

Remove and stir in the scallions and celery. Allow to stand for 20 minutes at room temperature to develop flavor.

Yield: 1⅓ cups

Yogurt Sauces

YOGURT AND TOMATO SAUCE WITH CURRY

1 cup plain yogurt
2 shallots, finely minced (young spring onions may be used)
4 tablespoons Basic Tomato Sauce (see Index)
2 teaspoons orange juice
1 teaspoon curry powder
1 teaspoon mild honey
¼ teaspoon black pepper

Mix all ingredients together. Refrigerate until ready to use. Serve cold.

Yield: 1½ cups

YOGURT AND HORSERADISH SAUCE WITH MUSTARD SEED

1½ cups plain yogurt
3 to 4 tablespoons horseradish root, grated (or drained, if bottled)
½ teaspoon mustard seeds, toasted

Mix yogurt with horseradish.

In a small, dry, heavy skillet, toast the mustard seeds until they start to pop. Cover pan with a strainer turned upside down so the seeds won't jump out of the pan. Shake pan while toasting.

When seeds are toasted, crush and add half to sauce and sprinkle remainder on top of sauce before serving. Chill for 15 minutes to develop flavor. Serve cold.

Yield: 1¾ cups

Note: Many dieters are turning to yogurt sauces in place of sour cream sauces. They get the rich texture and flavor and they avoid the calories.

Natural Versions of Some Commercial Sauces

Too Hot to Handle

We always grow several different kinds of hot peppers in our garden at Fire Island—two plants of yellow hot peppers, two of green *jalapeno* peppers, and two of small red peppers—these few plants supply our family with enough hot peppers for an entire year. We merely dry them, string them from the ceiling, and then use a small amount for sauces and condiments. They also look quite beautiful when they hang from the rafters, an exotic decorative touch.

Any of the hot pepper sauces that follow can be used in place of bottled, commercial Tabasco Sauce for a better, purer, more interesting flavor. Throughout South America and Mexico these sauces are served in sauce boats right at the table. They should be used most sparingly to pick up and enhance the taste of certain foods. In South America, the *yellow* peppers are made into a sauce called *marisol,* and the red chilies become *salsa piquante* or *aji.*

Fresh chili peppers can add pungency and give an extra lift and zest to otherwise bland food. They're also a natural aid to digestion, since they stimulate the gastric juices, make you salivate, and thus help you get the most benefit from what you eat. Some countries, like Hungary, dry and grind their peppers into a powder to produce paprika, a seasoning that comes in a variety of flavors ranging from sweet to hot. Cayenne pepper is another form of powdered hot chili pepper. The large, sweet red and green peppers are also mild forms of the same family.

Generally, the larger the pepper, the *milder* it is; the smaller the pepper, the *hotter* it is. Keep in mind that there are volatile oils in the hot chili peppers, so wear rubber gloves and be careful not to touch your face and eyes with your fingers while you work with them.

Preparing Chili Peppers

Cut off the tops of the peppers, then cut them in half lengthwise, using only the tip of a sharp knife. Brush out the seeds and rinse the peppers under cold water. They may be used at once or soaked in cold water for one hour to make them milder.

Dried chili peppers are prepared in exactly the same way, but they must be soaked in cold water for at least three hours to reconstitute them. They may also be used crushed-dry and then sprinkled over the food.

If you are not used to hot, peppery food, proceed with caution and remember that a little goes a long way.

CHINESE HOT PEPPER OIL

2 heaping tablespoons dried, red, hot
   chili peppers
½ cup peanut oil

Grind hot chili peppers to a powder in a coffee grinder or a blender. Heat oil over high heat, add powdered chili peppers and cook for 1 minute. Let oil cool and pour into a bottle to keep and use when needed. Keep in refrigerator.

Use to spark sauces or add a few drops to the cooking oil when frying fish.

Yield: ½ cup

CORIANDER CHUTNEY WITH YOGURT
(AN INDIAN CONDIMENT FOR FISH)

3 tablespoons shredded fresh coconut
¾ cup plain yogurt
1 bunch fresh Chinese parsley (or
   cilantro)
2 small, green, hot chili peppers, seeded
½ teaspoon tamari soy sauce
½ teaspoon honey
1 teaspoon lemon juice

Mix the coconut and yogurt together and let stand at room temperature for 1 hour. Then place all the ingredients in a blender and blend at high speed until pureed. Add more lemon juice, if necessary. Chill in refrigerator for 1 hour before serving.

Yield: about 1 cup

COCONUT
MILK

2 coconuts
  enough milk to make 3 cups of liquid
    when combined with coconut milk

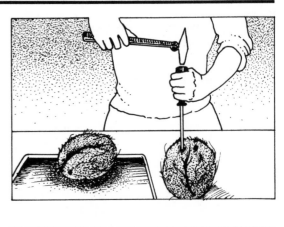

To Open a Coconut: Puncture two "eyes" at the end of the coconut with a screwdriver. You may have to tap the top of the screwdriver lightly with a hammer. Pour off the liquid into a cup, strain, and reserve. Add enough milk to the coconut liquid to make 3 cups, stir and set aside.

Preheat the oven to 375°F.

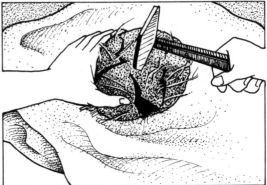

Place the coconuts in a shallow pan and bake for 20 minutes in order to loosen the meat from the shell. Place a folded towel on the bottom of your kitchen sink and place the coconuts on top of it. Tap the shell all over with a hammer, then crack open and pry the meat from the shell. It should come away easily when you insert a flexible knife between meat and shell. Use a swivel-bladed vegetable peeler to cut off the thin, brown skin from the white meat. This, too, should come off easily.

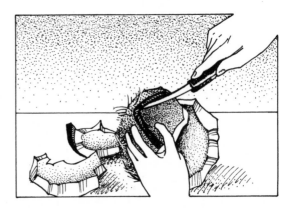

Rinse the meat under cold water and cut it into cubes. There should be about 3 to 3½ cups (depending upon size of coconuts). Heat the liquid in a saucepan just to the boiling point. Using an electric blender, puree 1/3 of the coconut cubes with 1/3 of the hot liquid at high speed for 1 minute.

Pour into a large pitcher and continue to blend the remaining liquid and coconut cubes. Let the puree stand in a pitcher for 30 minutes, then line a strainer with a double thickness of cheesecloth and place over a bowl. Pour the liquid and coconut mixture from the pitcher through, then squeeze and twist the cloth hard to extract all the milk from it. Discard the pulp.

Refrigerate until ready to use. If you like, you can also freeze this coconut milk. When freshly made, it will keep for several hours if refrigerated—when frozen, it will keep for about 3 weeks.

Yield: 3 to 3½ cups

VARIATION

COCONUT CREAM

3 coconuts
   enough water to make 3 cups of liquid
      when combined with coconut milk

Follow the procedure for Coconut Milk, but refrigerate mixture for 4 hours. Skim off the "cream" that rises to the top as coconut cream.

Yield: about 1 to 1½ cups

DRIED HOT PEPPER SAUCE

If you live in an area where you can only get *dried* red chili peppers, try this recipe as a substitute for commercial Tabasco Sauce.

½ cup dried, hot Japanese chili peppers (called *hontaka*)
1½ cups boiling water
3 tablespoons olive oil
½ small clove garlic, finely minced

Use rubber gloves! Break each dried chili pepper in half and shake out the seeds. If all seeds don't come out, rinse under cold running water. Put the dried chili peppers in a small bowl and add only 1 cup of the boiling water. Let soak for 3 hours, then drain in a strainer, and discard the soaking water. (If you don't have rubber gloves, wash your hands well after handling the peppers. Don't rub your eyes!)

Combine the chili peppers, oil, and garlic and the remaining ½ cup of boiling water. Blend for 1 minute at high speed in a blender, or until a smooth puree is formed. This paste will keep for months when closed tightly in a jar and refrigerated. To use, dilute with cold water—½ teaspoon of paste to ½ cup cold water (or use more water for a milder concoction).

Yield: 1 cup

Note: There are literally hundreds of different types of peppers available in the markets around the world, including many other varieties of dried, red chili peppers. The Latin American markets, in particular, display samples of red "dynamite" that are not grown anywhere else, and almost any of them can be used in dishes calling for hot peppers. The Japanese variety called for in this recipe is widely available in many parts of the United States and in Canadian markets.

FRESH HOT CHILI PEPPER LIQUID
(A SUBSTITUTE FOR COMMERCIAL TABASCO SAUCE)

1 or 2 tablespoons peeled, seeded, and minced fresh hot chili peppers*
1 teaspoon grated onion
¼ teaspoon finely minced garlic
3 tablespoons white wine vinegar or cider vinegar
¼ cup cold water
½ teaspoon tamari soy sauce
1 tablespoon olive oil

Combine chili peppers, onion, and garlic at high speed in a blender for 1 minute.

In a saucepan (not metal—use enamel or glass) bring the vinegar, water, and soy sauce to a boil. Pour the hot, diluted vinegar into the blender over the chili pepper mixture and blend for 1 minute more. Pour into a tightly covered glass jar or bottle that has been sterilized first. Pour oil on top, refrigerate, and use sparingly. It will keep well for a month or more.

*If you prefer a hotter sauce, use 2 tablespoons of the chili peppers, but we suggest that you make the sauce using 1 tablespoon first and then you can always adjust and add more if it's not hot enough for you.

PIRIPIRI OIL

This very peppery oil is used as a seasoning agent on fish. It can also be used with poultry, meat, or eggs as well, but use it very sparingly. It is hot!

¼ cup small, fresh, hot chili peppers
1 cup vegetable oil (peanut, olive or corn oil)
1 bay leaf
1 slice lemon rind

Remove stem ends of the peppers and discard. Place the peppers in a sterilized glass jar with a tightly fitting lid. Pour in the oil and add the bay leaf and lemon rind. Close bottle tightly and store for 1 month at room temperature.

Yield: 1 cup

HOMEMADE KETCHUP

1 pound tomatoes, cut in quarters
1 medium shallot, coarsely chopped
(young spring onion may be used)
1 medium clove garlic, chopped
¾ cup red wine vinegar
2 teaspoons finely minced, fresh thyme or
1 teaspoon dried
1 tablespoon chopped, fresh parsley
1 tablespoon chopped, fresh chervil or 2
teaspoons dried
2 teaspoons finely minced, fresh oregano
or 1 teaspoon dried
1 small bay leaf
1 teaspoon honey
¼ teaspoon black pepper

Using a food processor or blender, combine and chop the tomatoes, shallot, and garlic. Cook in a saucepan over moderate heat for 10 minutes, then force through a strainer, crushing the solids against the sides of the strainer back into the saucepan. Cook again, stirring frequently, for 15 to 20 minutes until a thick puree is formed and the tomato mixture is reduced to less than 1 cup. Stir constantly toward the end so that the tomatoes do not burn. Remove from heat.

In a small, heavy saucepan, combine vinegar and herbs. Bring to a boil and cook until reduced to 2 tablespoons. Strain and set aside.

Put honey in heavy pan and cook over low heat for 5 minutes, remove from heat, and add the reduced vinegar and herb mixture. Pour in the tomato puree and season with pepper to taste.

Yield: 1 cup

SAMBAL KETJAP
(AN INDONESIAN SOY SAUCE CONDIMENT)

½ cup tamari soy sauce
1 teaspoon dried, crushed, hot chili
    peppers
1 clove garlic, crushed and finely minced
1 teaspoon molasses

Combine ingredients and let stand for a few hours to develop flavor. Can be stored at room temperature.

Use as a condiment with any simply fried, broiled, or baked fish.

Yield: ¾ cup

TOMATO PASTE

4 tomatoes, pureed (about 2 cups)

Pour pureed tomatoes into a large skillet and cook over low heat, stirring occasionally, until liquid has boiled off leaving a thick tomato paste (about 1½ hours).

Yield: about ½ cup

Part 4: Soups, Stews, Bisques, and Chowders

Fish Brews to Delight the Senses

At our house, the freezer is always overflowing with containers of Fish Stock (see Index). We cannot pass up a fish skeleton, head, or scraps of meat left over after filleting. Our fisher friends have also learned to drop off the remains of their catch, whether it be *striped bass* or *weakfish*. The pot boils, the vegetables are prepared, and the cauldron yields a never-ending supply of the basic ingredients for superb soups, stews, bisques, and chowders. In fact, as this chapter was being written, our friend Ernie dropped an early morning skeleton from an 11½-pound weakfish on our doorstep and the freezer is richer by ten cups of stock.

Great fish soups and stews should develop spontaneously from what is regional and seasonal. In that way you'll be using only the freshest fish and seafood rather than frozen fish, and the resultant flavors will be more delicate and more briny. If you like, you may substitute other fish for those selected in the recipes, but just keep in mind which fish are lean and which are fatty (see Index).

For recipes that serve six, you should use a six-quart soup pot or Dutch oven to prevent overflow. Make sure the pot is heavy weight to insure even heat without burning. (See Index under "Equipment" for other utensils that may be used for cooking and serving.)

Incidentally, if your family is too small to finish six servings at one meal, it's good to know that all of the recipes given here freeze well for future dining. Next to our supply of Fish Stock (see Index), we also have a bounty of various left-over stews and soups for quick lunches and unexpected guests.

Soups, Stews, Bisques, and Chowders 125

The Fish in Bouillabaisse

Since the names of fish vary so much (as you have no doubt discovered), we list below, in French, the fish used in Bouillabaisse, and then we provide the equivalent in English, or suggest a fish that will do just as well in this most marvelous of seafood dishes.

rouget	goatfish or red mullet
merlan	whiting
St. Pierre	John Dory
grondin	sea robin
rascasse	sculpin or rockfish
congre	conger eel
lotte	burbot
vive	tautog or blackfish

BOUILLABAISSE AMERICAN STYLE WITH ROUILLE

The various ingredients used and the different methods of preparing this elegant soup-stew from the Marseilles area of France have provoked national conflict. Rather than join the controversy, this American version was created to make use of the fish that are plentiful in this part of the world.

A cup of wine is used in the French version. We substitute lemon juice in this recipe.

A zesty condiment called *Rouille* is passed and added at the table. Although this recipe looks long and elaborate, it takes no more than 40 to 45 minutes to cook after all the ingredients have been assembled and prepared.

ROUILLE

 1 small, sweet red pepper, seeded and coarsely chopped
 2 small, fresh, hot chili peppers, seeded
 3 cloves garlic
⅓ cup olive oil
¼ cup broth from the Bouillabaisse, hot
 1 egg yolk, beaten
¼ cup dry, whole grain bread crumbs

Combine all ingredients in a blender and process until smooth. Let stand at room temperature for 30 minutes or more to develop and blend flavors.

THE SOUP

⅓ cup olive oil
 2 cloves garlic, coarsely chopped
 2 large onions, coarsely chopped
 2 to 3 medium leeks, washed well and thinly sliced
 4 large tomatoes, peeled and cut into cubes
¼ cup plus 2 tablespoons finely minced, fresh parsley
 1 teaspoon finely minced, fresh thyme or ½ teaspoon dried
½ teaspoon dried summer savory
½ teaspoon fresh rosemary or ¼ teaspoon dried
 1 bay leaf
 1 teaspoon crushed saffron strands
1-to-3-inch strip of orange rind, white scraped off
½ teaspoon crushed fennel seed
¼ teaspoon black pepper
¼ teaspoon Dried Hot Pepper Sauce (see Index)

 2 pounds assorted *firm-fleshed* fish, such as halibut, scrod or cod, haddock, red snapper, monkfish, tilefish, or sculpin, cleaned, dressed, and sliced into 1½-inch slices
1½ pounds eel, skinned, boned, and cut into small chunks
 6 cups boiling Fish Stock (see Index)
 4 cups boiling water (or more to cover) juice of 2 lemons
 2 pounds assorted *soft-fleshed* fish, such as sole, mullet, whiting, perch, or sea trout, cleaned, dressed, and cut into 1½-inch slices
 1 lobster, about 1¼ pounds, with shell left on, chopped with a cleaver into 2-inch pieces
½ pound shrimp, shelled and deveined, with tails left on

Please turn the page for procedure.

Heat olive oil in large, stove-to-table pot, about 8 to 10 quarts (to avoid spillover). Add garlic, onions, and leeks. Saute slowly for 8 minutes, stirring occasionally until soft. Add the tomatoes and cook 5 minutes more. Add the 2 tablespoons parsley, thyme, savory, rosemary, bay leaf, saffron, orange rind, fennel seed, pepper, and Dried Hot Pepper Sauce and stir.

Lay the firm-fleshed fish in a layer over the vegetables and also tuck in the pieces of eel. Add the boiling Fish Stock and water to cover and the lemon juice. Cover pot and bring to a boil. Then uncover pot and cook over medium heat for 5 minutes. Then add the soft-fleshed fish and pieces of lobster and shrimp. (If more water is necessary, add it now.) Simmer for 10 minutes more, and test fish to see if it needs additional cooking time. Sprinkle with the remaining ¼ cup parsley.

Saute thick slices of whole grain bread in olive oil until dry and crisp.

Arrange fish on a platter and pass the vegetable-rich broth to be ladled out over the fish in individual bowls. The toasted bread can be served in a basket or floated on top if you wish. Pass the *Rouille* at the table.

Serves 10 to 12

A Tale of Bouillabaisse

There are places in the world that we have been trying to get to for years. The Statue of Liberty, even though it lies within two miles of our home, is one attraction that we have yet to visit. Another is Niagara Falls, though we have been within three miles of the roaring water twice in our travels. The most frustrating "miss," however, has been Marseilles. We, who love Bouillabaisse in all its forms, who have cooked it ourselves, tried it in restaurants in France, Belgium, and the United States, have *never* eaten it in Marseilles, its national home. On three recent trips to France, we have come within ten miles of the city and we could practically smell the aroma wafting past our car. But business and deadlines prevented us from getting there. One day, we will certainly go—and on that day we will order Bouillabaisse—and we are certain that it will be like no other Bouillabaisse anywhere else in the world!

CARIBBEAN
CODFISH-HEAD STEW
WITH BEANS AND VEGETABLES

5- to 6-pound codfish head, eyes and
    gills removed—the fish head can
    be cut into 4-inch chunks
2 quarts Court Bouillon (see Index)
1 bay leaf
    juice of 1 lemon
4 peppercorns
2 sprigs parsley
½ cup cooked chick-peas
1 cup cooked navy or pea beans
½ cup cooked lima beans
2 medium-size potatoes, peeled and
    diced into 1-inch cubes
1 small, yellow turnip or rutabaga,
    peeled and diced into 1-inch cubes
2 onions, coarsely chopped
2 stalks celery, sliced ½ inch thick
½ of small cabbage, coarsely chopped
2 small, yellow, unpeeled summer
    squashes, cut into 1-inch slices
2 ears young, fresh corn, husked and
    broken into 1½-inch pieces
⅔ cup fresh, green peas
1 bunch watercress, coarsely cut
    Indian Tomato Onion Sauce (see Index)

Add the fish head to the Court Bouillon in a large, 8-quart soup pot. Then add the bay leaf, lemon juice, peppercorns, and parsley. Bring to a boil. Lower heat and simmer for 20 minutes. Then strain.

Let the fish cool to the touch. Pick off the fish from the bones and reserve. Pour ½ cup of the broth over the reserved fish and refrigerate while the soup cooks.

Return the rest of the liquid to the pot and add the chick-peas, navy or pea beans, lima beans, potatoes, turnip, onions, and celery. Bring to a boil, lower heat, and simmer for 15 minutes. Then add the cabbage, summer squashes, and corn and simmer for 8 more minutes. Add the green peas and the fish. Cook for 3 minutes. Add the watercress on top. Cover pot and cook for 1 to 2 minutes until the watercress is wilted and the fish is heated through.

Serve with Indian Tomato Onion Sauce, to be added at the table so each person can season the soup to taste.

Serves 6 to 8

CHINESE
HOT AND SOUR
WHOLE FISH SOUP

6 dried Chinese mushrooms (½ pound
    small, whole, button mushrooms
    may be used)
5 cups water
8 peppercorns
½ cup rice wine vinegar
1 onion, sliced
1 whole, scaled, gutted fish, about 3½
    pounds, with head on (sea trout,
    bream, mullet, snapper, or sea bass)
2 cloves garlic
3 dried, hot chili peppers
1 tablespoon tamari soy sauce
1 tablespoon cornstarch
1 tablespoon water
1 egg, beaten
1 green scallion, sliced

Soak the dried mushrooms in lukewarm water to cover for 1 hour. Drain, reserve, and strain liquid; remove stems and discard. Then slice the tops of the mushrooms into ¼-inch slices.

In a large, oval pot or roaster, add the water, peppercorns, vinegar, and onion. Bring to a boil. Add the whole fish. Reduce the heat, cover, and simmer for 15 minutes, or until fish flakes. Remove fish from pot, bone and reserve. Crush the garlic with the hot chilies and add the soy sauce. Mix the cornstarch and water and add to the garlic-chili mixture. Blend well and add to the pot. Add the mushrooms and reserved liquid or the tiny, fresh mushrooms and simmer for 5 minutes more.

Let the beaten egg trickle slowly into the hot soup. Sprinkle soup with the green scallions.

Serve the soup and fish at the same time but in separate bowls.

Serves 6

CIOPPINO

This seafood soup is the California version of the Italian fisherman's answer to the French fisherman's Bouillabaisse. In ethnic communities, 2 cups of dry, red wine would be added to this soup, in place of the vinegar and water.

¼ cup olive oil
1 large onion, finely chopped
1 green pepper, finely chopped
3 to 4 cloves garlic, minced
¼ pound mushrooms, thinly sliced
6 to 8 fresh, coarsely chopped plum
   tomatoes, or a 1-pound, 10-ounce
   can Italian plum tomatoes
2 cups Fish Stock (see Index)
2 cups water
¼ cup vinegar
1 small lemon, thinly sliced
4 tablespoons Tomato Paste (see Index)
½ cup finely minced, fresh parsley
2 tablespoons fresh basil, leaves
   shredded, or ½ teaspoon dried
1 teaspoon finely minced, fresh oregano
   or ½ teaspoon dried
1 small bay leaf
¼ teaspoon black pepper
2 pounds sea bass and halibut fillets, cut
   into 2-inch pieces
½ pound shrimp, shelled and deveined
1 Dungeness crab, broken into pieces, or
   ½ pound lump crab meat, picked
   over to remove cartilage
2 lobster tails, cut into 1-inch-wide pieces
   and left in shells

Heat olive oil in an 8-quart, heavy soup pot. Add onion, pepper, and garlic. Stir and saute over medium heat until soft. Add the mushrooms and stir and cook for 1 minute. Then add the plum tomatoes, Fish Stock, water, and vinegar. Bring to a boil. Lower heat and add the sliced lemon.

Spoon out ½ cup of the broth, mix with the Tomato Paste, and return to the pot. Add ¼ cup parsley, the basil, oregano, bay leaf, and pepper. Simmer for 25 to 30 minutes. Add the fish fillets and simmer for 5 minutes. Then add the shrimp, crab, and lobster tails. Cook for 8 minutes more, and test to see if cooked through. Sprinkle with remaining parsley.

Serve ladled out evenly in large, deep, soup bowls. Serve with a crusty, whole grain, sourdough bread.

Serves 6 to 8

COLD ARABIC FISH STEW
WITH SWEET RED PEPPERS

1½ pounds mackerel steaks, skinned
       (kingfish or bluefish can be used)
¼ cup olive oil
1 large onion, chopped
1½ sweet red peppers, seeded and cut
       into thin strips
3 cloves garlic, minced
2 cups Fish Stock (see Index)
2 tablespoons chopped, fresh coriander
       leaves
⅛ teaspoon ground cumin
2 tablespoons lemon juice plus the
       grated rind of 1 lemon
⅛ teaspoon Dried Hot Pepper Sauce (see
       Index)

Put the fish steaks into olive oil, heated in a very hot skillet; then lower heat and fry for 3 to 5 minutes on both sides until almost cooked through. Remove with a slotted spoon and set aside.

In the same skillet, add the onions, red peppers, and the garlic. Cook, stirring until the onions and peppers are soft, but not brown. Heat the Fish Stock and add the fish and onion and pepper mixture. Sprinkle with the chopped coriander, cumin, and lemon juice. Simmer for 2 minutes and add the pepper sauce. Spoon into a serving dish and chill for several hours. Serve cold with the lemon rind sprinkled over all.

Serves 6

COLD LOBSTER, CUCUMBER, AND YOGURT SOUP

4 cups plain yogurt, beaten lightly with a
       whisk
2 cups cold water
1 medium cucumber, peeled and
       chopped
3 cooked lobster tails (about 1 pound),
       removed from the shells and cut
       into 1-inch pieces
½ cup finely minced scallions
¼ teaspoon white pepper
2 tablespoons finely minced, fresh mint
1 teaspoon lemon juice
1 tablespoon raisins
½ cup boiling water
⅛ teaspoon allspice
6 sprigs mint for garnish

Mix yogurt with cold water. Add the chopped cucumber. Add the cooked lobster.

In a separate bowl, stir the scallions, pepper, mint, and lemon juice together. Add to the yogurt mixture.

Put the raisins into a cup and pour boiling water over them. When they are softened and plumped, add to the soup along with scallion mixture. Add allspice and chill soup for several hours to blend flavors. Serve ice cold with a sprig of mint.

Serves 6

COLD
SHRIMP AND TOMATO
BISQUE

1 pound shrimp, shelled and deveined
   (reserve shells)
3½ cups Fish Stock (see Index)
4 tablespoons softened butter
1 cup whole grain bread crumbs
1 whole onion, peeled and stuck with a
   whole clove
1 bay leaf
1 tablespoon Tomato Paste (see Index)
2 cups milk
1 cup heavy cream
2 egg yolks
¼ teaspoon white pepper
⅛ teaspoon nutmeg
   lemon wedges for garnish

Tie reserved shells in a cheesecloth bag. Split three or four shrimp lengthwise for garnish, depending on number to be served; reserve them. Puree the rest of the shrimp with 2 cups of heated stock in a food processor or blender. Add the butter to the shrimp in the processor or blender and blend. Pour ½ cup heated Fish Stock over the bread crumbs. Let soften, squeeze dry, and add to the blender. In a large, 6-quart pot, heat the remaining Fish Stock, the onion, bay leaf, and reserved shrimp shells and the shrimp garnish to boil. Lower heat and after simmering for 2 minutes, lift out shrimp garnish and reserve; then continue cooking for 15 minutes more.

Strain broth and return to pot. Add the shrimp, butter, and bread crumb mixture from the blender to the stock. Add the Tomato Paste and stir. Cook for 5 minutes. Add the milk and cream and simmer for 5 minutes.

Return soup to food processor or blender and puree, a few batches at a time, and return to pot again. Heat and slowly add the egg yolks, beating with a whisk. Cook for 1 minute more. Add pepper and nutmeg.

Chill soup until cold and float the halved, cooked shrimp garnish on top with an extra grating of nutmeg. Serve with lemon wedges.

Serves 6 to 8

FRENCH PROVINCIAL BOURRIDE

This is a Mediterranean-style feast, redolent with a garlic sauce and more to be passed at the table. The difference between *Bourride* and Bouillabaisse is that *Bourride* has no shellfish and has a garlic-mayonnaise sauce *(Aioli)* that is added. Bouillabaisse has a red pepper condiment, *Rouille*, that is used with it. Again, the French traditionally use 2 cups of white wine in place of 2 of the 8 cups of water.

4 to 6 Italian plum tomatoes, fresh or canned, peeled and coarsely chopped
1 large onion, finely chopped
1 small clove garlic, finely minced
1 bay leaf
½ teaspoon finely minced, fresh thyme or ¼ teaspoon dried
1 strip (each ½-inch wide) orange and lemon rind
⅛ teaspoon crushed saffron strands
2 tablespoons olive oil
8 cups water
2½ pounds assorted small fish, such as monkfish, porgy, butterfish, smelts, and the like, cleaned, dressed, and cut into 2-inch pieces
2 egg yolks
1 cup *Aioli* Sauce (see Index)
6 slices whole grain bread, cut ½ inch thick, sauteed in olive oil until golden

Use a 6-quart, heavy pot. Add the tomatoes, onion, garlic, herbs, orange and lemon rinds, saffron, olive oil, and water. Bring to a rolling boil. Reduce the heat to simmer and add the pieces of fish. Simmer covered for 12 to 15 minutes.

In a mixing bowl, beat the egg yolks well with a whisk. Ladle out 1 cup of the liquid from the pot and gradually pour the hot broth into the yolks, beating constantly.

With a slotted spoon, lift out the fish and transfer to a serving bowl.

Strain the broth into a soup tureen. Add the egg yolk mixture to the broth and whisk it for a few seconds to blend. Then add ½ cup of the *Aioli* Sauce to this broth.

Serve the soup ladled over the toast and pass the fish separately with the rest of the *Aioli* Sauce.

Serves 6

ITALIAN PASTA, LETTUCE, AND FISH SOUP

This thick and hearty soup-stew is a wonderful, whole summer meal when green, leafy vegetables are in season. You can use lettuce such as romaine, escarole, spinach, or even Swiss chard. Any kind of fish that is in season can be used as well.

¼ cup olive oil
3 cloves garlic, finely minced
1 medium onion, finely chopped
½ small, fresh, red chili pepper, seeded
1 carrot, finely chopped
1 stalk celery with leaves, finely chopped
1 leek, washed and finely chopped
2 leaves fresh basil, finely chopped, or ½ dried leaf basil
1 bay leaf
1 large potato, peeled and cut into ½-inch cubes
6 to 8 fresh, coarsely chopped plum tomatoes, or a 1-pound, 10-ounce can Italian plum tomatoes
4 cups Fish Stock (see Index)
2 cups water
¼ pound whole wheat pasta, such as spaghetti, broken into pieces, or small macaroni
1 pound any kind of fish fillets, such as sea trout or striped bass, cut into 1½-inch pieces
2 cups any fresh, green, broadleaf vegetables, shredded
½ cup finely minced, fresh parsley
½ cup grated Parmesan cheese

Heat oil in bottom of heavy 6-quart pot. Add garlic and cook until soft. If you have a food processor or blender, use it to chop the onion, chili pepper, carrot, celery, and leek together and add to the oil. Stir and cook over medium heat until wilted. Add the basil, bay leaf, the cubed potato, and tomatoes and stir. Add the Fish Stock and water. Bring to a boil, lower heat, and simmer for 10 minutes. Remove the bay leaf. Add the pasta and cook for 10 minutes more. Add the fish and continue to simmer for 8 minutes. Then add the shredded, leafy greens, stir carefully, and cook 3 minutes. Sprinkle with the parsley and cheese right before serving. Additional cheese can be passed at the table.

Serves 6 to 8

NEW ENGLAND
SCROD CHOWDER

A *chaudiere* is a kind of French kettle or cauldron. The French settlers who came to Newfoundland and then down the coast to New England were fishermen who brought with them these *chaudieres*. It was the custom for each fisherman to contribute part of his catch to the community pot. Vegetables were added to complete this soup. Eventually *chaudiere* became the word "chowder," the popular fish soup we enjoy in America today.

```
 3  tablespoons butter
 2  large onions, coarsely chopped
2½  cups peeled and diced potatoes
 2  pounds scrod fillets, cut into 2½-inch
      pieces (any firm white-fleshed fish,
      such as cod or halibut can be used
      as well)
 2  cups boiling Fish Stock (see Index)
 1  cup heavy cream
 3  cups whole milk
¼  teaspoon hot paprika, or ⅛ teaspoon
      paprika and ⅛ teaspoon cayenne
      pepper
 1  teaspoon finely minced, fresh thyme
      or ½ teaspoon dried
¼  teaspoon white pepper
 1  teaspoon finely minced, fresh tarragon
      or ¼ teaspoon dried
```

In a large pot heat the butter and saute onions in it until wilted. Add the potatoes and stir with a wooden spoon. Layer the fish over the potato-onion mixture and pour the boiling Fish Stock gently over and bring to a boil. Reduce heat, cover, and simmer for 10 minutes. Add the cream, milk, paprika, thyme, pepper, and tarragon. Cover and simmer for 10 minutes more or until potatoes are tender. Serve piping hot.

Serves 6 to 8

PERUVIAN
SHRIMP AND SEA BASS STEW
WITH POACHED EGGS

2 tablespoons butter
1 medium onion, finely chopped
½ teaspoon hot, dried, chili pepper, crushed
1 large clove garlic, finely minced
2 large tomatoes, peeled and cut into chunks
2 tablespoons Tomato Paste (see Index)
1 teaspoon finely minced, fresh marjoram or ½ teaspoon dried
1 small bay leaf, crushed
10 whole, small, new potatoes
2 tablespoons uncooked brown rice
5 cups boiling water
2½ pounds sea bass fillets, skinned and cut into 1½-inch chunks (sea trout or striped bass can also be used)
1½ dozen shrimp, shelled and deveined
2 ears young, fresh corn, husked and broken into 2-inch pieces
1 cup fresh or frozen green peas
¼ cup small curd cottage cheese
2 cups light cream
6 to 8 eggs, depending on number to be served
½ cup pimiento or sweet red pepper, rinsed, dried on paper, and coarsely chopped

In a skillet heat butter and when hot, add onion, hot pepper, garlic, tomatoes, paste, herbs, potatoes, and rice. Stir and cook for a few minutes and then add boiling water. Bring to a boil, lower heat, and simmer for 15 minutes. Add the fish, shrimp, and corn and cook for 5 minutes more. Add the peas and cook for 5 minutes, or until potatoes are done. Add the cottage cheese and cream and bring soup just under boiling.

Poach the eggs in boiling water.

Ladle the soup with seafood and vegetables into deep, individual bowls, top each with a poached egg, and sprinkle with pimiento or sweet red pepper.

Serves 6 to 8

SMALL FISH, BIG FISH SOUP

This Spanish soup is thickened with bread and sparked with orange. Traditionally, Spaniards add ¼ cup of brandy, flamed and poured into the soup at the end.

3 tablespoons tamari soy sauce
1½ pounds assorted small fish, such as butterfish, ciscos, smelts, crappies, and the like, cleaned, dressed, but left whole
1½ pounds assorted larger fish, such as haddock, halibut, hake, cod, mullet, or similar fish, cleaned, dressed, and cut into 2-inch pieces
3 tablespoons olive oil
3 cloves garlic, crushed
1 large onion, finely chopped
2 cups boiling water
4 cups boiling Fish Stock (see Index)
1 bay leaf
8 peppercorns
⅔ cup whole grain bread crumbs
¼ cup orange juice
¼ cup lemon juice
1 tablespoon grated orange rind
1 teaspoon grated lemon rind

Pour soy sauce over fish and let marinate in the refrigerator for 1½ hours. Then drain and pat dry.

Heat the oil in a 6-quart soup pot and saute crushed garlic until it gets slightly tan. Do not let it burn or it will be bitter. Remove garlic with a slotted spoon and add the onion. Saute until wilted. Add the boiling water and the boiling stock. Tie bay leaf and peppercorns together in a cheesecloth bag, and cook over high heat for 5 minutes. Reduce heat, add fish, cover pot, and simmer for about 10 minutes or until fish is cooked. Remove cheesecloth bag.

While fish is cooking, mix the bread crumbs with the orange and lemon juice and the grated rinds until it becomes a sort of paste. Add to soup and stir gently. Cook for 1 more minute. Serve hot.

Serves 6 to 8

VIETNAMESE SWEET AND SOUR SOUP

1 tablespoon mild honey
1½ cups fresh pineapple, cut into small cubes
4 tablespoons peanut oil
1 large onion, finely minced
3 scallions, thinly sliced
1 large clove garlic, finely minced
3 star anise pods* or 1 teaspoon anise seed, crushed
1 bay leaf
⅛ teaspoon Dried Hot Pepper Sauce (see Index)
1 tablespoon grated tangerine or orange rind
¼ teaspoon crushed saffron strands
3 tablespoons cider vinegar
8 cups water
1 pound fish fillets, such as snook, red snapper, or sea bass, cut into 1½-inch pieces
1 pound shrimp, shelled and deveined, with tails left on (reserve shells)
2 tablespoons tamari soy sauce
2 tablespoons cornstarch

Pour the honey over the pineapple cubes and toss. Set aside.

Heat the oil in a 6-quart soup pot and add the onion, scallions, and garlic. Stir and cook for 5 minutes. Add the anise, bay leaf, Dried Hot Pepper Sauce, grated rind, saffron, vinegar, and water. Bring to a boil. Add the fish and shrimp. Then add the shrimp shells which have been tied in a cheesecloth bag. Lower heat and cook, covered, for 8 minutes.

Mix the soy sauce and cornstarch into a paste and stir into the soup. Add the pineapple. Stir until soup is clear and slightly thickened, about 2 to 3 minutes or more. Add more Dried Hot Pepper Sauce to taste. Remove cheesecloth bag, bay leaf, and star anise pods, if used.

Serve hot over cooked, brown rice.

Serves 6

*Star anise pods can be bought in shops that sell Oriental groceries.

Part 5: Stuffings For Fish

Basic Techniques for Stuffing Fish

Stuffing a Whole Fish

1. Wash and dry a gutted, whole fish with paper towels. Cut a still deeper pocket in the body cavity by slicing almost to the tail section.

2. Prepare stuffing. (See Index for various recipes for stuffing fish.)

3. Sprinkle lemon juice in cavity of fish and add the stuffing.

4. Insert small, oiled, metal skewers through both sides of the fish and lace and tie like a boot, using heavy white cord.

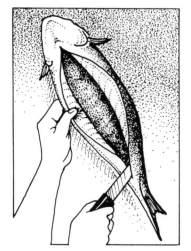 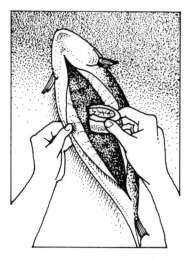 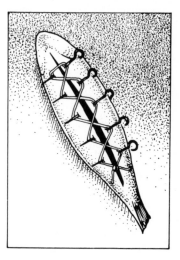

5. Brush both sides of the fish lavishly with melted butter and then place on a long, doubled piece of cheesecloth.

6. Wrap the cheesecloth around the fish, allowing the skewers to pierce the cloth. Fold the ends over to encase the fish.

7. Poach or bake the fish according to instructions. (See Index.)

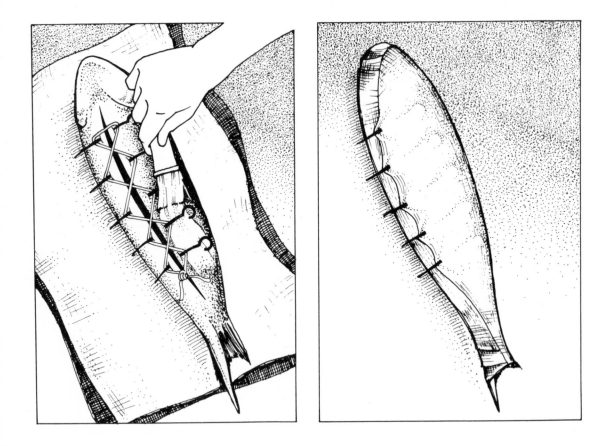

Stuffing a Flatfish

1. Using kitchen shears, trim off the fins and then scale the fish by using a scaler or a knife. You might want to place the fish on some newspaper before scaling it just to make the job a bit neater. If fish was not cleaned and gutted at the market or in the boat, remove gills.

2. Using a thin knife or a flexible filleting knife, cut along the center bone and, using a slicing motion, begin to separate the flesh from the bone. Do the same to the opposite side, and then flip the fish over and repeat the same process on the bottom of the fish.

3. Using the kitchen shears, cut the bone near the head of the fish and along the sides of the fillets. You will now be able to lift the bone right out of the fish. Cut it at the tail to remove it.

4. The four fillets are now connected only at the head and tail of the fish. It is now ready to be stuffed.

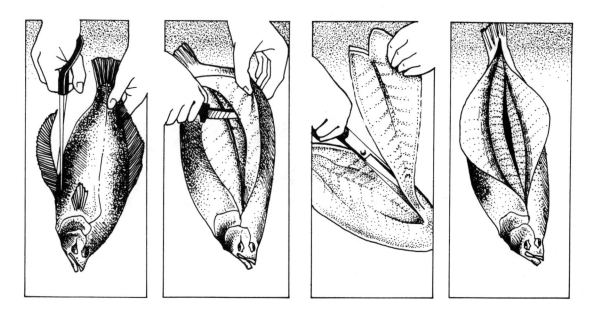

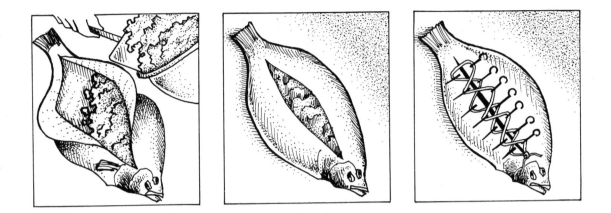

Stuffing Fillets

1. Pan dress the fish and use the thickest center cut. This is best for long, thin fish that won't fit in the pan, such as *mackerel*, *pike*, or *pompano*.

2. Stuff the fish like a sandwich and skewer both sides closed.

3. Lace with string to retain the stuffing.

Note: For stuffing *shrimp*, *lobster*, or *crab*, see Index.

How Much Stuffing to Make

Pike, bass, trout, salmon, weakfish, flounder, sole, and *mackerel* are all different size fish and each has a different size body cavity. Therefore, the amount of stuffing needed will, of course, vary. When using the following recipes, if you have any stuffing left over, it can be baked either around the fish as a garnish or in a separate baking dish to be served alongside the fish.

Bouillabaisse American Style with Rouille   For this recipe, see page 126

Peruvian Shrimp and Sea Bass Stew with Poached Eggs   For this recipe, see page 137

ARABIC
RICE AND PINE NUT
STUFFING

2 tablespoons olive oil
1 large onion, finely chopped
1 cup cooked, brown rice
2 tablespoons pine nuts, toasted
2 tablespoons currants, soaked in boiling
   water and then drained
½ teaspoon allspice
1 tablespoon lemon juice
¼ teaspoon black pepper
1 tablespoon minced, fresh parsley

Heat the oil and saute the onions until wilted. Add the rice and cook for 2 minutes. Remove from heat. Add the toasted pine nuts, drained currants, and the remaining ingredients. Stir, and then cool for 20 minutes for flavor to develop before stuffing fish.

Yield: 2 cups

CASHEW NUT
STUFFING

6 tablespoons butter
1 stalk celery with leaves, finely chopped
2 scallions, finely minced
½ clove garlic, finely minced
1 cup fine, dry, whole grain bread crumbs
½ teaspoon black pepper
1 cup coarsely chopped cashew nuts
4 sprigs thyme or ½ teaspoon dried
¼ teaspoon nutmeg
¼ cup finely chopped, fresh parsley
1 teaspoon grated lemon rind
½ teaspoon tamari soy sauce

Melt better in skillet and saute celery, scallions, and garlic until wilted. Add all remaining ingredients. Stir and cool before stuffing fish.

Yield: 2 cups

CRAB MEAT STUFFING

4 tablespoons butter
½ cup finely minced celery
½ cup finely minced onion
¼ cup finely minced green pepper
½ pound fresh crab meat (chopped, raw shrimp or lobster can also be used)
1 tablespoon lemon juice
1 cup fresh, whole grain bread crumbs
2 eggs, lightly beaten
1 tablespoon finely minced, fresh parsley
¼ teaspoon black pepper
½ teaspoon paprika
1 teaspoon dry mustard

Melt butter in a skillet and saute celery, onion, and green pepper until wilted, but not brown. Stir to prevent burning. Add crab meat and stir a few seconds. Then add lemon juice.

Remove from stove and add the bread crumbs and the beaten eggs. Then add all the remaining ingredients. Let cool slightly before stuffing fish.

Yield: 2 cups

Note: If there is any extra stuffing, place a few tablespoons in ramekins or some scallop shells, dot with butter, and sprinkle with cheese. Bake along with stuffed fish for about 5 minutes and serve as a decorative garnish.

CUCUMBER AND ALMOND STUFFING

4 tablespoons butter
1 large onion, finely chopped
1 large clove garlic, finely minced
2 cups fine, dry, rye bread crumbs
1 medium cucumber, peeled and finely chopped
½ cup slivered almonds, toasted
2 tablespoons minced, fresh mint
juice of 1 lemon
¼ teaspoon black pepper

Melt butter in a large skillet. Add onion and saute until wilted. Add garlic and cook 1 minute more. Add the bread crumbs, cucumber, almonds, mint, lemon juice, and pepper. If stuffing seems dry, add a few tablespoons of water or Fish Stock (see Index).

Yield: about 3 cups

CUCUMBER, MUSHROOM, AND DILL STUFFING

2 green scallions, thinly sliced
¼ pound mushrooms
2 large cucumbers, peeled and cut into chunks
2 tablespoons butter, melted
4 cups soft, crumbled, whole grain bread
2 eggs, beaten
1 tablespoon lemon juice
½ teaspoon black pepper
1 tablespoon finely minced, fresh dill

Chop the scallions, mushrooms, and cucumbers together in a food processor or blender to make them very fine. Add the melted butter and the soft bread. Add beaten eggs. Then add the lemon juice, pepper, and dill.

Yield: about 3 cups

FISH MOUSSE STUFFING

2 cups soft, whole grain bread crumbs
½ cup milk
1 pound pike fillets or any other white-fleshed fish
1 whole egg
4 egg yolks
1 teaspoon finely minced, fresh tarragon or ¼ teaspoon dried and crushed
¼ teaspoon finely minced, fresh thyme or ⅛ teaspoon dried and crushed
¼ teaspoon white pepper
2 to 4 tablespoons very cold, heavy cream

In a deep bowl, soak the bread crumbs in the milk until the crumbs absorb all the liquid.

Puree the fish in a blender or food processor until it becomes very pastelike in consistency. Add the wet bread crumbs, egg, egg yolks, and all the seasoning to the blender or food processor and blend with enough cold, heavy cream to make the mixture smooth and very fine in texture.

You may use this to stuff a whole fish, or wet your hands and form the mixture into tiny fish balls and poach them in a Court Bouillon (see Index). You may also use this mousse, spread like thick butter on a fish fillet such as flounder or sole. Roll up the fish and secure with a toothpick, then bake or poach it.

Yield: about 4 cups

Part 6: How Can Anything That Ugly Taste That Good?

Introducing Those Underutilized, Tasty, Nutritious, Lower-Cost, Homely Beauties

We were having dinner at one of our favorite Spanish restaurants, accompanied by a close friend. We love the place because their seafood dishes are beyond compare, the unusual preparation and sauces are not to be found anywhere else in New York City. Excitedly, we ordered the *pulpo* for an appetizer and, when it came, our friend tasted it tentatively and a smile broke out as he exclaimed, "It's delicious!" And, indeed, it was.

About five minutes into the feast, he looked up and asked, "What do you call this in English?" To which we answered, "Octopus." The smile faded and he muttered, "Please go back to the Spanish name. It tastes so much better that way!"

Throughout America, there are unfounded prejudices about fish and seafood in general. Not only is this most nutritious food avoided because of the usual complaints—a smell associated with it, lack of knowledge about preparation—but if the creature looks the least bit unusual or if we tend to shrink from it because it's ugly, that fish is immediately relegated to the purgatory of the rejected and the "inedible." For the most part, this prejudice is pure American. Over the centuries our neighbors overseas have tasted of seafood delicacies that we have yet to discover or, at best, are just beginning to know.

In these days of high prices—both of meat and of seafood—it is time we took a good hard look at some of the nutritious, tasty, reasonably priced fish and seafood that are becoming more readily available, though they have yet to win the prize for "The Most Popular Fish on the Block." They may look unusual (ugly), but that is no reason to reject them out of hand.

Of course, the *octopus* mentioned above gets its unsavory reputation from the sea movies of the 1930s and, without doubt, this most docile of sea creatures has gotten a bad press. The *monkfish* is not particularly lovely to look at and neither is the *skate* (or *ray*). We have unfounded prejudice against the *eel, squid, shark, blowfish,* the *frog* (or at least its legs)—and if a fish has a name that is unfamiliar, we just don't buy it. There it lies at the fishmonger's, untouched and unloved.

The classic example of these past few years is the succulent *tilefish,* a deep water treat that has been selling for about half the price of other, more popular fillets. Recently we have noticed an increase in its popularity, which has been accompanied by an increase in price, of course.

We want to emphasize these lesser known fish, or at least pay more attention to them than do most books now on the market. We have them often at our house—*skate, eel, octopus, tilefish.* So the next time *you* visit your fish market, take a look at the unusual fish that are displayed. Ask about them, check the prices, and you'll probably find that they're much lower in price than the popular fish. More important, you and your family will enjoy a taste treat that is quite unexpected.

And—if anyone at the table wants to know the name of the fish they're eating, tell it to them in Spanish or French.

**Blowfish Tails, Steamed in Butter,
Lemon, and Mint
Blowfish Tails, Marinated and Broiled
Blowfish Tails *Provencale***

We see these fish all through the summer, caught by disappointed fishermen who were really out for *bluefish* and *weakfish* and *fluke*. They come up puffed full with air or water until they reach a size almost three times normal and the reason for their name, *blowfish*, becomes apparent. (They're also called *puffers*, *toadfish*, *ocean squab*, *globefish* and, most commonly, *sea squab*.)

Unfortunately, many fishermen throw them back, unaware that they contain some of the most delectable morsels to be found on any fish anywhere. Since only the meat along the spine is edible, and when prepared they taste much like delicate chicken, the blowfish is displayed in your local fish market as sea squab—and the change in name brings with it a subsequent upward change in price. Blowfish, after all, is cheap. Sea squab can be rather expensive!

If You Catch a Blowfish . . .

Don't throw it back! Two to four blowfish will make a perfect portion for one person. To clean it, you'll need a sharp knife and a piece of cloth or towel. The blowfish skin is quite abrasive, so you'll need to protect your hand.

Grasp the blowfish in your left hand and cut through the spine in back of the head and down past the front fins. Using the knife, insert the blade between skin and flesh just enough so that you can grasp the skin between your thumb and forefinger (using the cloth for protection). Pull the skin back from the flesh just like taking off your glove. When the skin has been pulled back, hook the forefinger of one hand right under the fin bone and pull hard. The fleshy back, looking much like a chicken thigh, will be pulled loose from the rest of the body. The head and entrails are discarded since nothing is edible except the back meat along the spine.

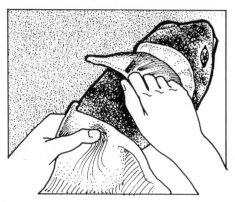 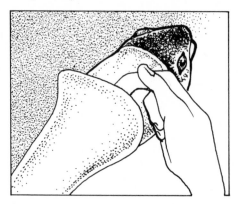

BLOWFISH TAILS, STEAMED IN BUTTER, LEMON, AND MINT

1 cup butter
12 to 24 blowfish tails, depending on size (about 3 pounds)
½ teaspoon black pepper
2 tablespoons lemon juice
2½ tablespoons finely chopped, fresh mint (reserve ½ teaspoon for garnish)

Melt butter slowly in a large, heavy skillet (or an electric frying pan). Add the blowfish tails and, with tongs, turn to coat evenly with the butter. Sprinkle with pepper, lemon juice, and mint. Cover the skillet tightly, raise the heat to medium, and steam for 6 to 8 minutes. Remove tails with tongs, and pour the lemon-mint butter sauce in the pan over the blowfish tails and garnish with reserved mint.

Serves 6

BLOWFISH TAILS, MARINATED AND BROILED

12 to 24 blowfish tails, depending on size
    (about 3 pounds)
¾ cup corn oil
3 tablespoons wine vinegar
2 teaspoons finely minced, fresh thyme or
    1 teaspoon dried
1 small sprig rosemary or ¼ teaspoon
    dried
2 shallots, finely minced (young spring
    onions may be used)
½ teaspoon black pepper
1 tablespoon minced, fresh chives
1 tablespoon minced, fresh parsley

Place blowfish tails in a shallow, glass pan in one layer. Mix other ingredients, except chives and parsley, and pour over. Marinate unrefrigerated 1 hour, turning once.

Lift tails out of the glass pan and place them on an aluminum-foil-lined broiler pan. Broil 2 to 3 inches from source of heat for about 5 to 6 minutes on each side. Brush with marinade while broiling.

Mix chives and parsley together and sprinkle over tails just before serving.

Serves 6

BLOWFISH TAILS PROVENCALE

12 to 24 blowfish tails, depending on
    size (about 3 pounds)
½ teaspoon black pepper
½ cup whole wheat flour
½ cup olive oil
3 cloves garlic, finely minced
2 small shallots, finely minced (young
    spring onions may be used)
    juice of ½ lemon
1 teaspoon honey
2 tablespoons water
4 medium tomatoes, peeled and
    chopped
1 small bay leaf
3 sprigs thyme or ½ teaspoon dried
3 tablespoons minced, fresh parsley

Season the blowfish tails with pepper and coat lightly with flour. Heat the olive oil in a large skillet and saute fish in the oil for 3 to 4 minutes on each side. Lift out with tongs and set aside.

In the same skillet, add the garlic and shallots to the oil, stir and cook until wilted. Do not allow to burn. Add the lemon juice, honey, and water and cook for 1 minute; then add the tomatoes, bay leaf, and thyme. Simmer uncovered for 20 minutes.

Just before serving, place the blowfish tails in the sauce in the pan and heat briefly. Remove to shallow, heated serving platter and add parsley.

Serves 6

The Great Belzoni Catfish Festival

Wherever we travel in the world, we generally arrive in town to be told "You should have been here *last* week, we had a great festival!" But for one time in our lives, we arrived at just the right time. We were on our way south through Mississippi to do a film for a client in Biloxi, and we made a detour near Yazoo City to visit the Arcola Catfish Farms. With aquaculture becoming big business, we wanted to see a fish farm for ourselves. *Trout, perch, carp, bass,* and *bluegill* are all being raised from eggs to mature fish, and even *lobster* and *shrimp* are being raised experimentally. One of the most interesting farms is devoted to the *tilapia* for home breeding (see page 162).

The day was capped, however, by the fact that nearby Belzoni was right in the midst of its annual Catfish Festival, so we left the farm and drove the short distance just in time to see the crowning of the Catfish Queen. As with all good festivals, there was music, dancing, and a "Who-Can-Eat-the-Most-Catfish-Contest."

Filled to the top with good fun, music, more knowledge about aquaculture and about 15 fried, baby *catfish* with hush puppies, we headed south again toward Biloxi.

**Broiled, Barbecued Catfish Fillets
Catfish, Oriental Style
Traditional Southern Fried Catfish
(with Hush Puppies)**

We remember reading an article some time ago which stated that the first freshwater fish an eastern youngster catches is often the catfish. Mel had penciled in along the margin: "True!" His fishing "career" began at a mountain lake in the Catskills and the hooks on bamboo poles were baited with "night crawlers," the big worms that crawl on the lawn after a rainstorm. Those were the days before so much pollution, when the lakes and the rivers were fairly clean (or maybe we just didn't know how dirty they really were), and the bottom-scavenging catfish could be eaten with impunity.

Those were the years when the poor catfish was much maligned. It was looked down upon by northerners as a southern dish served with hush puppies. It was ignored, even called by a variety of other names—*Rocky Mountain trout*, for example—to disguise its real identification.

Today, though many catfish are still caught both in fresh water and in salt water, over ten million pounds a year are commercially farmed in 34 states, and this delicate-flavored, superb fish can be found not only in the South, but in supermarkets and restaurants in cities as diverse as New York and San Francisco.

In the catfish family, the name *bullhead* is synonymous with the more common name. In fact, Mel says it is exactly what the kids called these fish when he caught them at that little lake. However, there are 28 varieties of catfish (or bullheads) — some of them very tiny—ranging up to the giant, blue catfish, well over a hundred pounds. In fact, there are catfish in the Amazon and in Europe that weigh as much as 600 pounds! For the purposes of this book, we will ignore the larger ones and discuss only the catfish that can be cleaned easily and will fit in your kitchen frying pan or stew pot.

Though your market may only carry the fish under the heading of "catfish," here are some other common names that you might come across: *black bullhead, brown bullhead, flat bullhead, green bullhead, horned pout, spotted bullhead,* or *yellow bullhead.*

The catfish has no scales, so it is not dressed as other fish are. It has sharp, almost lethal spines on the dorsal and pectoral fins and they must be handled with care. Some catfish carry a numbing poison at the base of these spines and the sensation of pain from a puncture can stay with you for several hours. But even this did not stop Mel and his friends from avidly skinning them as kids. In fact, they carried the red marks from the spines on their fingers like military decorations.

How to Skin a Catfish

The easiest method is to drive a nail into a heavy board, point up. Impale the catfish on the nail through the lower lip and then grasp it firmly with your hand, making sure to avoid the pointed spines. Make a cut behind the head and around the fish and then cut around the dorsal and anal fins.

Flip up the skin right behind the top of the head and grasp it solidly with a pair of pliers, pulling firmly downward. The skin should come off in one inside-out piece. Then finish the gutting and take the head off. The fish can also be held in the hands for skinning, but this method is a bit trickier.

The marvelous thing about the catfish is that there is only one large spine in the fish, leaving the meat boneless and tender.

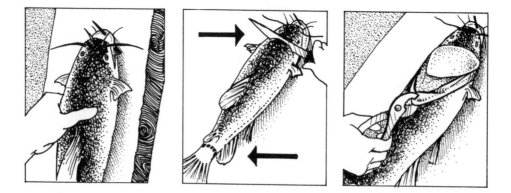

BROILED, BARBECUED CATFISH FILLETS

½ cup Basic Tomato Sauce (see Index)
½ medium onion, grated
½ clove garlic, finely minced
¼ teaspoon Dried Hot Pepper Sauce (see Index)
¼ cup water
3 tablespoons lemon juice
1 teaspoon honey
½ teaspoon finely minced, fresh thyme or ¼ teaspoon dried
2½ pounds catfish fillets

Combine all ingredients, except for catfish, in a saucepan, simmer slowly, stirring frequently for 8 minutes. Cool and use as a marinade.

Use a glass dish. Spread some of the marinade on the bottom, lay catfish in layers, then spoon more marinade on top. Refrigerate the dish for 30 minutes, turning fish once.

Oil a heat-proof baking dish. Lift out fillets making sure they have sauce clinging to them. Broil for 2 to 3 minutes on each side, adding more of the marinade and basting with it so fish is moist and coated.

Serves 6

CATFISH, ORIENTAL STYLE

3 pounds catfish fillets, skinned and cut into 4-inch pieces
1 cup stone-ground cornmeal
½ cup sesame seeds, coarsely ground
1 small, fresh, hot chili pepper, seeded
¾ cup tamari soy sauce
2 teaspoons rice wine vinegar
½ teaspoon sesame seed oil
2 scallions, green part only, minced
¾ cup peanut oil

Wash and dry the fillets on paper towels. Mix the cornmeal and sesame seeds together and put in a plastic bag with the fish fillets. Shake to coat evenly, a few pieces at a time. Spread on wax paper and chill for 1 hour.   Meanwhile, put the hot chili pepper in a blender with the soy sauce, vinegar, and sesame seed oil. Blend at high speed for a few seconds until the hot pepper is pureed. Pour into individual small bowls and sprinkle with the scallions as a dipping sauce.   Then heat the oil to 370°F., add the fish pieces a few at a time and cook for 3 minutes on each side. Drain well and serve hot with the dipping sauce.

Serves 6

TRADITIONAL SOUTHERN FRIED CATFISH
(WITH HUSH PUPPIES)

The combination of tender, sweet, white flesh encased in a light coating of crisp, golden cornmeal is an irresistible temptation. Some southern cooks may use lard rather than oil. Some will use fillets or small, whole, baby catfish that are pan dressed. The skeletal structure of the catfish is very simple; therefore, it's easy to lift out the center bone.

Catfish are traditionally accompanied by Hush Puppies (see page 161), onion-scented cornmeal puffs that are fried in the same pan after the fish is removed. Coleslaw is another traditional accompaniment.

2½ pounds catfish fillets, skinned, or 12 whole, small, baby catfish, dressed
1 cup stone-ground white cornmeal
¼ teaspoon black pepper
corn oil for frying

Wash and dry fillets on paper towels. Cut into 3-inch pieces or keep whole and dressed. Place cornmeal and pepper in a plastic bag. Add fish, a few pieces at a time, and shake well to coat. Spread in single layer on sheet of wax paper and place in the refrigerator to chill for 1 hour before frying. In a deep, 12-inch, heavy iron skillet or Chinese wok, heat oil (about 1 inch deep) to 370°F. Add fish, a few pieces at a time, and cook for 2 to 3 minutes on each side until brown. Drain well on paper towels and serve hot.

Serves 6

Note: We have known people to gorge themselves on huge amounts of catfish. In fact, the authors are notorious in parts of the South for eating more than their fill when the menu reads, "All you can eat" for a given price. The amount stated in this recipe is adequate for the average eater, but for those who must have more (like Mel), you may have to increase the amount accordingly. A fish as sweet and delicious as catfish seems to demand overeating!

HUSH PUPPIES

Catfish and hush puppies are inseparable when served in the traditional method—they go together like "love and marriage." In Mel's book *Bread Winners* (Emmaus, Pa.: Rodale Press, 1979), he included a superb recipe that we found at the Shelby Motel, just north of Memphis. Since he has already published his secret ingredients, we thought there would be no harm in repeating the recipe here for those of our readers who would like to try them with their catfish feast.

½ cup whole wheat flour
1½ cups stone-ground white cornmeal
2 teaspoons baking powder
1 teaspoon baking soda
¼ teaspoon black pepper
1 egg, beaten
½ cup beer
½ cup buttermilk
1 large onion, grated
    oil for frying

Sift all the dry ingredients. Heat the oil for deep fat frying to about 375°F. and heat the oven to 400°F. to keep the hush puppies warm while making the rest of the batter.

Beat the egg and add the beer and buttermilk. Combine with the dry ingredients, add the grated onion and mix. The batter should be slightly stiff—if it is not, add a bit more flour.

Drop the batter by the teaspoonful into the oil and fry the hush puppies 3 or 4 at a time so that the temperature of the oil is maintained. They will float to the top when they're brown and done.

Lift out with a slotted spoon, drain on paper and keep hot in the oven.

Serves 6

Tip: Whenever we work in the South, we find that the best way to discover the finest local catfish haunts is to ask among our native friends about them. Most are the kind of place that you might never find if you were passing by in your car—little cabins run by efficient women, river-edge restaurants that serve only catfish, hush puppies, and coleslaw, and nothing else. Since writing this chapter, we have discovered several more places that we have added to our growing list—one in Mississippi, a great one in North Carolina, and a third in Tennessee. Both of us place catfish and hush puppies among the world's great treats.

Fish Farming for the Family

Though commercial farming of fish has become big business (see story on catfish farming, page 156), an exciting experiment is currently going on in Maxatawny, Pennsylvania, at the Organic Gardening and Farming Research Center. The logic is simple: since fish can be raised commercially and since more and more people are buying home aquariums, why not combine the two to make fish farming possible on a smaller scale, right in the home basement? It's quite possible that some day soon, fish will be raised that way for family consumption, and at a lower cost than the supermarket price for fish. Eating homegrown fish will certainly be less expensive than buying beef or chicken for the table.

Unlike cattle, fish convert food into flesh very efficiently, and some fish, like the experimental *tilapia* at the farm, are 50 times cheaper to produce per pound than beef, 35 times cheaper than chicken, and 4 times cheaper than soybeans! So, theoretically, we might all one day be raising tilapia for our dinner tables in a 12 × 12-foot space in the basement, with controlled temperature, controlled feeding, and controlled filtration.

Though the experimental farm is also breeding catfish and Israeli *carp*, the tilapia is the most interesting fish of the group, a species that can produce up to 100,000 fish in six months, just from one mating pair! It comes from Africa, where it has been known as a food fish for many years and in the past few years it has been introduced into Florida waters. It's easy to raise—can be fed on duckweed, lettuce, coffee pulp, and algae—and it grows equally well in fresh or salt water.

If you're ever near the Pennsylvania Dutch Country, the Organic Gardening and Farming Research Center is right in the heart of the area. In the summer, conducted tours are given throughout the day and even after dinner. We loved it!

Baked, Skewered Eel with Bay Leaves
Broiled Eel with Rosemary, Sage,
Thyme, and Watercress
Eel with Vegetable Sauce

The *eel*, very much like the *octopus* and *squid* (see Index), is a fish that is either very much loved or completely ignored. There seems to be no in-between. Those of us who love them can't understand those who don't, and those who don't can't understand how the rest of us can bear to eat them!

In Europe and the Orient, the eel is simply another food to be eaten and enjoyed. But here in North America, eels are considered quite exotic, appearing only as a delicacy in expensive gourmet restaurants or on the tables of ethnic families who still constitute a strong market for the fish. No traditional Italian family, for example, would be without a dish of eel at Christmastime. Eel is, in fact, a delicious and relatively inexpensive food and, once you know it and know how to prepare it, you are likely to join the ranks of eel fanciers.

In spite of the fact that it's not the most popular fish in the vicinity, *Larousse Gastronomique*, the guide used for the professional chef, lists 48 recipes for eel. And even Irma Rombauer's *The Joy of Cooking*, the cookbook that almost every new bride receives as a gift, provides eel recipes. So people somewhere in America must certainly be eating it. We find that many of our friends, after traveling in foreign countries, bring back a newfound taste for eel.

The eel is a most unusual creature in that all of these fish begin and end their lives in the Sargasso Sea, south of Bermuda. They're both saltwater and freshwater creatures, and the European eels find their way back to Europe after spawning, while the American eels return to the freshwater areas on our own continent.

Eels are caught throughout all the seasons—at night from boats using underwater guide lights, with nets and traps, hook and line, and by spearing either in open water or through holes in the winter ice. Most eel lovers feel that winter provides the best-tasting catch. The fish range from 10 to 16 inches in length; they're rich and fatty and they take beautifully to fresh herbs. They can be sauteed, baked, broiled, simmered in stew or soup, fried, or poached.

Buying Eel

If you don't catch your own eels, as some of our local fishermen do, you can generally purchase them in local fish markets, particularly those in ethnic neighborhoods. Eels are especially abundant at Christmastime. If your market ordinarily doesn't carry them, they can usually be ordered in advance. Many specialty and gourmet shops also stock eel.

The best way, of course, is to buy your eel *live*, right from the tank. Choose large, fat eels for broiling. The fishmonger will kill it, clean it, and skin it for you. If you buy an eel that is not alive, just make certain that it's free of slime and has a pleasant, fresh, briny smell.

Uncooked eel will keep for a day in a covered container in the refrigerator. After cooking, however, it can keep for three to four days. For best flavor, cook as soon as possible.

Allow three pounds for six people. The sizes will, of course, vary:

   small—under one pound
   medium—one to two pounds
   large—two pounds or more

How to Clean, Gut, and Keep an Eel

Eels are, to put it mildly, wriggly creatures and it's best to keep them alive until you're ready to cook them if you want the most delicate flavor. If you catch them yourself by netting them, you can keep them alive in a small bucket of wet seaweed without any water for about two or three days. Keep them in a cool place.

The commercial fishermen kill them immediately by placing them in plastic bags and freezing them at once. You can use this method too, if your catch is large and you want to keep a supply on hand.

If you cook the eels, unskinned, they should be scrubbed well with a stiff brush to remove any covering of slime. If you're on the beach or on a dock, rub a handful of sand down the length of the eel's body to remove the slime, so that you can get a better grip.

How to Remove the Skin

Method One: Hook or nail the eel by the head to the dock or to an upright board. Cut the skin in a circle around the neck and peel the skin down and off with the help of a pair of pliers to give you a more secure grip.

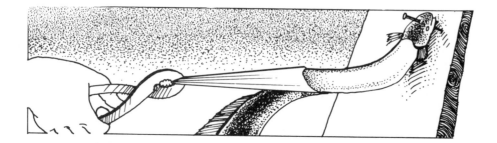

Method Two: Eels may also be skinned by placing them in a hot broiler for a few minutes. Turn the eel with tongs to expose all sides to the source of heat. This blisters the skin and it's easy to remove with pliers or a knife.

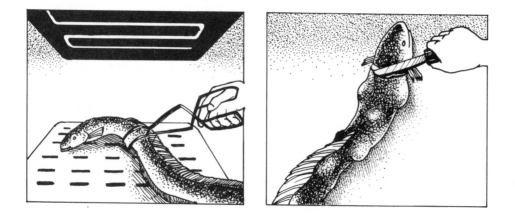

How to Gut and Dress

The eel is gutted by making a cut in the abdominal wall from the vent, carefully cutting up to the gill region. Turn the eel over and make a cut through the backbone at gill level. Hold the body firmly, stomach side up, and grasp the head and pull it up. The head and the intestines should be removed in one motion. Lying against either side of the backbone are two dark red structures. These are the kidneys. Scrape them out and then wash the eel well again in cold, running water.

Remove the bone if the eel is to be used as part of a soup or sauce recipe.

If you've never tried eel, now is the time for a new gustatory adventure!

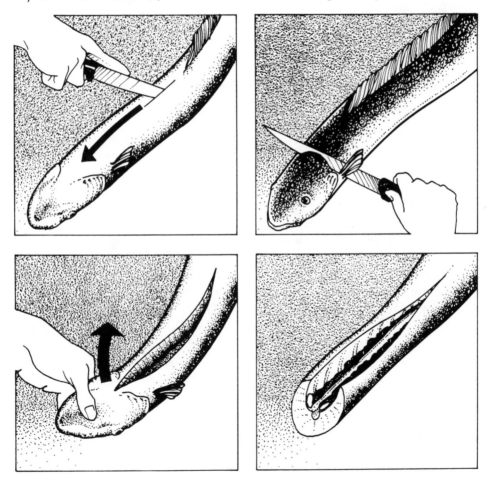

BAKED, SKEWERED EEL
WITH BAY LEAVES

2 cloves garlic, slivered
½ cup olive oil
¼ teaspoon black pepper
1 tablespoon rye bread crumbs
2 tablespoons vinegar
8 bay leaves
3 pounds thick, meaty eel, skinned,
    cleaned, and cut into 4-inch pieces

Mix garlic, oil, pepper, bread crumbs, vinegar, and 2 of the bay leaves, crushed. Add the eel and marinate for 3 hours, turning occasionally.

Preheat oven to 375°F.

Oil a baking pan. Place pieces of eel on skewers, alternating with a bay leaf between pieces. If some of the bay leaves crumble, don't worry. Just scatter them over the top of the eel.

Bake the eel for 20 to 25 minutes, turning frequently and basting with any remaining marinade. Serve hot.

Serves 6

BROILED EEL
WITH ROSEMARY, SAGE, THYME, AND WATERCRESS

3 pounds thick, meaty eel, skinned,
    cleaned, and cut into 4-inch pieces
¼ teaspoon dried rosemary*
½ teaspoon dried thyme*
¼ teaspoon black pepper
¼ teaspoon dried, crushed sage*
¼ teaspoon paprika
3 tablespoons fine, dry, whole grain
    bread crumbs
¼ cup olive oil

Garnish
1 bunch watercress
  lemon wedges

Dry eel well and roll in mixture of all the herbs and seasonings and bread crumbs that have been mixed with the olive oil, coating each piece evenly. Broil 4 inches below source of heat for 5 minutes. Turn and baste with the oil if necessary and broil on the other side until golden and flesh flakes easily. Serve hot with a bunch of watercress in the center with the lemon wedges and the hot eel around the rim of the platter.

Serves 6

*Do not use fresh herbs for this recipe. Broiling will burn them.

EEL WITH
VEGETABLE SAUCE

1½ cups vinegar
3 cloves garlic, slivered
1 medium carrot, cut in strips
1 medium onion, peeled and stuck with
    3 whole cloves
2 thin leeks, washed well and cut in
    strips lengthwise
1 stalk celery, cut in strips
¼ teaspoon black pepper
1 teaspoon finely minced, fresh thyme
    or ½ teaspoon dried
4 sprigs parsley
3 pounds thick, meaty eel, skinned,
    cleaned, and cut into 3-inch pieces

Mix all ingredients together for a marinade and add the pieces of eel. Marinate for 30 minutes.

Pour out half of the vinegar, leaving the vegetables. Add enough water just to cover and poach the eel in the vegetable broth for 15 minutes. When tender, remove the pieces of eel with tongs to a serving dish.

Bring the liquid to a boil and reduce to half the amount. Pour the broth through a strainer into a bowl.

Remove the cloves from the onion and puree all the vegetable solids and add to the broth.

Return the vegetable sauce to a deep, oven-to-table serving dish. Add the eel and reheat to serving temperature.

Serves 6

Note: We specify the thick, meaty eel whenever possible. It's more pleasant to bite into without encountering bone with every mouthful.

Frogs' Legs with Garlic Butter and Pine Nuts
Sauteed Frogs' Legs with Garlic

Ask any cook to describe the flavor of something you've never eaten, and the answer is likely to be: "Well, I'd say it tastes like a cross between chicken and lobster!" Finally, we have frogs' legs, a food that really does taste like that combination.

There was a time in our earlier days of struggle when we ate frogs' legs every day for lunch and dinner over a period of months, in spite of the fact that its price even then put it into the "gourmet" category. Mel was directing a cooking show on television and two of the sponsors were a frozen frogs' legs company and a firm that made blintzes (an ethnic crepe filled with cheese). The free samples filled the freezer to overflowing and, though we made very little money in those early days, the meals of frogs' legs and blintzes were filling— if eventually quite boring. In spite of this, we have never lost our appetite for these delicious little morsels.

Frogs' legs are grown and marketed commercially all over this country, and many more are imported. Generally, you'll find them frozen on the supermarket freezer shelves, and we'd strongly suggest that you choose the small-to-medium size for the best taste and texture. Some years ago we found frogs' legs on the menu of a roadside restaurant in the Midwest and, unfortunately, ordered them as a change from the ubiquitous steak and french fries that infest our countryside. Out came two chicken-leg-size frogs' legs, drenched in garlic powder and as tough as nylon rope. We went back to steak the next day.

However, if you love garlic as we do, frogs' legs love garlic too, and they make a perfect marriage. Frogs' legs are also fine when soaked in milk, which improves their flavor, and then sauteed and served with herbs and simple sauces. For six people, allow 18 pairs—or 3 pairs of frogs' legs per person.

FROGS' LEGS
WITH GARLIC BUTTER
AND PINE NUTS

1 tablespoon thinly sliced shallots
(young spring onions may be
used)
3 sprigs parsley
½ cup water
2 tablespoons lemon juice
18 pairs frozen frogs' legs, thawed
¾ cup softened butter
1 tablespoon finely minced shallots
(young spring onions may be
used)
2 teaspoons finely minced garlic
¼ cup finely minced, fresh parsley
¼ cup pine nuts, toasted (sunflower
seeds may be used)
lemon slices for garnish

In a skillet, mix sliced shallots, parsley, water, and lemon juice and bring to a boil. Add the frogs' legs, cover, and simmer for 5 minutes. Lift out with a slotted spoon and remove to a broiler plate. Reduce the liquid to 1 tablespoon. Strain and reserve.

In a separate bowl, mash the butter, minced shallots, garlic, and parsley with the 1 tablespoon of reserved liquid. Smear lavishly over the top of the frogs' legs. Broil at least 6 inches from the heat source for 4 minutes or less, until butter melts into a sauce. Sprinkle with toasted pine nuts. Garnish with lemon slices.

Serves 6

SAUTEED
FROGS' LEGS
WITH GARLIC

18 pairs frozen frogs' legs
 4 cups milk
 2 tablespoons tamari soy sauce
¾ cup whole wheat flour
¾ teaspoon black pepper
 4 tablespoons olive oil
¾ cup butter
 6 large cloves garlic, finely minced
   juice of ½ lemon
½ cup finely minced, fresh parsley

Place the frogs' legs in a bowl and add the milk and soy sauce. Let them defrost in the milk either overnight in the refrigerator, which is best, or at room temperature for several hours. About 20 minutes before serving, lift out the defrosted frogs' legs, place them in a pie pan with the flour and pepper, and turn to coat evenly.

Heat the olive oil until very hot and add the frogs' legs, a few pair at a time. Saute for 4 to 5 minutes, turning so they brown and become crisp quickly without drying out. Drain on paper towels and place on a heated platter and keep warm in the oven. More oil can be added if necessary to saute all the frogs' legs.

While the frogs' legs are cooking, cut the butter into pieces and melt it in a second skillet over low heat; then add the minced garlic. Cook the garlic just long enough to turn a golden color. Add the lemon juice. Pour sauce over the frogs' legs and sprinkle with the parsley.

Serves 6

Note: The people of rural southern France prepare frogs' legs in a traditional herbed tomato sauce. If you care to try this dish, make Sauce *Provencale* (see Index), and follow the recipe above, but eliminate the garlic. After the frogs' legs have been sauteed, pour this sauce over them.

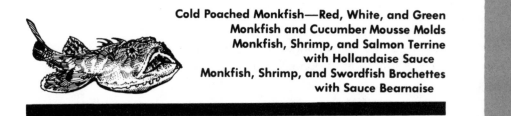

Cold Poached Monkfish—Red, White, and Green
Monkfish and Cucumber Mousse Molds
Monkfish, Shrimp, and Salmon Terrine
with Hollandaise Sauce
Monkfish, Shrimp, and Swordfish Brochettes
with Sauce Bearnaise

This is another superb fish that is left out of nearly every cookbook we've ever used—even when we check the cross-index under its other names: *anglerfish*, *goosefish*, *bellyfish*, or *rockfish*. Because it tastes bad? Don't be foolish. Because it's *ugly*! It is, in fact, one of nature's most interesting fish, if we are willing to look at it long enough to study its habits and assess its food value.

The *monkfish* has a huge head, atop which is an undulating antenna that attracts the passersby—*any* passersby, including small baitfish, crustacea, birds, anything that comes into its path. Once lured by the waving, agitating antenna, the intruder is gobbled up quickly by a mouth that slams shut, to open again only when ready for the next morsel. The fact that it practically "fishes" for its food is what gives the monkfish its other common name, anglerfish. And its constant eating of everything that swims or crawls by seems to give the monkfish the succulent lobsterlike taste that distinguishes this unusual creature. In parts of the United States and Canada, it's actually known as "Poor Man's Lobster."

Like the blowfish, only a part of the monkfish is eaten—in this case, the tail section. And, by whatever name, you'll find it on tables all over the world. It's *coda di rospo* in Venice, it's called *rape* in Spain, where it's poached, cooled, and served with a sauce in a salad. It appears in France as *lotte* in the classic *bouillabaisse* and *bourride*.

Monkfish

Tip: Monkfish must be cooked a bit longer than other fish, so test frequently with a skewer to be certain that it's done.

Tip: Monkfish takes beautifully to poaching and to buttery or enriched cream sauces.

Tip: Unless you baste it frequently when you broil it, or serve it with a sauce if you fry it, monkfish tends to dry out and toughen.

COLD POACHED MONKFISH— RED, WHITE, AND GREEN

2 pounds monkfish fillets (whiting or sole may be used)
4 sweet, red peppers, roasted, peeled, and seeded (pimientos may be used)
3 egg yolks
1 to 2 tablespoons oil
juice of 1½ lemons
½ pound fresh or frozen green peas, cooked
3 hard-cooked eggs, cut into quarters

Poach the monkfish in barely simmering water for 25 minutes. Remove and let cool, then break into chunks, and place in a large seashell or other serving dish.

With a mortar and pestle or food processor, make a paste of the red peppers and gradually add to the egg yolks. Then gradually add oil and beat with a wire whisk until a fairly thick sauce is formed. Then beat in the lemon juice.

Pour the red sauce over the center of the fish. Surround with the green peas and place the egg quarters on the top to form a pleasing design.

Serves 6

MONKFISH AND CUCUMBER MOUSSE MOLDS

1 pound monkfish fillets, chopped into
    small pieces (whiting or sole may
    be used)
2 eggs
2 medium cucumbers, peeled, seeded,
    chopped, and well drained
¾ cup Basic *Creme Fraiche* (see Index)
½ teaspoon white pepper
⅛ teaspoon cumin
1 tablespoon minced, fresh dill

Using a food processor or a blender, place the fish, eggs, and cucumbers in the container and process to a smooth puree. Transfer to a bowl and refrigerate for 1 hour.

Preheat oven to 375°F.

Butter 6 timbale molds (or custard cups).

Boil a kettle of water.

Remove the puree from the refrigerator and stir the Basic *Creme Fraiche* into it with a rubber spatula. Stir in the white pepper, cumin, and dill.

Evenly distribute the mousse mixture among the 6 molds and place them in a shallow baking pan. Pour the boiling water into the baking pan until it reaches two-thirds of the way up the sides of the mold. Bake for 20 minutes. Then remove from oven, lift molds out of their water bath, and let rest for 5 minutes.

Unmold onto a plate. If liquid accumulates after unmolding, blot up with paper towels. Serve plain, or with a *Beurre Blanc Sauce* (see Index).

Serves 6

MONKFISH, SHRIMP, AND SALMON TERRINE
WITH HOLLANDAISE SAUCE

½ pound single salmon steak
4 tablespoons butter
¼ cup finely minced shallots (or scallions)
2 teaspoons finely minced, fresh tarragon or ½ teaspoon dried
¼ cup whole wheat pastry flour
1½ cups light cream (or half-and-half)
½ pound tiny raw shrimp, shelled and cleaned
1 pound monkfish fillets, chopped into small pieces (whiting or sole may be used)
3 eggs, slightly beaten
1 recipe Basic Hollandaise Sauce (see Index)
watercress for garnish

Carefully cut around the bones of the salmon steak, discard skin and bones, and separate fish into 2 long strips. Set aside.

In a skillet, melt the butter and add the shallots, cooking and stirring until they are soft. Add the tarragon. Blend in the flour and cook until mixture is bubbly over medium heat. Remove the skillet from heat and gradually stir in the cream with a whisk. Return to heat and stir and cook until the sauce reaches the boiling point and thickens. Remove from heat and stir in the shrimp, monkfish, and the eggs.

Preheat the oven to 350°F.

Boil a kettle of water.

Whirl half the mixture in a blender and pour into the bottom of a buttered mold. (Use an 8½ × 4½-inch loaf pan or a 6-cup, straight-sided, deep terrine mold.) Arrange the 2 salmon pieces end to end, down the center of the mold. Process the remaining fish and shrimp mixture in the blender and spread evenly over the salmon steak.

Place mold in a larger pan and pour boiling water around the loaf to 1 inch deep. Bake for 30 minutes or until the center of the loaf is firmly set. Cool in the mold, on a rack. Then chill well.

(continued on following page)

Before serving, bring to room temperature and unmold.

Prepare Basic Hollandaise Sauce.

Slice the loaf into serving portions and place a sprig of watercress beside the slice on the plate. Spoon some Basic Hollandaise Sauce over each slice.

Serves 6

Note: This is a layered loaf which has a layer of pureed whitefish and pink shrimp and a center of coral-colored salmon. It is served at room temperature. When sliced, it is beautiful served with a golden, lemony, slightly warm Hollandaise Sauce.

MONKFISH, SHRIMP, AND SWORDFISH BROCHETTES
WITH SAUCE BEARNAISE

Sauce Bearnaise (see Index)
12 jumbo shrimp, peeled and deveined
1 pound monkfish fillets, cut into 24 cubes, each 1½ inches (whiting or sole may be used)
about ½ pound swordfish, cut into 12 cubes, each 1½ inches
2 tablespoons tamari soy sauce
2 tablespoons olive oil or corn oil
1 tablespoon lemon juice
½ teaspoon black pepper

Prepare Sauce Bearnaise.

Arrange alternate pieces of shrimp, monkfish, and swordfish equally on 6 metal skewers.

Mix the soy sauce, oil, and lemon juice together. Place the skewers so that the ends rest on the edge of a baking pan. Pour 1 inch of water in the bottom of the pan. Brush the fish brochettes with the soy sauce, oil, and lemon. Baste and sprinkle with pepper. Broil 3 inches from the source of heat for 4 to 5 minutes on each side, or until fish tests done, basting frequently to keep it moist. Lift skewers out and serve one to each person. Serve with Sauce Bearnaise.

Serves 6

The Hunt for Jaws III

While taking the ferry over to our island, we've watched the small boats leave the bay marinas bound for the ocean, the people aboard determined that theirs will be the group that brings back the largest or the meanest shark. Then late in the afternoon they return for the weighing-in and the docks are crowded with spectators. The shark tournaments take place all along the coastlines of the Atlantic and the Pacific and the sport can be both exciting and dangerous. In fact, one of the entry brochures warns:

> All entrants are cautioned to use care in handling sharks. They do not die as fast as other fish and are dangerous for several hours after landing, even if gaffed and tailroped. . . .

The *mako* is the most edible variety, but one of the interesting sidelights to the shark tournaments is the scientific study conducted by Ocean Science Laboratories. *All* fish caught are examined for the purpose of promoting marine research, but the proudest fishermen are the ones who come back flying the blue flag that denotes that they've caught a *mako!*

Monkfish, Shrimp, and Salmon Terrine with Hollandaise Sauce   For this recipe, see page 176

Dogfish and Squash Kabobs   For this recipe, see page 183

**Dogfish and Squash Kabobs
Fried Shark Tempura with Tamari
and Ginger Sauce
Mako Remoulade**

It could not be listed among the best-loved fish in the world. It has had an evil reputation throughout history as a spooky and fearful creature, as a "man-eater," dangerous, a monster capable of being provoked into violent action by the mere presence of another living thing too close in the water. Jacques Cousteau assures us that the *shark* is merely misunderstood, and we tend to agree—certainly that is true from a culinary point of view.

The shark is good sport as well as good eating—and it is time that the tables were turned. Instead of the shark's eating man, it is high time that man began more aggressively eating the shark. Actually, it has been eaten for centuries in Europe. It is the traditional fish of "Fish and Chips" and it is part of Mexico's *seviche*. It is popular in Africa and the Orient. Only in the United States does an ill-founded prejudice against the shark as a prime eating fish seem to be alive and well.

There is a good chance that you have eaten shark even if you think you never have. It has been sold as *swordfish,* fillet of *sole,* and *halibut*. There are even stories (probably true) that during World War II, it was dyed and sold as *salmon* and *tuna*. However you may have eaten it—knowingly or unknowingly—you have eaten one of the most nutritious fish in the sea.

One-third of a pound of raw shark meat yields four ounces of lean, cooked fish that is all but cholesterol-free, holds more than 20 grams of high-quality protein, and contains only about 100 calories per serving. And if you want to talk about cost, shark is half the price of halibut or swordfish, two fish it closely resembles.

Despite the fact that shark was once thrown back as a trash fish, it is being rediscovered very rapidly by fish-lovers and is now available in the markets the year round. (This new-found popularity will eventually raise its price, no doubt—the same thing that has happened with the newly "discovered" *tilefish*.)

Shark flesh is solid and holds its shape well, making it particularly good for stews, for deep frying, or for cooking as kabobs. Although most shark meat is similar in texture and appearance, each kind has its own distinctive characteristics. *Mako* is a deep water species which is very tasty and is highly prized by sports fishermen. This is the shark that has a taste that is most similar to swordfish. *Dogfish* and *sandbar* have a finer grain than mako, as well as a more tender texture. The meat soaks up sauces well. *Tiger shark* has a fairly bland flesh with distinct circular white bands visible on the steaks. The meat can be tenderized nicely with marinades.

The larger the shark, the coarser the texture. The smaller ones are very tender. Shark must be very fresh and it must be cooked at once to insure the best flavor. Try marinating it for a few hours in lemon juice diluted with water to keep the taste fresh until you cook it.

Since a growing population has been looking toward the sea for its future food needs, the shark may well be one of the answers that swims beneath the waters all around us. If you've become acquainted with shark before now, you need no further encouragement to get into the recipes. If not, we can only suggest that you "try it—you'll like it!"

DOGFISH
AND SQUASH
KABOBS

2 pounds dogfish fillets, cut into 1-inch
    cubes
¼ cup olive oil
4 tablespoons lemon juice
1 teaspoon finely minced, fresh dill
1 teaspoon finely minced, fresh chervil or
    parsley, or ½ teaspoon dried chervil
2 small, yellow, summer squashes, cut
    into 1½-inch chunks
2 sweet red peppers, seeded and cut into
    1-inch squares
1 green pepper, seeded and cut into
    1-inch squares
½ teaspoon paprika
⅛ teaspoon cayenne pepper
    lemon wedges for garnish

Rinse and dry the fish cubes. In a glass bowl mix together the oil, lemon juice, and herbs and marinate the fish for 1 hour. Drain and reserve marinade.

Take all the cut vegetables and toss them in the marinade and then drain the vegetables as well. Reserve the marinade as a basting sauce.

Skewer the fish and vegetables, alternating the colors, on long, metal skewers. Sprinkle the kabobs with the paprika and cayenne and broil about 3 inches from source of heat for about 10 minutes, or until fish flakes, turning the fish often to cook on all sides and basting with the marinade while it cooks. Garnish with lemon wedges and serve with hot brown rice.

Serves 6

FRIED SHARK TEMPURA
WITH TAMARI AND GINGER SAUCE

2 pounds shark, cut into ¼-inch-thick fillets*
1 cup whole wheat pastry flour
1 cup cornstarch
¼ teaspoon baking soda
1⅔ cups cold water
1 egg, beaten
¼ teaspoon cayenne pepper
    peanut oil for frying
    tamari soy sauce for dipping
1 teaspoon peeled and grated fresh ginger root or 1 teaspoon ground ginger

Pound the thin shark fillets slightly with the back of a meat cleaver or heavy skillet and cut into 1 × 3-inch strips. Dry well on paper towels.

In a bowl, sift the flour, cornstarch, and baking soda.

In another bowl, mix the water, egg, and cayenne together and, using a wire whisk, combine thoroughly with the flour mixture. Now you must work quickly to get a lacy crust.

In a deep skillet, heat the oil to 370°F. Dip fingers in batter and trail a lacy bed of batter in the hot oil. Dip the fish strips in the batter and lay a few pieces at a time into the lacy puddles of batter. Then sprinkle more batter sparingly on top of each fish strip in a back and forth motion. Fry only 2 at a time and cook for only 1 minute until very lightly tan. Remove with wide, slotted spatula and drain on paper towels. Handle gingerly as they are fragile. When all are cooked, serve hot with a sauce of soy sauce mixed with ginger.

Serves 6

*Shark meat will not fall apart easily as other fish would. They retain their shape even though they are cut into small thin strips.

MAKO
REMOULADE

2½ pounds mako fillets (swordfish may be used)
1 large onion, sliced
water
2 tablespoons tarragon vinegar
juice of ½ lemon
2 tablespoons dry mustard
2 tablespoons water
1 to 2 tablespoons grated horseradish, drained
1 tablespoon finely minced, fresh parsley
1 teaspoon paprika
¼ teaspoon cayenne pepper
2 egg yolks
1 cup peanut oil
1 small stalk celery, finely minced
1 green scallion, finely minced

Preheat oven to 400°F.

Place mako fillets in a deep baking pan. Top with onion slices. Pour enough water around the fish so pan is half full. Bake for 35 to 40 minutes. Remove fish with slotted spoon and drain on paper towels and let cool slightly. Discard the onion and water.

While fish is poaching, make sauce or prepare sauce first and allow flavors to blend. Mix vinegar and lemon juice together. Mix mustard with water and let stand for 10 minutes. Add to vinegar and lemon juice, beating with a whisk. Then add horseradish, parsley, paprika, cayenne, and egg yolks. Gradually add the oil, a few drops at a time, whisking well until it thickens. Add the remaining oil and beat well. Then stir in the celery and scallion. Serve the fish and sauce at room temperature.

Serves 6

Baked Skate with Onions
Italian *Scapece* from Abruzzi
(Fried and Marinated)
Spanish Skate, Malaga Style

Skate is possibly one of the most underutilized of all fish, and yet travelers come back from France raving about a dish that was as tender and sweet as scallops, served to them in a little Paris restaurant. It was called, they write to food editors, *raie au beurre noir*—and the letters end: ". . . does this fish exist in the United States?"

Well, it does indeed exist, and it does remind us of the taste of scallops, but as with all underutilized species, the skate is relatively inexpensive, and costs about one-fourth as much as scallops. The "wings" of the skate that make this fish look like a kite in full sail, rather than a creature of the sea, are the edible part. The skate is one fish that improves by refrigerating it for 48 to 72 hours before cooking, and then it should be marinated overnight in a solution of one-half cup of vinegar to one gallon of water. (Lemon juice can be used in place of vinegar.)

How to Prepare a Skate for Cooking

Skate can be skinned before cooking, or the skin can be peeled off after cooking, depending upon the recipe you use. To remove the skin beforehand, put the "wings" in a large pot and cover them with water. Bring the water to a boil and simmer for about three minutes. Remove the skate to a board or counter and place on paper towels. Scrape the skin away with a sharp knife, turn the "wing" and repeat the procedure with the other side. Trim off the bones that are on the outside of the "wings." Then place the meat in the marinade and refrigerate it until you're ready to cook it.

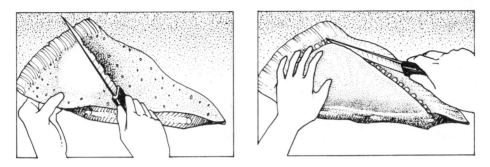

Remember, several days in the refrigerator will improve the texture of skate. You'll also find that the gelatinous bones of the skate are perfect for producing a naturally thickened and full-flavored soup stock.

When you eat skate, simply strip the long strands of flesh from the bone by using a knife. It is a most unusual, tasty, and economical fish.

BAKED SKATE
WITH ONIONS

¼ cup milk
1 egg, beaten
2 pounds skate chunks or wings, skinned (dogfish or mako may be used)
1¼ cups fine, whole grain cracker crumbs
¾ cup butter, melted
½ teaspoon paprika
¼ teaspoon black pepper
1 large sweet onion, thinly sliced
lemon wedges dipped in minced, fresh parsley for garnish

Preheat oven to 375°F.

Beat the milk and egg together and dip each piece of fish into this mixture, then into the cracker crumbs. Lay the chunks of fish in a shallow baking pan that has been buttered with 1 tablespoon of the butter. Mix paprika and pepper together. Top each piece of fish with a slice of onion and sprinkle with the paprika-pepper mixture; then pour some of the melted butter over each piece. Bake for 20 to 25 minutes and serve with lemon wedges dipped in parsley.

Serves 6

ITALIAN SCAPECE FROM ABRUZZI
(FRIED AND MARINATED)

½ teaspoon crushed saffron strands
3 cups white wine vinegar
1 tablespoon honey
2 cups water
2 bay leaves
6 peppercorns
1 or 2 small, dried, hot chili peppers
3 pounds skate wings, skinned and
      cut into serving pieces (dogfish
      or mako may be used)
½ cup whole wheat flour
½ cup olive oil
¾ cup corn oil
2 tablespoons finely minced, fresh
      parsley

Dissolve the saffron in a few tablespoons of the vinegar with the honey. Set aside.

In a saucepan that is nonmetallic, combine the saffron mixture, the vinegar, water, bay leaves, peppercorns, and hot pepper. Bring the liquid just to the boiling point. Set aside to cool.

Dip the pieces of skate wings into the flour. Heat the olive oil and corn oil together in a deep, heavy skillet to 370°F. Fry a few pieces of the fish at a time until golden brown. Lift out and drain on paper towels.

Serve the hot fish pieces with the vinegar sauce to be sprinkled on as a seasoning. Sprinkle with parsley.

Serves 6

SPANISH SKATE, MALAGA STYLE

2 pounds skate wings, skinned and cut into serving pieces (dogfish or mako may be used)
½ cup olive oil
¼ cup whole grain bread cubes
12 whole, skinned almonds
2 tablespoons finely minced, fresh parsley
2 medium onions, chopped
2 cloves garlic, chopped
3 tomatoes, peeled and chopped
½ teaspoon crushed saffron strands
2 tablespoons hot water
¼ teaspoon black pepper
1 tablespoon minced, fresh parsley

Preheat the oven to 350°F.

Oil a large, oven-to-table baking dish and place the pieces of skate wings in the dish.

Heat 2 tablespoons of the oil in a skillet and toast the bread cubes and almonds until golden in color. Add the parsley and remove from heat. Put the almond-bread mixture into a blender and blend until fine. Set aside.

In the same skillet, add the remaining oil and heat. Add the onions and garlic and saute until wilted. Add the tomatoes and simmer for 10 minutes. Mix the saffron with the hot water and let stand for 10 minutes while sauce is simmering. Then add the saffron to the sauce and continue to simmer for 5 minutes more. Remove from heat and let cool slightly, then strain the tomato-onion mixture, pressing the solids against the strainer. Mix with the almond-bread mixture, pour over the skate, and sprinkle with pepper. Bake for 10 to 15 minutes. Some of the sauce should be absorbed by the fish. Sprinkle with parsley before serving.

Serves 6

Broiled Squid with Rosemary Butter
Simple Sauteed Squid
Squid *Marinara* with Linguine
Squid Stuffed with Spinach
and Ricotta Cheese
Squid and Tomato Salad

Thousands of years ago, the Romans considered *squid* a delicacy, and they still do, even today. On the menus of Italian restaurants, you may see a dish called "Calamari." If you order it, you'll be eating squid. Since *calamari,* or squid, contain fine pen-shaped skeletons, the Italian name was derived from the Latin *calamus,* meaning reed or pen.

Squid are caught in the Monterey Bay region of California as well as on the East Coast. They're night feeders, though they live in the depths of the ocean. In darkness, they surface to feed on smaller fish. During the day, boats take depth soundings to locate them and then, at dusk, attracting lights are turned on to lure them when they can be seen coming to the surface. Squid are caught by netting them and they're found ranging in size from one inch to six feet. However, the smaller squid, those under ten inches, are more tender.

A squid has eight legs and two tentacles. All of the body parts are edible, and the very tiny squid is eaten whole. Squid gets tough and rubbery when overcooked, but it is delicately flavored and tender when cooked quickly.

If you've never tried this high-protein, low-calorie cephalopod because you don't know what to do with it—or you think it's ugly—forget your undeserved prejudice and, with an adventurous spirit, try this food of the ancients.

U.S. markets for squid are growing as consumers become more aware of their versatility and nutrition. They are high in phosphorus and protein and they contain traces of calcium, thiamine, and riboflavin. Whole squid are marketed fresh or frozen and they're also inexpensive enough to help keep your food budget down.

Here is a short guide, plus several recipes, to introduce you to this enticing, unique creature. If you have already tried squid, you don't need to be sold on its delicacy.

First of all, squid looks like this: somewhat like a swimming ice cream cone with fat whiskers! And you eat parts one and two. That's about 80 percent food with very little waste!

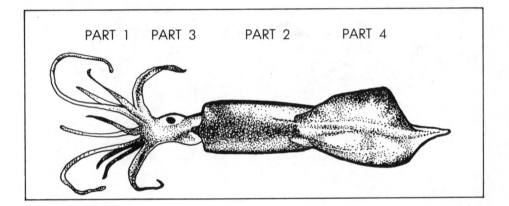

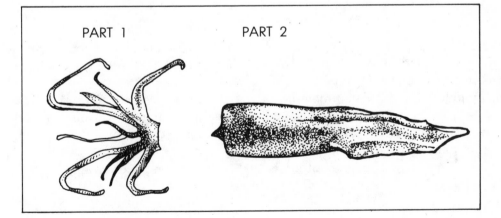

How to Clean a Squid

1. Grasp the squid firmly by the head (Part 3) and pull gently. This separates the insides from the body that contains the reedlike, transparent spine, which is then discarded.

2. Cut off the legs and tentacles (Part 1)

from the head (Part 3). These can be cooked whole or cut up. Discard the head. Open the tentacle (Part 1), laying it out flat like an open flower. In the center of this "flower," you will find a small knob like the stamen of a flower. Cut this out and discard it.

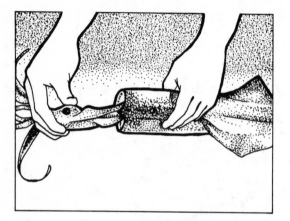
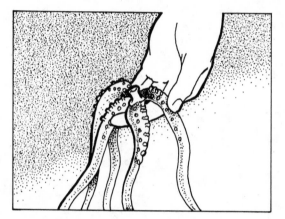

3. Tear off the triangular, floppy fins at the rear of the main body (Part 4) and discard them. Then peel off the dark grayish purple, thin, outer skin membrane that covers the body. Turn inside out, pull off loose white membrane and rinse well under cold running water to get rid of any sand. Turn it back and rinse the outside as

well. You will now have the pristine white, cone-shaped, hollow body (Part 2).

4. Hold the tentacles (Part 1) under cold running water and rub off the dark skin with your fingernails.

5. Dry well on paper towels.

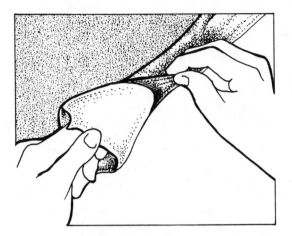 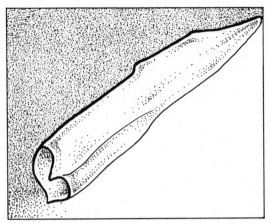

Tip: A six-inch squid weighs about one-quarter pound. Allow approximately two pounds for six people.

Tip: Remember, when cooked properly, squid will not be rubbery in texture, but tender enough so that you can cut it with a fork. Therefore, when frying or sauteing, use medium heat and cook for about 1 to 2 minutes. If cooked in a sauce on top of the stove, use medium heat and 10 minutes should be enough cooking time. If you use the oven and the squid is in a liquid sauce, use moderate oven temperature (about 375°F.); 15 to 20 minutes cooking time should be sufficient.

BROILED SQUID
WITH ROSEMARY BUTTER

2 pounds squid, cleaned*
½ cup sweet butter
1 sprig rosemary or ¼ teaspoon dried
    lemon wedges for garnish

Prepare squid.

Melt butter with the rosemary. (Heat gently so butter does not brown until rosemary is wilted and very soft.)

Place squid in oven-proof serving dish. Brush squid with butter mixture and broil for 3 minutes under high heat. Turn squid with tongs and broil again for 3 minutes. Serve with lemon wedges.

Serves 6

*Cut the main body into ¼-inch rings. Keep the tentacles and legs whole. (See page 192.)

SIMPLE SAUTEED
SQUID

2 pounds small squid, cleaned*
¼ cup whole wheat flour
1 egg, beaten
½ cup milk
¼ teaspoon black pepper
¾ cup fine, dry, whole grain bread
    crumbs
1 teaspoon wheat germ
¼ cup corn oil
    lemon wedges for garnish

Prepare squid.

Coat squid with flour. Then mix egg and milk, and dip squid in mixture. Add pepper to bread crumbs mixed with wheat germ, and coat squid with this mixture. Set aside until egg absorbs crumbs.

Heat oil and saute a few pieces at a time turning once when brown on outside (about 1 minute on each side). Serve hot with wedges of lemon to be squeezed at the table.

Serves 6

*Cut the main body into ¼-inch rings. Keep the tentacles and legs whole or cut up. (See page 192.)

SQUID MARINARA
WITH LINGUINE

2 pounds 6-inch squid, cleaned*
2 tablespoons olive oil
1 medium onion, coarsely chopped
3 to 4 large cloves garlic, finely minced
2 pounds plum tomatoes, pureed in
    blender
2 tablespoons Tomato Paste (see Index)
1 carrot, shredded
6 fresh basil leaves, coarsely chopped, or
    1 teaspoon dried
1 teaspoon finely minced, fresh thyme or
    ½ teaspoon dried
2 teaspoons finely minced, fresh oregano
    or 1 teaspoon dried
⅛ teaspoon dried, red, hot pepper flakes
½ teaspoon black pepper
½ bay leaf
½ cup water
1 pound whole wheat linguine (or thin,
    whole wheat spaghettini)

Garnish
2 tablespoons finely minced, fresh
    parsley
1 teaspoon grated lemon rind

Prepare squid and set aside.

Heat oil over medium heat in a heavy pot with deep sides. Add the onion and garlic. Cook and stir occasionally until soft, about 2 minutes. Add the tomatoes, Tomato Paste, carrot, basil, thyme, oregano, hot and black pepper, and bay leaf. Lower heat and simmer uncovered, stirring occasionally for 15 minutes. Add the water and cook for 10 minutes more. Set sauce aside.

Cook linguine according to package directions.

While linguine is cooking, add the squid to the sauce. Return sauce to medium heat and cook for the length of time it takes for the linguine—about 8 to 10 minutes.

Drain linguine and serve very hot with the sauce spooned over it. Garnish with the minced parsley and lemon rind. Toss at the table to distribute the sauce.

Serves 6

*Cut the main body into ¼-inch rings. Cut the tentacles and legs into ½-inch pieces. (See page 192.)

SQUID
STUFFED WITH SPINACH
AND RICOTTA CHEESE

12 squid, about 6 inches each, cleaned*

*Stuffing***

½ pound ricotta cheese

2 pounds fresh spinach, steamed lightly, and liquid squeezed out

¼ cup grated Parmesan cheese

½ teaspoon black pepper

¼ teaspoon grated nutmeg

2 tablespoons finely minced, fresh parsley

1 egg, slightly beaten

Sauce

2 tablespoons olive oil

2 cloves garlic, finely minced

1½ pounds plum tomatoes, pureed in blender

1 tablespoon Tomato Paste (see Index)

½ teaspoon fresh rosemary or ¼ teaspoon dried

Garnish

1½ tablespoons butter

3 tablespoons pine nuts (sunflower seeds may be used)

Prepare squid and set aside.

Mix all the ingredients for the stuffing together. Set aside.

To prepare sauce, heat the oil at medium heat in a large, heavy skillet. Add the garlic. Stir and cook for a few seconds. Then add tomatoes. Bring to the boiling point and add the Tomato Paste. Lower heat and add the rosemary. Simmer sauce for 25 minutes, stirring occasionally.

While the sauce is simmering, stuff the body of each squid only about one-third full with the spinach and cheese mixture. (The squid shrinks somewhat in cooking and the filling expands slightly. The bodies will burst if overstuffed.) Fasten the opening of each stuffed squid with a toothpick.

After the sauce has cooked, place the stuffed squid in the simmering sauce and tuck the tentacles and legs around in the sauce. Simmer for 3 to 4 minutes. Then turn carefully and simmer for an additional 3 minutes.

While the squid is cooking, melt the butter in a clean pan and toss the pine nuts in the butter and toast until slightly tan in color. Watch carefully, shaking the pan while cooking so they do not burn.

(continued on following page)

Lift out stuffed squid to a warm, flat serving dish with sides. Spoon sauce around and garnish with pine nuts.

*Keep the bodies whole for stuffing; remove tentacles and legs and reserve. (See page 192.)
**You can also stuff the squid with Arabic Rice and Pine Nut Stuffing (see Index) as a variation of this recipe.

Serves 6

SQUID AND TOMATO SALAD

2 pounds small squid, cleaned*
¼ cup olive oil
1 clove garlic, finely minced
1 medium onion, finely chopped
½ teaspoon dried, red, hot pepper flakes, crushed
2 cups peeled and chopped plum tomatoes
¼ teaspoon black pepper
3 tablespoons lemon juice
1 tablespoon finely minced, fresh parsley for garnish

Prepare squid.

In a skillet, heat olive oil and saute the garlic and onion until wilted. Add the squid rings, tentacles, and legs and continue to saute for 2 to 3 minutes. Add the remaining ingredients, except parsley, and cook for 5 minutes more.

Cool to room temperature or serve chilled from the refrigerator. Add minced parsley as a garnish. Looks lovely in a large, clean, seashell.

Serves 6

*Cut the main body into ¼-inch rings. Cut the tentacles and legs into small pieces. (See page 192.)

**Baked Tilefish with Mushrooms,
Scallions, and Dill
Tilefish Steamed with Vegetables
and Horseradish Yogurt Sauce
Steamed Tilefish, Broiled with Spinach
and Parmesan Cheese
Tilefish with Yogurt and Spices**

This is another species which, because of its unfortunate name, has only just begun to find its way to the dinner tables, markets, and palates of North America. We first tried *tilefish* at one of our local seafood restaurants, and we noted that every other fish seemed to be twice as expensive in its menu listing. To our surprise, the tilefish turned out to have a firm, tender flesh, flaky white, and an incredibly delicious flavor. Its popularity is spreading and people everywhere are beginning to find out that it broils superbly, can be poached, baked, deep fried, or used in chowders or *sashimi*.

It is a large fish, with a particularly huge head. One of our secrets is to ask our fishmonger for the head (generally we get it free of charge); then we carry the prize home and make it the prime ingredient in a devastatingly good fish stock. The residual flesh on the head is used later for cold salads. Try the tilefish. You'll be pleasantly surprised. When tilefish is simply poached, baked, or broiled, serve it with these sauces (see Index):

Green Peppercorn Butter
Crab Meat and Shallot Sauce
Mornay Sauce (with Gruyere Cheese)

For cold tilefish salads, use these sauces (see Index):

Almond Ginger Sauce
Hard-Cooked Egg Yolk and Herb Sauce

BAKED TILEFISH
WITH MUSHROOMS, SCALLIONS, AND DILL

2 pounds tilefish fillets, cut into 6 pieces
¼ teaspoon black pepper
½ cup softened butter
8 to 10 scallions, thinly sliced (about 1 cup)
1 pound small, fresh, button mushrooms
¼ cup minced, fresh dill

Place fish in a buttered, oven-to-table baking pan, season with the pepper, and smear 2 tablespoons butter over the fish. Set aside.

Preheat oven to 400°F.

In a skillet, melt 3 tablespoons of the butter and add the scallions. Cook stirring for 1 minute; add the remaining butter to the pan, and add the mushrooms. Continue cooking, shaking the pan until all the butter is absorbed; then add the dill and stir. Spoon over the fish and bake, basting several times with the accumulated pan juices, about 8 to 10 minutes per inch of fish thickness.

Serves 6

TILEFISH
STEAMED WITH VEGETABLES
AND HORSERADISH YOGURT SAUCE

12 small, red potatoes; peel only center
    strip
 6 medium white onions, peeled
    water
 6 wedges green cabbage
 2 pounds tilefish fillets, cut into 6
    serving-size pieces
    grated lemon rind

Place potatoes and onions on the rack of a steamer. Boil the water, add the rack of vegetables, cover pot, and steam for 15 minutes. For the last 2 minutes, add the cabbage to the rack. Transfer to a larger serving casserole with a lid and pour 2 inches of the steaming liquid over the vegetables. Place the fish over the vegetables and sprinkle with lemon rind. Cover tightly and steam 8 more minutes or until fish flakes easily.

Serves 6

HORSERADISH
YOGURT SAUCE

1 cup plain yogurt
1 teaspoon horseradish, drained
1 tablespoon minced, fresh dill

Mix all ingredients together. Serve in a separate dish with the fish.

STEAMED TILEFISH,
BROILED WITH SPINACH AND PARMESAN CHEESE

1½ pounds tilefish fillets, cut into serving
portions
2 packages, 10 ounces each, frozen,
chopped spinach, cooked
1 egg yolk, beaten
1 small onion, grated
⅛ teaspoon grated nutmeg
¼ teaspoon black pepper
¼ cup plain yogurt
2 teaspoons lemon juice
½ cup grated Parmesan cheese

Using a vegetable steamer, steam the pieces of fish over boiling water for 5 to 8 minutes or until almost done. Remove skin. Transfer fish to a buttered, oven-to-table serving dish.

Squeeze any liquid out of the spinach. Mix the spinach with the egg yolk, onion, nutmeg, pepper, yogurt, lemon juice, and ¼ cup of the Parmesan cheese. Pour mixture over steamed fish chunks. Sprinkle with remaining Parmesan cheese and slip under the broiler until cheese is melted and slightly browned. Serve at once.

Serves 6

TILEFISH
WITH YOGURT AND SPICES

2 pounds tilefish steaks, about 1½ inches
thick
2 cups plain yogurt
1 teaspoon paprika
1 teaspoon ground cumin
1 teaspoon ground coriander
¼ teaspoon black pepper
1 tablespoon finely chopped, fresh mint

Place the fish in a nonmetallic flat dish. In a blender combine 1 cup yogurt, paprika, cumin, coriander, and pepper. Pour over fish and marinate in the refrigerator for at least 3 to 4 hours.

Place fish 4 inches from source of heat and broil according to thickness of fish, turning if necessary, about 8 to 10 minutes per inch of thickness. Serve while hot with a remaining cup of yogurt that has been sprinkled with mint.

Serves 6

Part 7: The Regulars and the Favorites

The Best Sellers

If you ask the counterman at your favorite fish store what sells best, he's sure to mention several of the types of fish featured in this section—*cod, halibut, flounder, salmon,* and the like. He'll also tell you that some customers willingly pay whatever it costs to get *lobster, shrimp,* or *crab* to mark a special occasion. "Sometimes people buy it just to prove to themselves that they can have a luxurious meal if they want it," fishmonger Lou DeMartino told us.

Some of the fish in this section may be unfamiliar to you, but to the fish-lovers in some regions they are the heart of a feast that means a special season, or to travelers, the taste that reminds them so much of home.

Mention *scrod* to a Boston native far from Massachusetts and you will see remembrance in his eyes. Talk about *carp* to anyone who knows the incomparable flavor of Gefilte Fish and you summon memories of solemn Friday evenings at the dinner table and a meal featuring this most traditional of fish dishes. And what Baltimorean can pass by a case of iced crabs without longing for the fabled crab cakes of his hometown?

So we're presenting a grand variety of recipes—some that will spark up your regular favorites, and others that we hope will induce you to try some of the fish that makes history in various parts of this wonderful land.

Atlantic Croaker Amandine

This is the most common of the *croaker* family and, like its close relations it's a member of the *drum* family, that noisy group of fish who vibrate their muscles against their bladders to produce a distinctive croaking sound. Biologists are aware of the fact that this sound is quite voluntary on the part of the fish, but they've never been able to discover just *why* the fish makes it! We've heard them make the sound right after they were caught in the Gulf of Mexico off the coast of Texas, where they proliferate (and the croaking increases during spawning season) but the exact function of the sound is still a mystery to marine scientists.

Nevertheless, croak and all, it is a small, delicious, and delicate fish, running in size from one-half pound up to three pounds, and it's an excellent pan fish with a high food value of 17 percent protein. It can also be cooked pan dressed and dipped in a moist batter to be deep fried. (See Index for Deep Frying and Moist Batter information.)

ATLANTIC CROAKER AMANDINE

2 pounds croaker fillets
¼ cup fine, dry, whole grain bread crumbs
¼ cup whole wheat flour
⅛ teaspoon black pepper
5 tablespoons Basic Clarified Butter (see Index)
2 tablespoons softened butter
½ cup sliced, not slivered almonds
juice of 2 lemons
1 tablespoon minced, fresh parsley

Dip the fillets into a mixture of the bread crumbs, flour, and black pepper. Melt the Basic Clarified Butter in a heavy skillet and saute the fish until golden for about 5 minutes. Turn and cook the other side. Test after 3 minutes with a skewer to see if it flakes easily. Remove to a warm serving platter.

Wipe out pan with paper towels. Melt the softened butter and add the almonds. Toast carefully, shaking the pan. Do not allow to burn. Remove from heat and add the lemon juice. Return to heat for 20 seconds. Pour over the fish and sprinkle with parsley.

Serves 6

Tip: This is one of those pan-fry recipes that all but demand the flavor of butter. It's a good chance to test our plan for the cholesterol-conscious: dilute the butter in the pan with an oil high in polyunsaturates (safflower or corn for example), which allows for the marvelous butter flavor and cuts cholesterol at the same time.

**Blackfish Fillets Sauteed in Herbed
Bread Crumbs
Blackfish with Orange, Lime, and Lovage
Rumanian Blackfish with Vegetables**

There's an old wreck in the bay just off our village, duly marked with a Coast Guard buoy, and each spring the area draws all kinds of boats—small motorboats, rowboats, and sophisticated radar-equipped, party boats—to fish around the wreck. For far below, the *tautog* swims, though we call it the *blackfish* around these parts. Because it frequents old wrecks, mussel bars, rocks, outcroppings, and anything else under which it can hide, fishing for the tautog is fairly tricky, since the number of lures snagged and lost can make a fisherman turn to some sane sport such as skateboarding or tennis.

The average size of the tautog is about two to three pounds, though it can run much larger. It has a silver gray flesh that turns white and firm when it's cooked and it's excellent broiled, baked with bread crumbs and butter, or poached and then served cold in a salad with the following Mayonnaise-Based Sauces (see Index):

Sorrel Mayonnaise
Remoulade Sauce
Tomato Tarragon Mayonnaise

Tip: Since the tautog keeps its shape well during cooking, it is also perfect for stews, soups, and chowders. If you don't know someone who has caught a tautog and will share it with you—or if you can't get it at your fishmonger's—you can substitute *codfish* or *hake* for it in the recipes that follow.

BLACKFISH FILLETS
SAUTEED IN HERBED BREAD CRUMBS

1 cup fresh, whole grain bread crumbs
½ teaspoon black pepper
1 tablespoon minced, fresh parsley
½ teaspoon minced, fresh dill
1 teaspoon minced, fresh chives
½ teaspoon minced, fresh tarragon or ⅛
    teaspoon dried
6 blackfish fillets of equal size, about 2½
    to 3 pounds
1 cup milk
½ cup whole wheat flour
6 tablespoons butter
3 tablespoons corn oil
    lemon wedges for garnish

Combine the bread crumbs with all the herbs and seasonings. Dip the fillets in milk, then in flour, then in the milk again and finally in the seasoned bread crumbs.

Heat the butter and oil in a heavy skillet and saute the crumbed fillets until they are brown on both sides (about 4 minutes on each side). Test with a skewer to see if the fish flakes easily. Then transfer with a wide, slotted spatula to a hot platter. Garnish with lemon wedges.

Serves 6

BLACKFISH
WITH ORANGE, LIME, AND LOVAGE

3 tablespoons oil
1 large Bermuda onion, thinly sliced
2½ pounds blackfish fillets, cut crosswise
    into ¾-inch strips
2 bay leaves, crushed
½ teaspoon dried, red, hot pepper flakes,
    crushed
⅛ teaspoon black pepper
1 teaspoon finely minced, fresh tarragon
    or ¼ teaspoon dried, crushed
1 clove garlic, finely minced
1 tablespoon white wine vinegar
½ cup lime juice
½ cup orange juice

Garnish
1 orange, thinly sliced
¼ cup chopped, fresh lovage or celery
    leaves

Heat oil in a stainless steel or enamel saucepan, and place a layer of the onion slices on the bottom and the fish strips over the onion. Sprinkle with all the remaining ingredients except orange slices and the lovage or celery leaves. Cover the saucepan and bring to a boil. Lower heat and simmer until fish flakes easily. Transfer to a nonmetallic serving dish.

Chill for at least 6 hours in the refrigerator or overnight. Garnish with sliced oranges and sprinkle with chopped lovage or celery leaves.

Serves 6

RUMANIAN
BLACKFISH
WITH VEGETABLES

1 cup each: cubed carrots, cubed turnips,
   cubed parsnips, and cubed knob,
   root celery, or sliced celery stalks
   with leaves
2 potatoes, peeled and cubed
2 tomatoes, peeled and cubed
1 clove garlic, thinly sliced
¼ pound fresh string beans, cut into
   1-inch pieces
½ green pepper, seeded and cut into
   rings
¼ head of cabbage, coarsely chopped
½ teaspoon black pepper
1 teaspoon finely minced, fresh oregano
   or ½ teaspoon dried
1 teaspoon minced, fresh basil or ½
   teaspoon dried
1 cup tomato juice
¼ pound fresh or frozen green peas
1½ pounds blackfish fillets, cut into 2-inch
   pieces
2 tablespoons olive oil
2 tablespoons whole grain rye flour
   lemon wedges for garnish

Cook the vegetables, except peas, and the
seasonings in tomato juice for 5 minutes.
Then sprinkle with the green peas. Brush
the pieces of fish with olive oil and dip into
flour. Oil a serving casserole and place the
bed of vegetables on the bottom and lay
the fish on this bed of vegetables. Cook on
top of the stove, basting with the
accumulated liquid until the fish is opaque
and flakes easily, about 10 to 15 minutes.
Test the vegetables to see if they are
cooked through but still retain their shapes.
Serve hot with wedges of lemon.

Serves 6 to 8

The *drum* might well be called the noisiest fish in the sea, but the poets among us prefer to think of this fish as a highly accomplished marine musician. The fish actually has a drumming muscle and, by contracting it against an air bladder, it makes a distinctive sound that can be heard on land on a quiet night. The smaller relatives of the drum are known to make a croaking sound (and, of course, are called croakers). The first time we heard these strange fish, we listened in awe as a fisherman landed them off the Texas coast and the sounds broke the stillness of the quiet channel outside Padre National Park. (See the Chapter on the Atlantic Croaker.) The *black drum* is related to the *sea drum* and also to the freshwater *sheepshead*.

Preparing the Black Drum

The smaller fish are about 8 to 20 inches in length and, because the flesh is very lean, they take nicely to any butter sauce. The smaller fish can be poached or broiled if you use lots of butter, but baking seems to dry them out.

Larger drums sometimes weigh up to 100 pounds and are marketed as steaks or chunks. The meat is white and can be cooked in a chowder. However, it should not be used in dishes such as *sashimi* (the raw, Japanese-style fish), or in *seviche* (raw fish marinated in citrus juice), since it falls apart easily. It is just not firm enough when raw to slice it thinly and it doesn't keep its shape well.

Two-and-one-half pounds of fillets serve six people. You can substitute for black drum with *weakfish, croaker,* or *striped bass.* Black drum takes well to the following sauces (see Index):

Green Peppercorn Butter
Bercy Butter
Orange Butter and Chive Sauce
Herbed Butter Sauce *(Beurre Nantais)*
Mint Butter Sauce

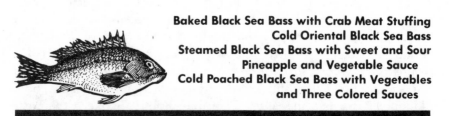

Baked Black Sea Bass with Crab Meat Stuffing
Cold Oriental Black Sea Bass
Steamed Black Sea Bass with Sweet and Sour
Pineapple and Vegetable Sauce
Cold Poached Black Sea Bass with Vegetables
and Three Colored Sauces

If you've eaten in a Chinese restaurant lately, and if you ordered a whole fish steamed or deep fried and served with a succulent sauce, surrounded by crisp, tasty vegetables, there's a good chance that the prize on the platter was a *black sea bass*. The Chinese discovered this treat, as they have so many others, centuries ago—the firm, white, delicate, juicy meat of the sea bass lends itself well to the spices of the Far East. Italian-Americans, too, have used this fish extensively because it closely resembles the *sea bream* of their native Italy.

Our readers on the West Coast are probably furrowing their brows with perplexity. Have they also tasted of this fish in their own Chinese restaurants? Of course. It's just that it's called *rockfish* in Washington, Oregon, and California. Basically it's the same tasty fish. The West Coast, though, provides this fish in a variety of colors, from orange to light green to deep red. On the East Coast, we have remained content with black. They all taste superb.

A whole, five pound fish will serve six people nicely, or you can buy two-and-one-half pounds of fillets. Black sea bass goes well with the following sauces (see Index):

Cold Walnut and Garlic Mayonnaise (Turkish *Tarator* Sauce)
Greek Egg and Lemon Sauce *(Avgolemono)*

BAKED
BLACK SEA BASS
WITH CRAB MEAT STUFFING

2 black sea bass, about 2½ pounds, or 1
    whole fish, about 4 to 5 pounds,
    with the head left on, cleaned and
    split open for stuffing
    juice of ½ lemon
¾ pound lump crab meat, picked over to
    remove cartilage
3 tablespoons whole grain bread crumbs
¼ teaspoon cayenne pepper
½ teaspoon finely minced, fresh thyme or
    ¼ teaspoon dried
1 tablespoon lemon juice
5 tablespoons butter, melted
    lemon wedges dipped in minced, fresh
    parsley for garnish

Preheat oven to 425°F.

Butter an oven-to-table, shallow baking pan, large enough to accommodate the whole fish. Lay the fish open, skin side down, and sprinkle with the juice of half the lemon. Let stand while preparing stuffing.

Toss cleaned crab meat lightly with the bread crumbs, cayenne, thyme, lemon juice, and 2 tablespoons of the melted butter. Spread the stuffing over one-half the fish, fold the fish over, skewer, and tie. (See Index on Stuffing a Whole Fish.) Pour remaining butter over fish and bake until fish flakes easily. Test with a skewer after 20 minutes. Baste several times with the butter sauce, or add some water to the pan to increase the basting liquid and keep the fish moist. Serve with parsley-dipped lemon wedges.

Serves 6

Note: If you wish to be budget wise, use the Cucumber, Dill, and Mushroom Stuffing (see Index), or increase the amount of bread crumbs in relation to crab meat. Crab meat in most areas of the country is expensive.

COLD ORIENTAL BLACK SEA BASS

2½ pounds black sea bass fillets, skinned and cut into 1-inch strips
1 tablespoon peanut oil
3 cloves garlic
1 medium onion, thinly sliced
5 thin slices peeled, fresh, ginger root
1 cup water
1½ cups rice wine vinegar
1 teaspoon turmeric
1 teaspoon tamari soy sauce

Dry fish well on paper towels. In a heavy skillet, heat the oil and saute garlic, onion, and ginger for 2 minutes, stirring constantly. Remove skillet from heat and add the water, vinegar, and the turmeric. Return to heat and bring the liquid to a boil. Add the fish, lower the heat to a very slow simmer, cover, and poach for 6 to 8 minutes. Cool in liquid and add soy sauce. Refrigerate for 24 hours in the liquid before serving. Serve with hot, brown rice and quickly steamed snow peas.

Serves 4 to 5

STEAMED BLACK SEA BASS
WITH SWEET AND SOUR PINEAPPLE AND VEGETABLE SAUCE

Sweet and Sour Pineapple and Vegetable Sauce (see Index)
3 pounds black sea bass fillets about 1 inch thick (keep fillets whole)
3 tablespoons tamari soy sauce
¼ teaspoon rice wine vinegar
4½ tablespoons peanut oil
2 scallions, cut into thin slices

Prepare sauce first and set aside.

Place the fish on a shallow, oven-proof plate. Mix the soy sauce and the vinegar and pour over the fillets, turning to coat evenly. Sprinkle fish with the peanut oil and scallions.

Pour about 2 inches of boiling water into a large baking pan with a lid. Put a rack in the water and place the plate on top. Cover the whole baking pan tightly and steam on the rack over boiling water for 15 minutes.

While fish is steaming, reheat the sauce. Remove the platter and spoon the sauce over the fish.

Serves 6

COLD POACHED
BLACK SEA BASS
WITH VEGETABLES AND
THREE COLORED SAUCES

The fish can be prepared ahead of time and chilled, and so can the vegetables. The whole thing can be assembled quickly for a festive and lavish looking feast.

2 black sea bass, about 2½ pounds each, or 1 whole fish, about 5 pounds
   Court Bouillon (see Index)
½ pound snow peas or sugar snap peas
½ pound small, whole carrots or carrot sticks
½ pound small, whole zucchini or zucchini sticks
¼ pound whole string beans
6 small pieces each broccoli and cauliflower florets
1 bunch watercress for garnish

Prepare the following 3 sauces (see Index) first and set aside:

   Aioli Sauce—yellow
   Tomato Tarragon Mayonnaise—pink
   Cold Green Sauce with Sage—green

Poach fish in Court Bouillon. (See Index for poaching directions.) Carefully remove to a platter lined with paper towels. When cool to the touch, peel off the skin leaving the head and tail intact. Turn the fish over carefully and peel the skin from the other side. Transfer fish to a serving platter and cover with plastic wrap.

Steam all the vegetables, except watercress, until crisp-tender and run under cold water to cool. This will only take 2 to 3 minutes of steaming. Arrange bunches of vegetables attractively surrounding the fish. Tuck in a few watercress sprigs for color. Serve cold or at room temperature accompanied by a choice of the 3 sauces of different colors, served in separate bowls.

Serves 6

Bluefish

Baked Bluefish with Zucchini and Sour Cream
Baked Bluefish with Potatoes, Garlic,
Sweet Marjoram, and Parsley
Bluefish *Seviche* with Red Onion
and Hot Pepper Flakes
Marinated and Broiled Bluefish
with Oranges and Mint

Besides being one of the tastiest fish that swims in our waters, the *bluefish* has a deserved reputation as being one of the most incredible battlers and superb game fish that ever swam in the sea. Pound for pound, ounce for ounce, this battling carnivore is a fisherman's dream. As far back as 1874, in a U.S. Commission of Fish and Fisheries report, the bluefish was described as ". . . an animated chopping machine, the business of which is to cut to pieces and otherwise destroy as many fish as possible in a given space of time." In fact, the bluefish—a frenzied feeder—has been known to fill itself with *menhaden (bunker)* or *sand eels,* disgorge its feast and then begin eating all over again. It is this trait that makes it such a remarkable game fish.

From spring through late fall, from Florida up to Nova Scotia, the bluefish travel in schools, eating as they go. For the fisherman, large flocks of shrieking terns signal the arrival of the blues, the water churning with activity, the birds diving to get at the scraps of half-eaten baitfish, each cast usually resulting in a fighting, thrashing, battling fury. And as suddenly as they appeared, they are gone, moving quickly up the coast or along the bay, while the boat or dock carries the results of the few minutes of a fisherman's dream.

Their teeth can be deadly and many a fisherman has accidentally gotten a finger between the steel-trap jaws. One acquaintance of ours was even bitten while carrying the "dead" fish home. He had taken it up by the gill, his finger wandering into the mouth, when the fish clamped shut and the teeth left their mark. The finger was bandaged for a week. There are stories, in fact, of bluefish "tasting" of swimmers who got too close.

These beautiful, feisty, bluish gray fish with their silvery undersides average from 2 to 25 pounds, though the early spring and early fall bring smaller blues into our waters. These range in size from the tiny *snappers*, excellent when quickly pan fried, to the baby blues, about 1 to 1½ pounds in weight. The latter are superb either stuffed and baked whole or filleted, with each side of the fish a perfect portion for one person. Generally, though, the bluefish has a strong and distinctively rich taste and it takes well to these strong sauces (see Index):

Cold Walnut and Garlic Mayonnaise (Turkish *Tarator*)
Green Peppercorn Butter
Basil, Eggplant, and Tomato Sauce
Tarragon-Lemon Butter Sauce
Herbed Butter Sauce *(Beurre Nantais)*
Pistachio Nut Butter

Small *mackerel* can be substituted for bluefish in any of the recipes that appear in this chapter. Remember, mackerel is an oilier, stronger-tasting fish.

BAKED BLUEFISH
WITH ZUCCHINI
AND SOUR CREAM

---

4 tablespoons butter

2½ pounds zucchini, cut into ¼-inch slices

1 medium onion, finely chopped

1 tablespoon curry powder

½ teaspoon black pepper

2½ pounds bluefish fillets

1 cup sour cream

1 tablespoon minced, fresh chives, or 2
   tablespoons minced, green onion

2 tablespoons fine, dry, whole grain
   bread crumbs

½ teaspoon paprika

In a large skillet, melt butter and add zucchini, onion, curry powder, and black pepper. Stir and cook over medium heat for 8 to 10 minutes until onion is soft and zucchini is crisply tender. Set aside.

Preheat oven to 400°F.

Arrange bluefish, skin side down, in a single layer in a lightly buttered, oven-to-table baking dish.

Drain the zucchini mixture in a strainer if any liquid has accumulated. Reserve liquid and mix the sour cream and chives with a bit of the reserved liquid to thin it. Spread the zucchini evenly over the fish and pour the diluted sour cream and chive sauce over all in the baking dish. Sprinkle with the bread crumbs mixed with the paprika and bake for 15 to 20 minutes, or until the fish flakes easily.

Serves 6 to 8

BAKED BLUEFISH
WITH POTATOES, GARLIC, SWEET MARJORAM, AND PARSLEY

2 bluefish fillets, about 1¼ pounds each
4 to 5 potatoes, preferably Idaho, about
     1½ pounds
⅓ cup olive oil
⅓ cup Basic Clarified Butter (see Index)
3 to 4 cloves garlic, finely minced
½ teaspoon black pepper
¼ cup finely minced, fresh parsley
1 teaspoon finely minced, fresh
    marjoram or ½ teaspoon dried
juice of 1 lemon

Preheat oven to 450°F.

Rinse and dry bluefish on paper towels and set aside.

Slice the potatoes into paper thin slices and dry on paper towels.

Use a large, heavy, shallow, oven-to-table baking dish. Pour in all the oil and the Basic Clarified Butter and make several overlapping layers of potato slices on the bed of butter and oil. Sprinkle the potatoes with all but ½ teaspoon of the garlic. Then sprinkle with the pepper, parsley, and marjoram. Bake in the top-most shelf of the oven for 20 minutes. Baste with a turkey baster by tilting the pan and squirting some of the butter-oil mixture on top. A delicate, brown, crisp crust will form on the bottom.

While the potatoes are baking, smear the remaining ½ teaspoon of garlic on top of the fish with a spatula. Then lay the fish fillets on top of the potatoes, baste with more butter-oil mixture from the bottom of the pan, and continue baking and basting for 8 to 10 minutes more until fish flakes with a skewer.

Remove from the oven and use a spatula to loosen the browned potatoes that may have stuck to the bottom of the dish. Pour the lemon juice over all and serve hot.

Serves 6

BLUEFISH SEVICHE
WITH RED ONION
AND HOT PEPPER FLAKES

This is a mixture of hot and cool—the hot peppers are cooled with fresh lime juice and mint to "cook" the fish.

1 bluefish, about 2 to 3 pounds, filleted, skin removed, and cut into ¾-inch-wide strips
1 tablespoon tamari soy sauce
1½ teaspoons dried, red, hot pepper flakes
1 large red onion, thinly sliced
1 cup fresh lime juice (juice of 6 to 8 limes)
1 tablespoon minced, fresh mint

Place fish strips in a bowl, pour soy sauce over the strips, and toss to coat evenly. Place a layer of fish pieces in the bottom of a ceramic crock, or any sort of deep bowl with straight sides (not metal), such as a small souffle dish. Over the layer of fish, sprinkle some of the hot pepper flakes and then make a layer of red onion rings. Repeat until all is used up, then pour lime juice over all to cover the fish. Cover tightly with plastic wrap and refrigerate overnight. Add mint when serving.

Serves 6

Tip: Pour boiling water over limes and let stand for 1 minute, then rinse under cold water. This procedure extracts more juice from the limes.

MARINATED AND
BROILED BLUEFISH
WITH ORANGES AND MINT

Marinade
- 1 bay leaf
- 1 teaspoon finely minced, fresh thyme or ½ teaspoon dried
- ½ cup mild vinegar
- ¼ cup cold water
- 2 large bluefish fillets, about 1½ pounds each

Bring all marinade ingredients to a boil. Allow to cool.

Place fish in a flat dish or platter with sides (not made of metal) and marinate for 30 minutes, turning once. Drain and wipe dry and proceed with recipe.

The Fish
- 3 tablespoons butter, melted
- ¾ cup orange juice
- 1 tablespoon grated orange rind
- ½-inch piece peeled and minced, fresh ginger root
- ½ teaspoon black pepper
- 2 small, whole oranges, cut into slices
- 2 medium red onions, cut into slices
- 1 tablespoon mild honey
- 2 tablespoons minced, fresh mint

Lay the fish in an oven-to-table broiling pan large enough to accommodate them in one layer.

Melt the butter and add the orange juice, rind, ginger, and pepper and pour this sauce over the fish. Place slices of orange on top of the fish and top the slices of orange with overlapping slices of red onion. Dribble honey evenly over the onions.

Broil for 10 to 12 minutes, according to the thickness of the fish, 3 inches from source of heat. Baste several times during broiling. If there is not enough basting sauce after 5 minutes, add some boiled water to the bottom of the pan and continue basting. Serve hot, sprinkled with chopped mint.

Serves 6

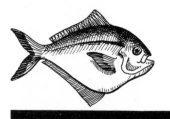

**Sauteed Butterfish with Sesame Seeds
and Oranges**

For some reason, this fish seems to be a favorite with children, possibly because of its small size (about six to ten inches, weighing about one-half pound) and its beautiful golden color when it's cooked. *Butterfish* has a buttery, melting, dark meat texture and, since it's a fatty fish, it lends itself well to pan frying, sauteing, or broiling.

It's a particularly popular fish in New England, where it's called *dollarfish* in Maine and *pumpkinseed* in Connecticut. For many years it was available only during the months from April to December, but increased fishing along the eastern seaboard has brought it to market almost every month of the year. However, if you can't get butterfish, fresh *herring* or *mackerel* can be used instead.

If you use a sauce, choose one that does not overpower the fish, but enhances its flavor (see Index):

Sauce Bearnaise
Hungarian Paprika Butter
Herbed Butter Sauce *(Beurre Nantais)*

Butterfish

SAUTEED
BUTTERFISH
WITH SESAME SEEDS
AND ORANGES

6 whole butterfish, about ½ pound each,
   gutted
¾ cup whole wheat flour
1 large egg, beaten
1 teaspoon lemon juice
¼ teaspoon black pepper
¾ cup sesame seeds
¼ cup Basic Clarified Butter (see Index)
1 large orange, thinly sliced
1 tablespoon finely minced, fresh mint

Dip the fish in the flour and place on wax paper. Reserve any flour that is left. Mix the egg with the lemon juice and pepper and pour into a pie plate.

Put the sesame seeds and ¼ cup of the reserved flour into another pie plate.

Dip the whole fish into the egg mixture and then into the sesame seed-flour mixture.

Melt the Basic Clarified Butter and when hot, quickly saute the fish for about 4 to 5 minutes on each side until it flakes easily. Remove to a warm serving platter with a wide spatula. Top each fish with a slice of orange and top orange with a sprinkle of the mint.

Serves 6

Hungarian Carp in Paprika Sauce
Pickled Carp
Momma's Gefilte Fish

carp

The *carp* is ancient. The carp is international. It is a fish of legend. For the Japanese, the *golden carp* is a symbol of courage and bravery and he or she who eats it is magically transformed into one who is also brave and has courage. (Would that it were just that simple!) Schubert wrote about it. And it swims live in a tank in our favorite Chinese fish store on Mott Street in New York just as it used to swim in the bathtub of Sheryl's grandmother before she made Gefilte Fish with it.

For thousands of years, fishermen cast their nets into the waters of the Sea of Galilee in Israel (it's really a lake—the carp is a freshwater fish), and the Israeli fishermen of today still bring in their catch and stock the carp ponds around the country.

As the peoples of the world left their homelands and resettled in other countries, the recipes for this ancient fish also traveled with them, for the carp can be found not only in central Europe, Asia, and Israel, but also across the United States and Canada, where it has bred most prolifically since its introduction to this continent in the mid-eighteen hundreds.

The people from Austria and Hungary cook carp with paprika. Oriental Jews from the Middle East use sesame paste in preparing it, while the middle Europeans from Poland, Germany, and Czechoslovakia use sweet and sour sauces or sour cream when making the fish. No matter which way the fish is prepared, however, it provides a protein content that is comparable to milk protein. One serving will supply about half the daily requirement for an adult!

One of the most famous recipes included in this chapter is the traditional Gefilte Fish, and many Jewish mothers include carp as a prime ingredient. Not only are there disagreements as to recipe amounts (depending upon whose mother made it), but the arguments really heat up when it comes to just whose mother made it best! To settle the argument once and for all, we include the best recipe in this book. Naturally, it comes from *Sheryl's* mother!

HUNGARIAN CARP
IN PAPRIKA SAUCE

2 pounds carp fillets, cut into serving
    portions
  juice of 1 lemon
¼ cup butter
½ cup coarsely chopped onion
1½ teaspoons paprika*
2 green peppers, diced
2 tomatoes, peeled and diced
  fresh dill for garnish

Preheat oven to 350°F.

Sprinkle fish with lemon juice. Then let sit for 20 minutes. Dry well.

In a small saucepan, melt butter and saute onions. Sprinkle with paprika. Add the green peppers and tomatoes and bring to a boil.

Place the pieces of fish on the bottom of an oval, shallow, buttered casserole. Pour the sauce over. Bake for 20 to 25 minutes, basting occasionally. Sprinkle with dill before serving.

Serves 6

*Hungarians use sweet, mild, or hot paprika, depending on the taste they want to achieve.

PICKLED
CARP

¾ cup white wine vinegar
½ cup water
2 tablespoons tamari soy sauce
2 bay leaves
6 peppercorns
1 whole clove
4 whole allspice
½ teaspoon celery seed
¼ teaspoon mustard seed
1 small, dried, hot chili pepper
2 onions, sliced
3 pounds freshwater carp or other
    freshwater fish, cut into 6 steaks

In a large pot, boil together the vinegar, water, soy sauce, all the spices, and the onions for 10 minutes. Add the fish steaks, lower heat at once to simmer, and cook for about 25 minutes. Allow the fish to cool in this broth, then lift out into a glass jar, bowl, or crock. Strain the liquid and pour over the fish. Refrigerate for at least 24 hours before serving, to enhance the flavor. Serve chilled.

Serves 6

MOMMA'S GEFILTE FISH

Things have really changed since momma placed the wooden chopping bowl and chopper in her lap and "chopped until her arms fell off." Her daughters get it all together in a food processor, but finish it traditionally in a wooden bowl to get the proper consistency—in deference to momma!

There are three kinds of freshwater fish that are combined and used in all traditional recipes—carp, whitefish, and yellow pike or pickerel. However, cooks change the balance by using different amounts of each fish according to their own preferences. When more carp is used (my friend Flora's mother used more carp), the dish is darker in appearance. When more whitefish is used, the dish is whiter in color. Sometimes momma even added a piece of "buffalo fish," a freshwater, small-mouthed bass, if the fishmonger had it.

Momma always made extra. She always expected a few unexpected guests. If you have any left-overs, do what momma did—plan to serve them within the next few days.

6 pounds freshwater fish filleted—made up of 2 pounds whitefish, 3 pounds yellow pike (pickerel or walleye), and 1 pound carp—cut into 1½-inch chunks (heads, skin, and bones reserved)
4 large onions, 3 coarsely chopped, 1 sliced for fish stock (reserve the skin of 1 onion*)
¼ cup cold water
3 eggs, beaten until foamy
1 teaspoon white pepper
2 tablespoons dry, whole grain bread crumbs
1 carrot diagonally sliced into ¼-inch slices
cold water to cover

(continued on following page)

Puree fillets, a few batches at a time, in a food processor. Remove to a wooden chopping bowl or large wooden chopping board. Add the chopped onions. Use a single blade chopper with a handle or a French knife, and chop mixture for 10 to 15 minutes, gradually incorporating the water, eggs, ¼ teaspoon pepper, and bread crumbs. Chop until mixture is a pasty consistency. Set in refrigerator to chill while preparing broth.

Use a large fish poacher and layer the scraps of fish and bones on the bottom. Stretch a cheesecloth or the pieces of fish skin over the bones and then add a layer of sliced onion and carrots. Pour 2 cups of cold water into poacher. Add onion skin and remaining pepper. Cover pot and bring to a boil, lower heat, and simmer for 20 minutes. While broth is simmering, prepare the fish ovals.

Wet hands under running water and spoon 2 or more tablespoons of fish between the hands. Keep hands wet while forming these ovals, about 3 to 4 inches long. As each is finished, place on wax paper.

Bring the broth to a boil and lower the fish ovals into the broth. Make sure the boiling broth comes up to cover two-thirds of the fish with liquid. Lower the heat at once and cover the poacher. Simmer on very low heat for 2 hours.

Let fish cool in broth and lift fish out to a platter when cool. Remove the cooked carrot slices and use to garnish the ovals. Strain the liquid, pressing solids against the strainer. Pour broth into a separate bowl. Refrigerate and chill separately for several hours. Serve with beetroot horseradish and the traditional *challah* (egg bread) to absorb the liquid which is spooned over the fish at serving time. The broth will gel into an aspic.

Yield: 3 to 4 ovals per person

*Momma claimed that the onion skins colored the fish stock a lovely amber color and gave it more eye appeal.

The Widow's Walk

They sailed from Provincetown, from Gloucester, from New Bedford, Newport, and Sag Harbor, and from all the little ports up and down the Northeast Coast. The boats seemed as frail as matchsticks when challenged by the sea, and sometimes—too often—the fishermen did not return to the harbor.

Left behind, the families waited and, when it was time for the fishing fleet to return, the wives went outside onto a little balcony that looked toward the ocean and they paced while trying to catch the first glimpse of the little bobbing dots afloat on the horizon. There were times that the wait was in vain and the lonely, hopeless lookout became "the widow's walk." Today, throughout New England, these walks are still a part of the lovely houses that stand along the coastline.

COD
**New England Codfish Cakes
and Two Variations
Poached Cod Fillets with Eggs and Onions
Whole Cod Poached in Milk and Dill with Greek
Egg and Lemon Sauce (Avgolemono)**

CUSK
Fried Cusk in Mustard Marinade

HADDOCK
**Haddock Ring
Milk Poached Haddock with Egg
and Parsley Sauce**

POLLACK
**Broiled Pollack with Paprika and Herbs
Pollack Curry with Eggplant,
Tomatoes, and Basil**

SCROD
**Baked Scrod in Coconut Cream Sauce
Baked Scrod with Potatoes,
Tomatoes, and Oregano
Savory Baked Scrod with Vegetables**

WHITING
**Fried Whiting with Fennel, Cinnamon,
Almonds, and Raisins
Marinated and Fried Whiting with Tomatoes**

Meet the members of the family: □ Atlantic cod □ burbot (freshwater) □ cusk □ haddock □ Pacific cod □ pollack □ scrod (cod weighing under three pounds) □ whiting (or silver hake).

Although over seven *billion* pounds a year are caught commercially and the *cod* may well be called the world's most important food fish, it is another of the ocean's proofs (as though further proof were necessary) that all fishermen are crazy. During the wildest winter months, when all sane people stay at home, a few saltwater anglers (dubbed "Codballs") set out in high seas and rough weather to catch the *Atlantic cod*. Of course, the fish is readily available in the markets already flaked, shredded, in slabs, in steaks, dried whole and frozen, but commercial availability never stopped anyone from fishing for his own.

For many years following a childhood that included daily doses of cod liver oil for vitamins and whatever else our mothers thought it contained, we had an unfounded aversion to anything associated with the name of that fish. It may have been a superb source of nutrition (even "brain food"), but as we recall, it tasted and smelled just awful. It took a lot of years and a lot of tasting to convince us, at last, that there are lots of good things about the codfish and its family.

The cod has an interesting history. It is most closely associated with New England and with the fishermen of that area whose ancestors came from Portugal. (See "The Blessing of the Fleet," page 6.) In fact, cod is so readily available in the Northeast that it is called "Cape Cod Turkey" up in Gloucester and it appears on a Nova Scotia banknote with the motto, "Success to the Fisheries." The cod's value to New England as a food source and as a resource in world trade is reflected by the model codfish cast in gold that hangs in the Massachusetts State House.

Though all of the family members are good eating and can be prepared in a variety of ways, the Atlantic cod, particularly, is a lean, low-fat, very digestible fish. It flakes easily and it's quite adaptable to almost any method of cooking. It takes well to grilling, frying, poaching, or stewing; it can be used in fish salads and fish patties, and it makes wonderful chowder. It also loves rich sauces.

Almost all the fish in this family are lean and flaky, but the flavors vary slightly from variety to variety. The average market size of the cod is about 10 pounds, though its kid brothers and sisters, the *scrod*, are under 3 pounds. Its youth makes for a more delicate texture. Larger cod, weighing up to 100 pounds, is packed commercially and flash frozen aboard the ships as steaks, sticks, and fillets.

Haddock, averaging two to six pounds, is popular as a fresh fillet, or as a frozen fillet, distributed throughout the country all year round. When smoked, haddock is used for finnan haddie, the traditional Scottish dish.

The *pollack* looks somewhat like a green codfish. However, it is meatier and firmer-fleshed than haddock or cod, though it tastes much the same. Sometimes it is sold as *Boston bluefish* or *deep sea fillets*. It's in season in winter, so it is less costly at that time. Pollack is excellent in chowders because its texture is so firm; it also takes well to herbs.

The opposite of pollack, but still part of the cod family, is *whiting*, or *silver hake*. It is slender, soft, snow-white, sweet and delicate in flavor. Whiting must be handled carefully in cooking because it breaks easily, but it can be cooked in any way you like. Another plus—it is relatively inexpensive.

No matter which member of the cod family is available at the fishmonger—haddock, Atlantic cod, or pollack—keep in mind that their basic characteristics are very much the same and, thus, the recipes that follow are quite interchangeable.

NEW ENGLAND
CODFISH CAKES
AND TWO VARIATIONS

2 pounds codfish fillets
2 cups cold, mashed potatoes
2 tablespoons minced, fresh parsley
3 tablespoons minced, fresh chives
¼ teaspoon mace
¼ teaspoon white pepper
⅛ teaspoon cayenne pepper
2 eggs, beaten
¾ cup fine, dry, whole grain bread
    crumbs
¼ cup Basic Clarified Butter (see Index)
    minced, fresh parsley for garnish

Chop the raw codfish very fine by hand, or use a food processor or blender. Add the mashed potatoes, parsley, chives, mace, pepper, and cayenne. Mix well with wooden spoon. Add the eggs and mix again. Form into 3-inch patties about ¾ inch thick and dip into bread crumbs to coat.

Heat the Basic Clarified Butter until hot in a heavy skillet and fry patties about 4 minutes on each side until brown and crisp. Remove to hot serving platter. Garnish with parsley or serve with any of the tomato sauces (see Index).

Serves 6

VARIATIONS

CODFISH
BALLS

Prepare the same recipe but roll into small 1-inch balls. Fry quickly in hot oil and serve as an hors d'oeuvre.

Yield: 18 balls

CODFISH
CASSEROLE

Prepare the same recipe but add ½ cup milk and 2 finely minced cloves of garlic. Spoon into a well-buttered, 2-quart casserole. Dot with butter and bake uncovered in a preheated 375°F. oven for 40 to 45 minutes or until edges are crisp and brown.

Serves 6

POACHED
COD FILLETS
WITH EGGS AND ONIONS

1½ cups water
½ cup lemon juice
1 small onion, cut in half
1 bay leaf
6 peppercorns
1 whole clove
2 sprigs parsley
2½ pounds codfish fillets or 3 packages
(12 ounces each) frozen cod fillets,
each portion cut in half
6 tablespoons butter, lightly browned
2 onions, thinly sliced
2 hard-cooked eggs, thinly sliced
2 tablespoons minced, fresh parsley

In a skillet mix the water, lemon juice, onion, bay leaf, peppercorns, clove, and parsley and bring to a boil. Simmer this broth until it is reduced to ¾ cup, strain and reserve.

Wipe out the skillet and arrange the fish in one layer and pour the reserved liquid over the fish. Cover the pan and simmer for 15 to 20 minutes or until fish flakes easily.

Meanwhile, heat the butter in a separate skillet and saute the onion slices until tender-crisp. Turn carefully with a spatula so the slices remain intact. Transfer the fish with a slotted wide spatula to a heated serving platter. Place onion slices on top of each portion and a slice of egg over the onion. Pour the browned butter over all and sprinkle with minced parsley.

Serves 6

Note: In place of the egg and onion topping, simply poached cod can be served with any of the following sauces (see Index):

Shallot and Garlic Butter
(also called "Escargot Butter")
Hungarian Paprika Butter
Orange Butter and Chive Sauce
Black Butter Sauce

Soy Sauce Butter
Egg and Parsley Sauce
Spanish Saffron *Veloute* Sauce
Sauce Maltaise (Orange Hollandaise)
Sorrel Mayonnaise

WHOLE COD POACHED IN MILK AND DILL
WITH GREEK EGG AND LEMON SAUCE

6 cups water
1 cup milk
½ lemon, thinly sliced
1 bay leaf
1 whole clove
12 sprigs dill, tied with string
1 whole codfish, 6 to 7 pounds, cleaned
and with head left on, but gills
removed
Greek Egg and Lemon Sauce
(Avgolemono) (see Index)

Combine all ingredients, except fish and sauce, in a fish poacher and bring to a boil. Lower heat and simmer for 15 minutes. Bring liquid to a boil again and add the codfish. Lower heat to simmer and cook for 20 to 30 minutes or until fish flakes with a skewer when tested.

While fish is poaching, prepare sauce and keep warm. Lift the fish out carefully to a warm platter. Spoon some sauce over the fish and pass the rest in a sauce boat.

Serves 6 to 8

FRIED CUSK
IN MUSTARD MARINADE

2 pounds cusk fillets
2 tablespoons lemon juice
2 tablespoons dry mustard
2 eggs, beaten
2 tablespoons cold water
¾ cup stone-ground cornmeal
corn oil for frying

Garnish
2 limes cut into wedges
1 tablespoon minced, fresh dill

Place the cusk fillets in a nonmetallic flat dish. Mix the lemon juice and mustard together and let stand to develop flavor for 10 minutes. Then spread on fish fillets and keep at room temperature for 30 minutes.

Dilute the eggs with the water and beat lightly in a pie pan. Spread the cornmeal on a piece of aluminum foil. Dip the fillets in the egg and then the cornmeal. Dry fish pieces on a wire rack for 15 minutes.

Heat oil to 370°F. and fry about 3 to 4 minutes on each side until golden and pieces flake with a skewer. Drain on paper towels and transfer to a warm serving dish. Dip lime wedges into minced dill and serve with wedges to be squeezed over fish.

Serves 6

HADDOCK
RING

Duxelles *Veloute* or Spanish Saffron
Veloute Sauce (see Index)
2 cups whole grain bread cubes
2 cups light cream
2 tablespoons lemon juice
¼ teaspoon white pepper
1 pound haddock fillets
1 medium onion, grated
4 egg whites
1 tablespoon minced, fresh tarragon or ¾
teaspoon dried

Prepare the sauce first and set aside.

Place bread cubes in a bowl with the
cream, lemon juice, and pepper. Let stand
for 20 minutes to absorb the liquid.

Preheat oven to 325°F.

Use a food processor or a blender and
puree the fish and onion very fine. Transfer
fish and onion mixture to a mixing bowl.
Add the soaked bread to the processor or
blender and chop very fine. Remove, blend
with the fish mixture, and refrigerate. Oil a
1-quart ring mold and set aside.

Beat the egg whites until stiff and add the
tarragon. Then fold into the fish puree.
Spoon into the mold, cover top with
buttered aluminum foil, and bake for 30 to
40 minutes or until firm. Let cool for 5
minutes before unmolding. Serve with
sauce in a glass bowl that fits into the
center of the ring mold.

Serves 6

MILK POACHED HADDOCK
WITH EGG AND PARSLEY SAUCE

Egg and Parsley Sauce (see Index)
1 haddock, about 4½ pounds, cleaned but with head left on, or 2 haddock fillets or steaks weighing 2½ to 3 pounds
3 cups milk
1½ cups water
1 large onion, peeled and stuck with 3 whole cloves
1 carrot, cut into strips
1 bay leaf
¼ teaspoon peppercorns
1 tablespoon butter

Prepare sauce first and set aside.

Wrap whole fish in cheesecloth, with extra cheesecloth left at ends for removal. Add milk and water to a fish poacher or roasting pan. Add the onion stuck with cloves to the milk. Add the carrot, bay leaf, and peppercorns. Bring to a boil, add the fish and lower heat to a very gentle simmer. Poach for 15 to 20 minutes and test with a fork. Remove and unwrap fish to a warm serving platter. Put the butter on the end of a fork and run it over the surface of the fish to glaze it slightly. Serve with the Egg and Parsley Sauce in a sauce boat to be passed at the table.

Serves 6

BROILED POLLACK
WITH PAPRIKA AND HERBS

1 tablespoon corn oil
6 pollack fillets, about 2½ pounds
1 teaspoon paprika
½ teaspoon black pepper
½ cup softened butter
2 tablespoons finely minced, fresh chives or minced green scallions
2 tablespoons finely minced, fresh parsley
1 tablespoon minced, fresh tarragon or ¾ teaspoon dried, crushed tarragon
1 tablespoon lemon juice

Oil a large piece of foil and place on a broiling rack. Lay the fillets on the foil and sprinkle with the paprika and pepper.

Cream the butter by beating with a wooden spoon or in a food processor. Spread butter lavishly on top of the fish and broil 4 inches from the source of heat, basting several times for about 5 to 8 minutes. Test with a skewer to see if fish flakes easily. Add the minced herbs and the lemon juice. Transfer to heated platter with wide spatula and pour sauce from the pan over all.

Serves 6

POLLACK CURRY
WITH EGGPLANT, TOMATOES, AND BASIL

⅓ cup olive oil
1 cup chopped onion
8 tomatoes, about 3 pounds, peeled and chopped
2 cloves garlic, finely minced
1 tablespoon finely minced, fresh basil or 2 teaspoons dried
½ teaspoon black pepper
1 eggplant, about 1½ pounds, peeled and diced (about 5 cups)
⅓ cup whole wheat pastry flour
2 tablespoons curry powder
2 pounds pollack fillets, cut into 2-inch pieces
¼ cup butter
¼ cup olive oil
2 tablespoons minced, fresh parsley or 1 tablespoon minced, fresh coriander leaves

Heat olive oil in a large skillet and saute onion until tender but not brown. Add tomatoes, garlic, basil, and pepper and cook over medium heat for 10 minutes. Add eggplant, cover skillet, and cook for 15 minutes more or until eggplant is tender. Stir occasionally.

Meanwhile, mix the flour and curry powder and coat the fish pieces with this mixture.

In another heavy skillet, heat the butter and oil until hot. Saute the fish over medium heat about 5 to 8 minutes, turning carefully and cooking until the fish flakes easily. Drain on paper towels and keep warm. Spoon the eggplant-tomato mixture into a serving dish. Top with the fish and sprinkle with the parsley or coriander. Serve with bowls of hot, brown rice for a complete meal.

Serves 6

BAKED SCROD
IN COCONUT CREAM SAUCE

1 tablespoon butter
3 tablespoons chopped onions
3 tablespoons chopped green pepper
1 cup Coconut Milk (see Index)
1½ tablespoons cornstarch
2 pounds boneless scrod fillets, cut into 1-inch cubes
½ cup grated cheddar cheese

To prepare the sauce, melt butter and saute onion and green pepper until wilted in a saucepan. Add ¼ cup of the Coconut Milk and bring to a boil. In a cup, blend another ¼ cup of the Coconut Milk with the cornstarch. Lower heat and add this mixture to the saucepan, add remaining Coconut Milk and simmer, stirring, for 3 to 4 minutes. Set aside.

Preheat oven to 350°F.

Arrange the fish in one layer in an oiled, oven-to-table baking pan. Pour the sauce over all and sprinkle with cheese and bake until cheese melts, about 25 minutes. Then brown lightly under broiler and serve.

Serves 6

BAKED SCROD
WITH POTATOES, TOMATOES, AND OREGANO

2½ pounds scrod or 2 fillets from a 5-pound fish
4 medium potatoes, sliced paper thin
½ teaspoon black pepper
1½ pounds plum tomatoes, peeled and coarsely cut
3 tablespoons olive oil
1 large onion, peeled, thinly sliced, and separated into rings
1 clove garlic, finely minced
1 teaspoon finely minced, fresh oregano or ½ teaspoon dried
1 cup minced, fresh parsley
1 lemon, thinly sliced

Preheat oven to 350°F.

Place the fish fillets in the center of a large, oven-to-table baking pan and arrange the potatoes, overlapping, around the fish. Sprinkle with black pepper. Toss tomatoes with 1 tablespoon olive oil and spread over fish. Toss onions with 1 tablespoon olive oil. Scatter the onion rings on top. Sprinkle with the minced garlic, oregano, and parsley. Toss lemon slices with 1 tablespoon olive oil. Arrange slices of lemon on top. Bake for 40 to 45 minutes, basting occasionally. Test after 40 minutes.

Serves 6 to 8

SAVORY
BAKED SCROD
WITH VEGETABLES

---

1 cup diced carrots
1 cup diced potatoes
¾ cup diced turnips
1½ cups water
4 tablespoons butter
½ cup diced celery
¾ cup coarsely chopped onion
¾ cup coarsely chopped leeks
½ pound mushrooms, coarsely chopped
2 pounds scrod fillets or steaks
½ teaspoon black pepper
3 tablespoons lemon juice
2 tablespoons minced, fresh parsley
3 tablespoons melted butter

Preheat oven to 425°F.

In a covered saucepan, simmer the carrots, potatoes, and turnips in the water until just tender, for about 8 minutes. Drain and reserve the vegetable liquid.

In a skillet, melt 2 tablespoons of the butter and saute the celery, onion, and leeks until tender but not brown. Stirring to prevent browning, add the remaining 2 tablespoons of butter and the mushrooms and cook and stir for 2 minutes more. Then stir in the drained, parboiled vegetables.

Butter an oven-to-table baking dish and arrange the fish in a single layer. Spoon the vegetable mixture over and around the fish. Add the pepper.

Boil the vegetable cooking liquid over high heat until it is reduced to ½ cup, add the lemon juice and pour over the fish and vegetables. Bake in the hot oven, basting with pan liquids for 15 to 20 minutes or until fish has turned opaque and flakes with a skewer. Sprinkle with parsley and pour the 3 tablespoons melted butter over all.

Serves 6

FRIED WHITING
WITH FENNEL, CINNAMON, ALMONDS, AND RAISINS

2 ½ to 3 pounds whiting fillets, cut into
    2-inch-thick slices
  juice of 1 lemon
½ teaspoon black pepper
½ teaspoon ground cinnamon
 1 cup whole wheat flour
 3 eggs, beaten
 2 tablespoons cold water
 2 cups fine, dry, whole grain bread
    crumbs
 1 tablespoon paprika
  about ½ cup corn oil for frying or
    enough to cover ¼ inch of pan
 1 bunch fennel sprigs or ½ teaspoon
    crushed fennel seeds
 2 tablespoons slivered almonds, toasted
 2 tablespoons raisins, soaked in hot
    water and drained
 1 lemon cut in wedges for garnish

In a nonmetallic dish, place the pieces of fish and pour the lemon juice over. Let marinate in the refrigerator for 1 hour, then drain and dry thoroughly. Add the pepper and cinnamon to the flour and place on a sheet of aluminum foil.

In a shallow pie pan, beat the eggs with the water. Combine the bread crumbs with the paprika and place on another sheet of aluminum foil.

Dredge each piece of fish lightly in flour. Dip in beaten egg and then dredge in the bread crumb mixture. Place the crumbed pieces of fish on a wire rack and let dry in the refrigerator for 30 minutes.

Use a deep, heavy skillet, such as a black, cast-iron one, and heat ¼ inch of corn oil until it registers 370°F. on a frying thermometer. Fry the fish in a single layer without crowding for 5 minutes. Turn when golden and fry on other side. Test after cooking 4 minutes more to see if it flakes easily with a skewer. Drain on paper towels. Spread half of the fennel sprigs on the bottom of a platter. Place the fish on top and the remaining fennel sprigs on top of the fish. Sprinkle with the almonds and raisins and let stand at room temperature for 1 hour before serving to absorb the fennel flavor. Garnish with lemon wedges.

Serves 6

MARINATED AND
FRIED WHITING
WITH TOMATOES

2½ pounds whiting fillets, cut into serving
  pieces
3 tablespoons lemon juice
3 tablespoons white wine vinegar
⅔ cup olive oil
1 medium onion, thinly sliced
1 clove garlic, finely minced
2 teaspoons chopped, fresh dill
2 teaspoons chopped, fresh parsley
1 bay leaf
¼ teaspoon black pepper
½ cup whole wheat flour
4 tomatoes, peeled and coarsely
  chopped

Garnish
1 lemon, cut into wedges
2 tablespoons finely minced, fresh
  parsley

Place the fish in a nonmetallic dish. Combine the lemon juice, vinegar, 5 tablespoons of the oil, onion, garlic, dill, parsley, and bay leaf and pour over the fish. Allow it to marinate for 1 hour at room temperature, then drain and dry the fish. Reserve the marinade.

Combine the pepper and the flour and coat the fish with this mixture. Heat remaining olive oil in a large skillet and fry the fish quickly over high heat, just 2 to 3 minutes on each side until golden. Lift out carefully and arrange on a serving platter and keep warm. Add the tomatoes and the reserved marinade to the same skillet and cook over medium heat, stirring until thickened slightly, about 5 minutes. Pour the sauce over the fish. Arrange the lemon wedges around the fish and sprinkle parsley over all.

Serves 6

Gruyere Cheese and Crab Meat Puff Casserole
Avocado-and-Crab Mousse
Baked Alaskan King Crab Legs with Shallot
and Garlic Butter
Baked Potatoes Stuffed with Crab Meat
Broiled Crab Cakes, Maryland Style
Cantonese Crab Fu-Yung
Hot Crab Salad Baked in Whole Wheat
Pita Bread
Crab Meat *Chausseur*
Sauteed Soft-Shell Crabs

We are devout lovers of *crab*. Every place we travel, we look for this tasty and unusual treat. We can remember orgies of steamed, peppered crabs on a back porch outside of Baltimore, a huge Queensland *mud crab* devoured seaside at a restaurant called Doyle's of Watson's Bay outside Sydney, Australia—it must have weighed fully eight pounds. There have been the feasts of the popular *blue crab* right in our Fire Island home and the finger-dipping, butter-dripping goodness of *stone crab* claws when we've worked in Florida. To put it mildly (and with pun intended), we're hooked on crab. If you have tried them, wherever you live, you need no further introduction. If you've been put off by the seeming difficulty of dismantling them into edible portions—read on.

Who Are the Crabs?

The type of crab you can buy (or sometimes catch) depends, of course, on where you live. Only in certain parts of the country can you find them fresh from the sea. Many varieties are never tasted as freshly caught delicacies, but it does not seem to affect their popularity. Here are some members of the family.

Blue Crab

These are probably the best known and most popular of the crabs and they're found all along the Atlantic and Gulf Coasts from Massachusetts to Texas. They're a shallow water crab and they live near the mouths of coastal rivers as well as in the bays and sounds. They are not, in fact, blue, for only the claws carry the distinctive blue tint. The body is generally brownish green or dark green in color, while the undersides of the body and the claws are white.

Soft-Shell Crab

These are actually blue crabs that have molted. Females shed their shells from 18 to 20 times until they reach full size, while males may molt as many as 23 times. The crab is called a "buster" when it begins molting—the shell cracks, and the soft-shelled delicacy backs out. They come into season in late April or early May and they're available well into summer if the weather is mild.

King Crab

This is the crab generally listed on the menu as *Alaskan King Crab*—and a large one it is! It ranges in size from about 10 to 20 pounds and only the claws, legs, and shoulders provide edible meat. They're caught in midwinter and the ships that catch them in huge crab pots, baited with fish, either flash freeze them at once, cook them aboard, or hold them in "live" tanks until they can be processed ashore. The legs are available to the shopper either frozen or canned.

Dungeness Crab

Our first question upon arriving in San Francisco is always, "Are *Dungeness crabs* in season?" Since the catch has varied from year to year, the answers have also varied and a "no" can be a great disappointment to every member of our film crew, all of whom adore Dungeness crabs. It is a versatile delicacy and if you've visited the West Coast (or if you live in that gloriously lovely city by the Golden Gate Bridge), you've seen the tourists devouring Dungeness crabs right from the shell at the stands on Fisherman's Wharf. We have also purchased a freshly boiled crab, a loaf of local sourdough bread, and then devoured our lunch while seated wharfside. And, we have also eaten it (at slightly higher prices) at such elegant San Francisco restaurants as Ernie's. The Dungeness crab is available in the shell, ready to be cooked at home, by the pound already cooked in the shell, or out of the shell as body and claw meat, or you can find it frozen or canned. It can be used interchangeably in any crab recipe.

Stone Crab

The popularity of this southern crab is attested to by the fact that the most popular restaurant in South Florida is called "Joe's Stone Crab" and the wait for a table is from one to three hours, even more on a Saturday night in season.

And we, too, have waited, for it is most worthwhile.

The *stone crab* is found from the Carolinas to Texas, but it is most prevalent on the Florida coast. Only the claws are edible and the fishermen have found a way to perpetuate their catch, for only one claw is twisted off when the crab is caught, and within 18 months the creature grows another claw to replace the stolen one. The new claw will be slightly smaller than the original, but it can be just as devastating a weapon.

For years, we wondered why Joe's stone crabs were better than any others we had tasted, why we waited two hours or more to eat there, why the other restaurants just were not as good. The secret is that the *fishermen* cook the crab claws on ship and *then freeze them*. If the claw is frozen first, thawed, and then cooked, the meat adheres to the inside of the shell and is difficult to remove. The claws are eaten cold with drawn butter or in a mustard sauce dip.

Snow Crab

Not too many years ago, the Pacific Coast and Alaskan fisheries depended almost entirely upon the Dungeness and the king crab. Now, an under-utilized species has begun to find its way into the markets across the country. The *snow crab* (part of a family that includes the *tanner crab* and *queen crab*) has a delicate flavor, is tender and succulent, and it's low in calories. It can be used interchangeably with any other crab meat and it's available fully cooked, frozen, or canned. The leg meat is white with bright red coloring on the surface and the body meat is pure white.

Jonah Crab

This crab owes its undeserved unpopularity to the fact that the same fishermen who would normally harvest it for market are the very people who catch the lobsters off the coast of New England. Since lobsters are the major cash crop, the *Jonah crab* has gone unnoticed and remains under-utilized. The processing capabilities are just not there, the lobstermen just don't care enough—and a potential industry has gone undeveloped. Since the Jonah crabs are caught right in the lobster pots, they have lent themselves to family-type processing, where the wives of the lobstermen often pick and pack the crab meat for the local general stores. The dealers, in turn, handle the Jonah crab as a convenience for steady customers. It can be found as far south as Long Island and an occasional fisherman goes out after them, catching them as they move inshore off the piers and the bridges during the spring. Other than that, they're generally a deep water crab, with the larger ones being found at the greater depths of the Continental Shelf.

How to Buy Crabs

Depending upon location, season, and availability, you may find the crabs sold live in the shell. The Chinese markets in our city generally have basketsful of the blue claws, and avid buyers pick over them for the liveliest of the bunch. However, if you don't want to prepare them whole, the meat of the blue claw is generally sold already cleaned and shelled and the grades are described below.

Lump Meat
This is the meat from the body of the crab and it comes in large, white chunks. It has no waste and a pound will serve four people generously. However, it is the most expensive of the choices.

Backfin
This has smaller chunks than the lump meat, but it's just as good for cooking or for stuffing.

Flaked Crab Meat
This is the meat from various parts of the body. It is the least expensive and it can be mixed with lump meat or backfin meat in the recipes.

Frozen or Canned Crab Meat
As we've mentioned in our descriptions of the crab family, most crab varieties are available frozen or in cans, usually fully cooked. However, no matter how you choose your crab meat, make certain that it does not smell fishy or of ammonia. As with all fresh seafood, crab should have a fresh, briny smell.

Sometimes fresh crab meat is pasteurized, and then packed in hermetically sealed cans to prevent spoilage. As long as you do not open the can, the meat will remain fresh. However, as soon as you get it home, refrigerate it—*but do not freeze.*

(continued on page 246)

The Happy Crabber

Calvert Parks sails out of Wingate, Maryland, and he is, indeed, a happy crabber. We were interested in how the professionals do it, since we have been only moderately successful with our amateur efforts at snagging the blue crabs. (See page 247.) Calvert uses an open boat, and a combination of a "trotline," a scoop net, and ordinary bushel baskets for keeping the catch.

The trotline is a twisted, long, double line with chains, a plastic float and an anchor at either end.

The line is baited with chicken heads, eel, beef tripe, or any other tough bait that can't be taken too quickly by the crabs. Bait is wedged between the twisted line at three- to four-foot intervals. The line is payed out as the

boat drifts with the tide and, as the boat reaches the end of the trotline, the second anchor is dropped overboard, and the crabber returns to the first buoy.

The line is pulled slowly to the surface and the feeding crab is netted—the trick being to bring the crab close enough to the net without frightening it off. The crabs are tossed into the basket and then sized later, with the undersized crabs being thrown back.

Crabs caught professionally are then eaten with as much gusto as those caught by us amateurs!

Soft-Shell Crab

The tenderest and softest are the earliest—usually in late April and early May. As they approach the end of August, they become a bit tougher (and, in fact, are called "leatherbacks" at that time). Soft-shell crabs should *always* be bought live. If they've been frozen, they have a tendency to become wrinkled and soggy. However, there are some flash frozen, soft-shell crabs that are available and, though they don't compare with the fresh ones, they're quite adequate and can be kept in the freezer at 0°F. for about six months. Incidentally, we used to wonder why we were buying fairly large soft-shell crabs, while our favorite restaurants were serving a tiny, delicious variety. We found out that by asking for "hotel size" when we buy crabs, we now can match the culinary acrobatics of the best chefs!

Telling Male from Female

As kids we used to joke that you could tell a male crab from a female crab by feeding it. If *he* ate it, it was a male—if *she* ate it, it was a female. Children's jokes aside, there is a very good reason for being able to tell the male from the female among the blue crabs particularly.

As with lobsters, the female roe is delicious. Though all blue crabs have the distinctive tint on their claws, the female will have bright, red-tipped claws while the claws of the male will be striped blue on white, with no red showing on the tip.

Turn the crab over on its back. The female will have a wide, rounded shield on its underside, while the male will have a delicate, elongated strip that widens out to the base.

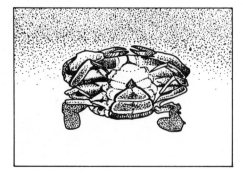 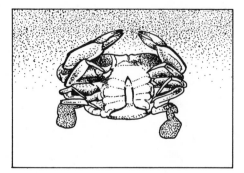

Can You Catch Your Own?

If you are near the place where they catch blue crabs and if you see the youngsters (and the not-so-young youngsters) dipping lines baited with meat or fish into the shallow waters, you may want to join them. The answer is, of course, yes, you certainly can catch your own. The best way is to ask some questions and then to follow directions, but there are two simple methods available to you.

Crabbing areas are usually quite accessible and you don't need expensive gear or years of experience. The simplest way is to wade out into the water and scoop up the crabs with a simple dip net. Or—you can use the dip method at night at a lighted pier. The crabs are attracted by the baitfish swimming in the water and an agile fisherman can net them as they swim by.

Another technique is the use of a bait line, or "trotline," and the dip net. (See The Happy Crabber, page 244, for more on this method.) You can keep the crabs you catch in an ordinary bushel basket, with wet burlap over them. Keep them out of sunlight and never put them in a closed container or in water, because they'll die from lack of oxygen.

There are more sophisticated methods of crabbing—the use of hand traps or crab pots, which can be left anchored to bridge abutments or piers for several days without losing the catch. If you plan to try these methods, you are already too far advanced for rank amateurs such as we are.

How to Cook Crabs Whole

The crabs should be kept alive before you cook them. The refrigerator or some other cool place will generally do nicely. If any of the crabs die before cooking them, throw them away! And keep in mind that only cooked crab meat should be frozen. Never freeze whole crabs, either cooked or un-cooked.

Live Hard-Shell Crabs
Use a large pot of boiling water (we use sea water for our crabs as we do for lobster) and add your favorite seasoning—any combination of cayenne pepper, basil, vinegar, or lemon. If you prefer, there are commercial "crab

boils" on the market that already contain ingredients such as mustard seed, coriander seed, cayenne pepper, bay leaves, allspice, and cloves. We have shopped for the commercial crab boil in New Orleans and we always keep a package or two of Rex Crab Boil or Zatarain's Crab Boil on our shelf awaiting the next influx of blue crabs into our bay. When the water comes to a rolling boil, plunge the crabs in and then let the water come to a boil again. Begin timing from this point. Cook the crabs for ten minutes and when they're done, turn to the next section of this chapter and eat them with gusto!

Live Soft-Shell Crabs

Find the apron that folds under the rear of the body. With a sharp knife, cut it off. Turn the crab and cut off the face at the point just behind the back of the eyes. Lift each point of the crab at the sides and, using your fingers, scrape away and discard the soft porous "lungs" underneath the shell. Then cook according to the recipe (see page 257).

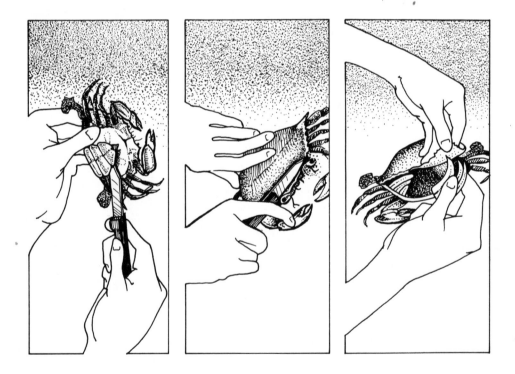

How to Eat a Whole Crab

First of all, the best way to eat a blue crab is to prepare yourself for a finger-licking good time. Forget the plates, the knives and forks. Just lay out last week's newspaper on the table, give each guest a small, heavy knife and a wooden mallet. Just follow the few simple steps we've given below and soon you'll become as adept as the professional crab pickers who work at the processing plants and who can pick out up to seven pounds an hour!

1. Remove the claws by pulling them away from the body of the crab. Put them aside. (If you prefer, eat them first. We always save them for last as we do with lobster.)

2. Lift up the "apron" or flap on the bottom side of the crab and in one motion take off the top shell, prying it loose with your fingers. Discard the shell and apron.

3. Use your fingers to pull away and discard the spongy white gills on the underside of the crab. These are inedible and are sometimes called "dead man's fingers" or "devils."

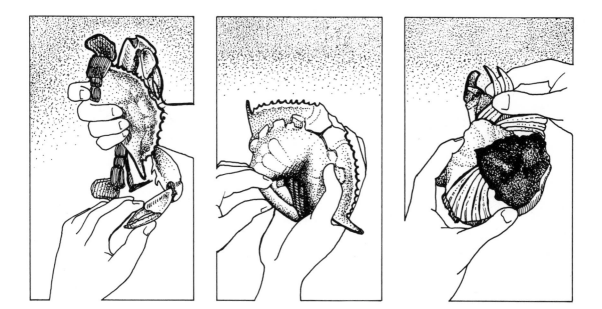

4. Break the body of the crab in half and then, using your fingers, extract the white, firm meat that you'll find all through the body as you peel away the sections. You can either eat these morsels directly or save them up to make a pile of crab meat.

5. With the wooden mallet, crack the claws and remove the meat from them by pulling on the pincer. The meat should come free in one succulent piece.

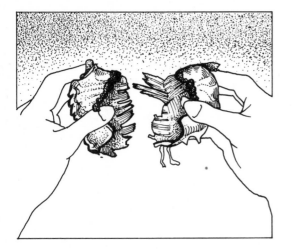 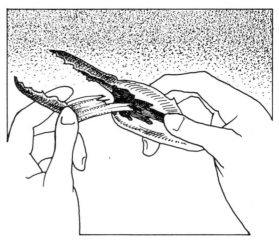

A Note about the Recipes

There are parts of the country where crab can be an expensive luxury and there are times of the year, even in areas where crab is plentiful, when the catch varies and the price goes up. As a result, most of the recipes that follow have been designed to stretch the crab-dollar as far as possible.

Sauces for Crab

For use with hot crab meat, try any of the following sauces (see Index):

Lemon Butter Sauce
Mint Butter Sauce
Lobster Sauce (Sauce Cardinal)

Spanish Saffron *Veloute* Sauce
Seafood Shell Sauce

For cold crab meat, use any of these sauces (see Index):

Sorrel Mayonnaise
Remoulade Sauce (Pungent Mayonnaise Sauce)
Tarragon Sauce
Cresson Mayonnaise (Watercress Mayonnaise)

GRUYERE CHEESE AND CRAB MEAT PUFF CASSEROLE

This dish is a light and lovely Sunday supper dish. It is easy to assemble beforehand, and takes only 30 minutes to bake. A crisp green salad would complete the supper.

6 large slices whole grain bread
8 slices Gruyere cheese, about ½ inch thick
½ pound fresh or frozen crab meat, picked over to remove cartilage (chopped shrimp or left-over, cooked fish may be used in place of crab)
4 eggs
1 teaspoon dry mustard
2 cups milk
1 tablespoon minced, fresh chives
¼ teaspoon cayenne pepper
2 tablespoons minced, fresh parsley

Butter a large, shallow, oven-to-table casserole and place the slices of bread on the bottom. Top the bread with the cheese and cover the cheese with the crab meat.

In a separate bowl, mix eggs, mustard, milk, chives, and pepper together using a wire whisk, and pour over the bread, cheese, and crab. Refrigerate for 1½ hours or until the bread has absorbed most of the liquid.

Preheat oven to 350°F.

Bake for about 25 to 35 minutes. Sprinkle with parsley and serve while hot and bubbly.

Serves 6

AVOCADO-AND-CRAB MOUSSE

2 large avocados, peeled, pitted, and cut
    in chunks
    juice of ½ lemon
2 envelopes unflavored gelatin
2 tablespoons water
1 tablespoon vinegar
1 egg yolk
2 tablespoons dry mustard mixed with 2
    tablespoons water to make a paste
½ cup sunflower oil or corn oil
¼ teaspoon cayenne pepper
¼ teaspoon black pepper
1 cup heavy cream
1 pound fresh or frozen crab meat, picked
    over to remove cartilage
½ cup Homemade Mayonnaise (see
    Index)
    watercress sprigs for garnish

Sprinkle avocado chunks with lemon juice. Place in a food processor or blender and blend until smooth.

In a saucepan, combine the gelatin, water, and vinegar; stir and warm over very low heat just until gelatin dissolves. Remove from heat and cool slightly.

Place the egg yolk and mustard in a slightly warmed bowl and start to beat with a wire whisk, while gradually adding the oil, drop by drop at first. Then beat in the gelatin mixture. Add the avocado puree and cayenne and black pepper.

Whip the cream until stiff and fold into the avocado mixture.

Lightly oil an 8-cup mold.

Shred the crab meat and mix it into the avocado mixture. Spoon all into the mold and chill overnight, or at least for 12 hours.

To unmold, fill your kitchen sink with hot water. Run a knife blade around the edge of the mold. Dip the mold in and out of the water quickly and then invert on a chilled plate and return to the refrigerator until serving time. Serve cold with mayonnaise and sprigs of watercress.

Serves 6

Note: If a ring mold is used, you might choose to mix only ½ pound of crab meat with the avocado and pile the remaining crab mixed with mayonnaise in the center.

BAKED
ALASKAN KING CRAB LEGS
WITH SHALLOT AND GARLIC BUTTER

6 pounds king crab legs, cut with a
    cleaver into 5-inch chunks
2 recipes softened Shallot and Garlic
    Butter (see Index) or any herbed
    butter sauce
    lemon wedges dipped in paprika for
    garnish

Preheat oven to 375°F.

Crack the crab shell every 2 inches with a
nutcracker, or split the crab shell
lengthwise, for easy removal of the flesh.
With a small spatula, force the softened
butter inside the shell covering the crab
meat. Put any extra butter in a small oven
dish to heat while the crab is baking. Place
in shallow, heavy, oven-to-table baking
pan and bake for 10 to 12 minutes. Serve
hot and bubbly with any extra butter and
with the lemon wedges to be squeezed on
at the table.

Serves 6

BAKED POTATOES
STUFFED WITH CRAB MEAT

6 potatoes, preferably Idaho, scrubbed
    and baked
1 tablespoon softened butter
¾ cup sour cream
1 small onion, grated
¼ teaspoon cayenne pepper
6 ounces fresh or frozen crab meat,
    picked over to remove cartilage
    dash of paprika
1 tablespoon minced, fresh chives or
    minced, fresh dill

Preheat oven to 375°F.

Cut baked potatoes in half lengthwise and
carefully scoop out the insides reserving
the skins. In a bowl with the potato pulp,
add the butter, sour cream, onion, and
cayenne pepper. Taste and adjust
seasoning. Beat with a potato masher until
smooth. Fold in the crab meat and then put
mixture back equally into the 12 potato
halves. Sprinkle with paprika and place on
a baking sheet. Bake for 10 to 15 minutes
until hot. If top is not browned and crusted,
put under broiler for 1 minute. Serve at
once, sprinkled with a few chives or dill.

Serves 6

BROILED CRAB CAKES, MARYLAND STYLE

1 cup Homemade Mayonnaise (see Index)
1 egg white
1 tablespoon finely minced, fresh parsley
1 teaspoon dry mustard
¼ teaspoon cayenne pepper
4 tablespoons fine, whole grain cracker crumbs
1½ pounds fresh or frozen crab meat, preferably backfin or lump, picked over to remove cartilage
¾ cup fine, dry, whole grain bread crumbs
4 tablespoons butter, melted
additional melted butter

Blend the Homemade Mayonnaise with the egg white, parsley, mustard, cayenne pepper, and cracker crumbs in a mixing bowl. Gently fold the crab meat into this mixture, but try not to break up lumps.

Wet the fingers and divide the mixture into 12 equal portions and shape each one into a patty. Coat the patties all over with the bread crumbs, pressing to make sure they adhere to the surface. Place on wax paper and chill for 15 minutes.

When ready to cook, dip the crab cakes in the melted butter to coat evenly and then place on a broiling pan. Broil 4 inches from the source of heat, turning once, until nicely browned on both sides, about 5 minutes. Allow 2 crab cakes per person. Additional melted butter may be passed at the table.

Serves 6

Note: Some Maryland cooks fry these cakes in hot oil, but we find this broiled version more delicate.

CANTONESE
CRAB FU-YUNG

6 eggs
2 tablespoons tamari soy sauce
¼ teaspoon black pepper
4 tablespoons peanut oil
1 small onion, finely minced
1 clove garlic, finely minced
2 thin slices peeled and shredded fresh
　　ginger root
½ pound fresh or frozen crab meat, picked
　　over to remove cartilage
2 medium tomatoes, peeled and cut in
　　large cubes

Beat the eggs with the soy sauce and pepper and reserve.

Heat 2 tablespoons of the oil and add the onion. Saute for 1 minute, stirring until slightly wilted. Add the garlic and ginger and cook, stirring for 30 seconds. Add the crab meat. Stir and cook for 1 minute and then remove from the heat and reserve.

In a second medium-size skillet, heat the remaining oil and add the tomatoes and the egg mixture so that it coats the bottom of the pan evenly and, with a fork, scramble lightly for a few seconds. At once, pour the crab meat mixture over the eggs, stirring quickly together. Serve promptly.

Serves 6

HOT CRAB SALAD
BAKED IN WHOLE WHEAT PITA BREAD

1 pound fresh or frozen lump crab meat,
　　picked over to remove cartilage
1 cup finely minced celery
1 cup fresh or frozen green peas, cooked
½ cup grated Swiss or Gruyere cheese
¼ cup finely minced, fresh parsley
¾ cup Homemade Mayonnaise (see
　　Index)
6 whole wheat pita pocket breads
¼ cup butter, melted

Preheat oven to 400°F.

Combine crab meat with celery, peas, cheese, and parsley. Fold in Homemade Mayonnaise.

Cut about ¾ inch off the top of the pocket bread with a pair of scissors and brush the inside with some of the melted butter. Fill each pocket equally with the crab meat mixture and wrap separately in aluminum foil. Lay foil-wrapped packages on a cookie sheet and bake for 15 minutes. Remove foil when cool to the fingers and serve sandwiches hot.

Serves 6

CRAB MEAT CHAUSSEUR

This dish can be prepared easily in a chafing dish or a skillet. Have all the ingredients assembled and ready to go if you make it in front of an audience. One rehearsal in the kitchen to test first on your family will make you look like a Cordon Bleu chef.

- 3 tablespoons butter
- 4 large mushrooms, sliced
- 1 tablespoon finely minced shallots (young spring onions may be used)
- 2 tablespoons Basic Tomato Sauce (see Index)
- 1¼ cups heavy cream
- 1 pound lump crab meat, picked over to remove cartilage (2 packages, 6 ounces each, frozen crab meat may be used)
- 2 egg yolks
- 1 teaspoon finely minced, fresh parsley
- 2 teaspoons finely minced, fresh tarragon or ½ teaspoon dried
- 1 teaspoon finely minced, fresh chives
- ¼ teaspoon paprika

Melt the butter and add the mushrooms and cook, stirring for 5 minutes. Add the shallots and stir and cook until most of the mushroom liquid has evaporated. Add the Basic Tomato Sauce and stir and cook 3 minutes more. Slowly pour in 1 cup of the cream, reserving the ¼ cup. Cook, stirring until ingredients are blended and mixture begins to simmer. Add the crab meat and carefully stir so the pieces don't break easily.

Mix the egg yolks with the remaining ¼ cup of cream in a bowl and add this mixture to the chafing dish or skillet. Stir gently and add all the herbs. Heat to thicken slightly, but do not allow to boil or it will curdle. Sprinkle with the paprika and serve with buttered toast points or over hot, brown rice.

Serves 6

SAUTEED
SOFT-SHELL CRABS

12 very small (about 2½ to 3 inches across
    the body in size), cleaned soft-shell
    crabs (see page 248 for cleaning
    directions)
½ cup whole wheat pastry flour
¼ teaspoon cayenne pepper
⅛ teaspoon black pepper
½ cup butter
1 small clove garlic, crushed
2 tablespoons lemon juice
1 tablespoon finely minced, fresh parsley

Dredge the crabs all over with the flour
which has been seasoned with the cayenne
and black pepper.

Heat the butter in a large, heavy skillet
and when hot, add the crabs. Cook until
golden brown on both sides, about 1 to 2
minutes on each side is all it should take.
Remove with tongs to a warm platter.

Add the garlic to the skillet and stir
quickly. Then add the lemon juice. Pour
this sauce over the crabs and sprinkle with
parsley.

Serves 6

VARIATION

Follow same recipe, but after removing
crabs with tongs, keep them warm. Have
ready Sauce *Provencale* (a Tomato-Garlic
Sauce). (See Index.) Heat the sauce to the
boiling point, add the sauteed crabs and
reheat for only a few seconds. Serve on
warm platter with finely minced parsley
sprinkled over all.

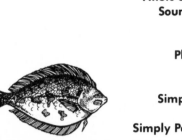

The Flatfish Family

If we had a tendency to pun (which we never do, of course), we might call this chapter "Sole Food!" However, there are many more members of the family and this chapter is dedicated to all of them, for whatever the flatfish are called in the usual confusion of marine terminology, the recipes in this section are perfect for all of them. The flatfish family is large, some members familiar, others not as well known. For example, the *witch flounder* is marketed in the United States as *gray sole*. Here are some other names in the flatfish family:

dabs	butter sole
summer flounder (fluke)	English sole (lemon sole)
winter flounder	petrale sole (brill)
Atlantic halibut	rex sole
California halibut	rock sole
Pacific halibut	diamond turbot
plaice	

Of course, if we begin to include the names of the flatfish served internationally, the list becomes endless, for these fish are as popular in Asia and Europe as they are in North America. Actually, the designation of "sole" on restaurant menus is frequently a misnomer, for you may be eating any one of a number of white flatfish that has been given that name by the people who create the menus. In fact, when you see the name *Dover Sole* listed and the word "fresh" precedes it, someone is not telling the truth, unless you are eating it in England. For there is no Dover Sole in North America and all of it is frozen when it arrives.

Actually, it is gray sole that is considered the best fish by gourmets and, as we mentioned earlier, the gray sole is actually a flounder.

This true *winter flounder* is the thickest and meatiest of the group, and is probably the best known and most popular flatfish. It has a marvelously firm texture and it's a lean fish with a sweet flavor. The baby flounder, like all flatfish, is born upright, but soon the eyes turn to the right and the fish begins to flatten out.

The *summer flounder* (or *fluke*), on the other hand, has eyes that move to the left side of the body as it flattens into its permanent shape.

Whether caught or bought, all the flatfish are quite popular because of their delicacy. Though most of these found in the markets are sold as fillets, they can be bought whole, and those of us who fish for them off our island certainly find them delicious stuffed and baked, or broiled as whole fish.

They live on the bottom, blending with the sand that they throw over their backs, only their eyes peering out in wait for baitfish. Fishermen usually troll the bottom for them (losing a lot of hooks and rigs in the process as they catch on underwater objects), and the description of catching them has generally been compared to hauling up a bath mat, for they are not particularly known as fighters. Some of our fishermen go out at night in the shallower water and, using a strong lantern, they spear the fish when they see the gleam of their eyes on the bottom. It is a most remarkable feat, for the parallax of the water makes it difficult to judge the distance and the placement of the fish.

The recipes that follow are based on the suggestion of using a ½-pound fillet per person, or two-and-a-half to three pounds to feed six people. If you are using a fairly rich sauce, you may want to decrease the amount of fish.

How to Fillet a Flatfish

The method of filleting a flatfish is almost exactly the same as for other fish. (See Index for How to Fillet.) However, since the flatfish has the center bone right down the middle, just cut the fillets from the middle out toward the edges of the fish. In that way you'll get four fillets per fish. Skin them in exactly the same way as for other fish or, if the fish is small, cook them with the skins on (scaled first, of course) and then remove the skin at the table.

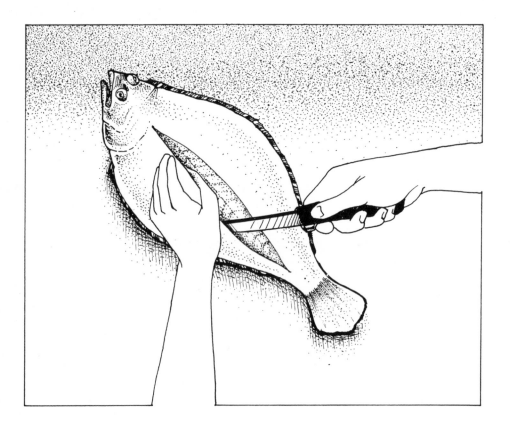

Note: For instructions on how to stuff a flatfish, refer to the chapter on Stuffings for Fish.

BROILED FLOUNDER
WITH CUCUMBER AND PARSLEY BUTTER

2 medium cucumbers, peeled and
    shredded
½ cup plus 2 tablespoons softened butter
1 tablespoon finely minced, fresh
    parsley
2 tablespoons lemon juice
2½ pounds flounder fillets (fillets of sole
    may be used)
¼ teaspoon white pepper
    pinch of cayenne pepper

Mix the cucumber with ½ cup of butter and set aside. Then mix the remaining 2 tablespoons of butter with the parsley and 1 tablespoon of the lemon juice and set aside.

Oil a shallow, oven-to-table broiling pan. Place the flounder in one layer and sprinkle it with the remaining tablespoon of lemon juice and the white pepper. With a small spatula, smear the cucumber butter evenly over the fillets. Broil 3 inches from source of heat for 5 to 8 minutes, depending on thickness of fish. Baste once. Dot the hot fish with the parsley butter and let it melt over the fish when serving. Sprinkle with cayenne pepper.

Serves 6

GINGER-SOY FRIED FLOUNDER
WITH MUSHROOMS

2 pounds flounder fillets, cut into 1- by
    2-inch squares
½ cup cornstarch
2 egg whites
¼ teaspoon black pepper
4 tablespoons peanut oil
2 teaspoons peeled and finely minced,
    fresh ginger root or 2 teaspoons
    ground ginger
1 cup thinly sliced mushrooms
1 cup chopped scallions
2 tablespoons tamari soy sauce

Dry fillets on paper towels, then toss together with cornstarch.

Beat the egg whites until foamy with the black pepper. Dip the cornstarch-coated fish pieces into the egg white mixture.

Heat the oil in a wok or heavy skillet until very hot. Fry coated pieces of fish, a few at a time, until golden. Remove, keep warm.

To the same wok or skillet, add the ginger, mushrooms, and scallions, constantly stirring and frying, and cook for about 1 minute. Add soy sauce and pour this mixture over the fish pieces. Serve hot.

Serves 6

FILLETS OF SOLE
WITH MUSHROOMS, TARRAGON, AND SOUR CREAM, BAKED IN BROWN PAPER BAGS

¼ pound mushrooms, thinly sliced
    juice of 2 lemons
2 pounds fillets of sole (flounder, fluke, or
    codfish may be used)
½ cup softened sweet butter
2 cloves garlic, finely minced
1 tablespoon minced, fresh tarragon or ¾
    teaspoon dried
6 tablespoons sour cream
1 tablespoon minced, fresh chives
¼ teaspoon black pepper
6 brown paper bags
    lemon slices for garnish

In a bowl, mix the mushrooms with juice of ½ lemon and let stand.

In another bowl, toss the fillets in juice of 1 lemon and let stand for 30 minutes. Then dry the fillets on paper towels and spread both sides with 2 tablespoons of butter.

In a saucepan, melt 2 tablespoons of remaining butter and add the garlic. Saute, stirring for 1 minute, then add the tarragon and cook, stirring for 3 minutes.

Spread some of this sauce on each fillet, then add 1 tablespoon of sour cream and some mushrooms to each fillet. Fold fillet in half across the width. Add some more butter, chives, and pepper to each one and the remaining lemon juice.

Preheat oven to 375°F.

Spread some remaining soft butter on the outside of each brown paper bag evenly. Place each fillet in its own bag. Fold over twice. Place bags on pan (use a flat pan with shallow sides, such as a jelly roll pan) and bake 25 to 30 minutes. The bags will puff up from the steam created by baking. Slash an X into each bag with a razor blade and open up the flaps. Serve in brown bag with slices of lemon.

Serves 6

LEMON SOLE
STUFFED
WITH SALMON
IN A LEMON DILL SAUCE

6 fillets lemon sole, about ½ pound
    each (gray sole, flounder, or fluke
    may be used)
¼ teaspoon black pepper
6 thin slices raw salmon, cut into 2- by
    4-inch pieces
6 tablespoons butter
1 tablespoon minced shallots (young
    spring onions may be used)
¾ cup Fish Stock (see Index)
1 cup Basic *Creme Fraiche* (see Index)
½ cup lemon juice
1 tablespoon minced, fresh dill

Preheat oven to 425°F.

Place the sole fillets on a flat surface. There is a tiny bone line in the center, running lengthwise down the fillets. With a sharp knife, remove this bone line and divide the sole in half lengthwise. Sprinkle with pepper. Lay 1 slice of salmon on each fillet, roll up like a jelly roll, and skewer with a toothpick.

Melt 2 tablespoons of the butter in a shallow baking dish and sprinkle with the shallots. Arrange the fish rolls so they show a pinwheel design and dot with 2 more tablespoons of butter.

Cut a piece of wax paper to fit the baking dish and butter one side heavily with the remaining butter. Add the Fish Stock around the pan. Place paper, butter side down, over fish. Bring liquid to a boil on top of stove. Then place in oven and bake for 10 minutes.

Remove paper and discard. Remove the fish rolls to a platter carefully, and keep warm. Place the pan they cooked in on top of the stove again. Bring to a boil and cook for 3 minutes; then add the Basic *Creme Fraiche*, and bring to a boil again. Remove from heat and stir in lemon juice and dill. Return fish to this sauce, spoon some on top, and serve.

Serves 6

PLAIN BROILED SOLE
WITH SAUCE VARIATIONS

2½ pounds fillets of sole*
¼ teaspoon black pepper
1 tablespoon lemon juice
2 tablespoons butter, melted
½ teaspoon paprika

Sprinkle the fish with pepper and lemon juice.

Heat the butter in a shallow, oven-proof serving dish. Add the fillets and turn them to coat evenly all over in the butter. Sprinkle with the paprika and broil about 4 inches from the source of heat until fish is opaque and flakes easily with a skewer.

Serves 6

Note: For any simple, broiled flatfish, use any of the following delicate, buttery sauces (see Index):

Bercy Butter
Orange Butter and Chive Sauce
Anise Butter
Chivry Butter

Lobster Butter
Tarragon-Lemon Butter Sauce
Pistachio Nut Butter

Note: Cooking time depends on the thickness of the particular fish. Lemon sole is very thin and may only need 2 to 3 minutes of broiling. A small flounder will take about 2 to 4 minutes. A 1-inch-thick slice of codfish will take 8 to 10 minutes, so be careful and do not overcook when broiling. When substituting fish, take this into account.

VARIATION

You may also add 1 tablespoon of thinly sliced, toasted almonds at the end of broiling. Or you may sprinkle with 1 tablespoon of grated Parmesan or sharp cheddar cheese 2 minutes before removing from oven, and let the cheese melt over the fish. Add a generous handful of toasted, buttered bread crumbs, basted once with the pan juices.

*The fish fillets that are seasonally available will be suitable for this method of cooking. Substitute flounder, haddock, whiting, grouper, codfish, striped bass—almost any white meat, lean fish.

ROLLED FILLETS OF FLOUNDER
WITH LEMON, RICE, AND BROCCOLI

⅓ cup butter, melted
⅓ cup lemon juice
¼ teaspoon white pepper
⅛ teaspoon paprika
1⅓ cups cooked brown rice
1 cup shredded, sharp cheddar cheese
½ pound fresh broccoli or 1 10-ounce
   package frozen, steamed, and
   coarsely chopped
2 pounds flounder fillets (sole or fluke
   may be used)*

Preheat oven to 375°F.

Mix butter with lemon juice, pepper, and paprika and set aside.

In a bowl, mix rice, cheese, and broccoli and add ¼ cup of the lemon butter. Reserve the rest.

On a large sheet of wax paper, lay the fillets flat. Divide the rice stuffing equally, and place portion on the wide end of each fillet. Gently roll up fillets and place seam side down in a large, shallow, oven-proof baking dish that has been coated with some of the lemon butter. Pour the rest of the butter sauce over the rolled, stuffed fish and bake for 20 minutes and then test with a skewer to see if it flakes easily.

Serves 6

Tip: When baking or poaching rolled fillets, measure the diameter of the fillet *after* rolling it and allow about 8 to 10 minutes per inch of cooking time.

*The thin, flatfish fillets, such as fluke, sole, and flounder, are the only ones that roll easily without falling apart.

SIMPLE
BATTER-FRIED
FILLETS
WITH FRESH HERBS AND CITRUS FRUIT

3 pounds flounder fillets
1 recipe dry or moist batter (see Index)
   vegetable oil for frying

Follow method for Deep Fry (see Index).

Serve with citrus fruit garnish and a finely minced fresh herb, such as tarragon, chervil, basil, parsley, or mint.

Serves 6

Tip: Try Cold Green Sauce with Sage or Yogurt and Horseradish Sauce with Mustard Seed (see Index) with fried fillets as a simple but distinctive dish.

SIMPLY POACHED
FLATFISH
WITH SUGGESTED SAUCES

This most versatile of fish is good served both hot and cold. If you have yet to try poaching fish, this is a good place to start. Allow 3 pounds of fillets for 6 people. Poach on top of the stove in milk, lemon, onion, and water, or any delicate stock (see Index). Then serve it with any of these sauces (see Index):

Sauces for Hot, Poached Flatfish
   Lobster Sauce (Sauce Cardinal)
   Mushroom, Shrimp, and Dill Sauce
   Spanish Saffron *Veloute* Sauce
   Mustard-Cheese Sauce
   Fresh Grape Sauce (Sauce *Veronique*)

Sauces for Cold, Poached Flatfish
   Sauce *Mousseline*
   Sauce *Maltaise* (Orange Hollandaise)
   Cold Green Sauce with Sage
   Cucumber Mayonnaise Sauce with Dill
   Remoulade Sauce (Pungent Mayonnaise Sauce)
   Tomato Tarragon Mayonnaise

**Deep Fried Grouper Fingers Stuffed
with Gruyere Cheese
Braised Grouper with Vegetables**

Reef fishermen love them because they take most any bait trolled over the rocks or the coral reefs. Scientists adore studying them because they might well be called the "Chameleons of the Sea," changing color to match their surroundings, "painting" their own stripes when they're near other fish, turning darker when they swim near the bottom, turning pale close to the top. And marine biologists love them because they're actually friendly enough to be handled by underwater swimmers. Most interesting of all, *groupers* have the strangest "sex life" of any fish in the ocean. They're hermaphroditic fish, all of them females from birth, then becoming males at a later age.

The grouper family are large fish who are related to *sea bass*, with the *red grouper* being the most common of the species. Its close relative, the *jewfish*, can be found in sizes up to *700 pounds* and the fishermen who go after them use ¼-inch Manila rope as their fishing tackle!

Groupers are usually marketed in large steaks or fillets that range in weight from 5 to 15 pounds. About 2 pounds of fillets will feed six people.

The larger steaks are best when broiled, but be careful that they don't dry out. Try baking them in sauce, deep frying, poaching, or in soups or stews.

Grouper heads make superb fish stock and they are the secret ingredient in many Carribbean conch and fish chowders.

The traditional way groupers are served in the West Indies is with rice and pigeon peas. But whichever way you choose to cook grouper, you'll find that it retains its shape nicely, since it has a thick, firm flesh. (See Index for poaching directions or soup and chowder recipes.)

Grouper

For poached grouper, hot or cold, try one of the following sauces (see Index):

Sauce *Mousseline*
Mustard-Horseradish Sauce
Cucumber Mayonnaise Sauce with Dill
Cresson Mayonnaise (Watercress Mayonnaise)
Spinach and Chive Sauce

DEEP FRIED GROUPER FINGERS STUFFED WITH GRUYERE CHEESE

2 pounds grouper fillets, cut into 1 x 3-inch fingers
¼ pound Gruyere cheese, cut into ½ x 2-inch pieces
   juice of 1 lemon
2 eggs, beaten
½ cup whole wheat flour
3 cups soft, whole grain bread crumbs
   corn oil for deep frying

Garnish
   small nosegays of parsley
   lemon wedges

Use a sharp, pointed knife and cut a slit on the side of each fish finger to make a pocket long enough to accommodate the sliver of cheese. Insert the cheese and close the pocket with a toothpick.

Beat the lemon juice and eggs together. Dip the fish fingers in the flour and then in the egg mixture. Roll them in bread crumbs. Chill on wax paper in the refrigerator for 30 minutes.

Heat the oil to 370°F. Use a fat thermometer to keep the temperature constant. Deep fry a few pieces at a time for 2 to 3 minutes until color is golden and fish flakes. Drain on paper towels and keep warm in a hot oven until all fingers are fried. Remove toothpicks and tuck nosegays of parsley and the lemon wedges between the fish.

Serves 6

BRAISED GROUPER
WITH VEGETABLES

1 tablespoon olive oil
2 tablespoons butter
1 large carrot, slivered
1 large onion, thinly sliced
2 stalks celery, slivered
4 sprigs parsley
1 teaspoon finely minced, fresh thyme or
    ½ teaspoon dried
1 sprig rosemary or ¼ teaspoon dried
1 bay leaf
2 cloves garlic, slivered
½ teaspoon black pepper
2 cups Fish Stock (see Index)
2 pounds grouper fillets, cut into 1½-inch
    cubes*
2 teaspoons arrowroot, mixed with 1
    tablespoon cold water
  juice of 2 lemons
1 tablespoon minced, fresh parsley

Use a Dutch oven or heavy casserole. Add the olive oil and butter and let butter melt over low heat. Make a bed of the carrots, onions, and celery. Then sprinkle with the parsley, thyme, rosemary, bay leaf, garlic, and pepper. Add the Fish Stock and bring to a boil. Add the fish cubes. Cover the pan and lower the heat and simmer for 15 minutes or until the fish is cooked.

Remove the fish cubes with a slotted spoon to the center of a warm serving dish. Strain the liquid into a saucepan and pick out the bay leaf and the sprigs of parsley. Spoon the vegetables around the fish.

Bring the liquid to a boil, and stir arrowroot into the liquid. Stir until thickened and pour over the fish and vegetables. Squeeze the lemon juice over all and sprinkle with parsley.

Serves 6

*Sea bass or snapper may be substituted, although grouper is a somewhat firmer textured fish that retains its shape best.

Grunt (or Pigfish)

**Crisp Fried Grunts with Garlic Butter
Grits and Grunts (Baked Cheese Grits
with Green Onions and Grunts)**

The sounds of the ocean are quite amazing. Not only do we hear the roar of the sea or the waves that lap at the shore, but we get the sounds of the creatures that inhabit the sea as well. Scientists believe the *dolphin* can speak and communicate through sound, the *drum* family are a noisy bunch that can be heard on shore on a still night. The little *croakers* "croak"—and the *grunt* "grunts" when it's caught. However, this little fish makes its noise by grinding its teeth when it's caught and the sound is reflected by an air bag inside its body.

The grunt is a moderately small fish, weighing from one-half to two pounds and it's superb pan fried or sauteed. In fact, A. J. McClane writing in *The Encyclopedia of Fish Cookery* (New York: Holt, Rinehart & Winston, 1977) delightfully suggests that they be picked up and eaten like corn on the cob, just making certain that you work your way around the bones.

CRISP
FRIED GRUNTS
WITH GARLIC BUTTER

6 grunts, about ½ pound each, pan
    dressed (snapper or catfish may be
    used)
½ teaspoon black pepper
½ cup rye flour
   oil for frying
½ cup butter
1 teaspoon finely minced garlic
1 tablespoon finely minced, fresh parsley
1 tablespoon lime juice

Dip the fish in a mixture of pepper and flour.

Heat the oil to 370°F. in a heavy, black iron skillet and fry fish about 2 to 3 minutes on each side. Drain on paper towels and keep warm.

In another skillet, melt the butter and add the garlic, parsley, and lime juice. Let cook for 2 minutes and pour over the grunts or use as a dipping sauce.

Serves 6

Note: Some of us like our garlic untouched and as is. Others of us find the flavor just a bit too strong. Though we are of the group who like garlic to be strong and very evident in our cooking, we do have a suggestion to tone it down a bit. Just split the garlic bud in half, and with the sharp point of a knife, remove the little green bud that runs down the middle. You'll find that you still will taste the garlic, but it won't be quite as pronounced. This is a trick you might well use in all of your cooking with garlic.

GRITS
AND GRUNTS
(BAKED CHEESE GRITS
WITH GREEN ONIONS AND GRUNTS)

These little pan fried or sauteed fish are as much of a staple in the South as the grits that go with them. For a complete, traditional southern dinner, include a pot full of collard greens flavored with hot pepper.

The Grits
- 1 cup stone-ground hominy grits
- 1½ cups shredded sharp cheddar cheese
- ½ cup softened butter
- ½ cup chopped green onions
- 1 teaspoon finely minced garlic
- 3 eggs, well beaten
- ½ cup milk
- ½ teaspoon black pepper

Cook the grits according to the package directions.

Preheat oven to 375°F.

Stir the cheese, butter, green onions, and garlic into the cooked grits. Beat the eggs, milk, and pepper together and stir in. Pour all into a well-buttered, deep, oven-to-table casserole. Bake for 1 hour.

About 10 minutes before grits are finished baking, prepare the fish.

The Grunts
- 6 grunts, about ½ pound each, pan dressed
- ½ teaspoon black pepper
- ¼ cup white cornmeal
- ½ cup whole wheat flour
- 6 tablespoons butter

Dip the fish in a mixture of pepper, cornmeal, and flour.

Melt the butter and when it starts to bubble, saute the fish a few at a time, about 3 to 4 minutes on each side. Drain on paper and lay on top of grits casserole.

Serves 6

**Cucumber Stuffed Halibut Steak Sandwich
with Peas
Sauteed Halibut Steaks with Duxelles
and Tarragon Cream
Halibut *Seviche*
Poached Halibut Steak with Minted
Lemon Cream Sauce
Halibut Casserole with Asparagus**

Though we have correctly listed the *halibut* as a member of The Flatfish Family (see Index), we have also decided to give it this special section all to itself because of its unusual qualities. It is, indeed, a flat fish and it does, indeed, have its eyes on only one side of the head (right side for Atlantic, Pacific, and Greenland varieties and left side for the California halibut). However, for those of us who revel in catching *fluke* or *flounder* of two or three pounds, the halibut is a veritable giant. As a result, the fish is available not only in superb fillets, but also in steaks.

The smallest of the halibut ("chicken" on the West Coast, "snapper" on the East Coast) run from 5 to 10 pounds and they go right up to the 125-pound "whales."

Halibut has a firm, white, flaky texture and it makes an excellent *seviche*. It's also marvelous when poached and served cold in a salad, and it is versatile enough to take rich sauces. Since it is so meaty a fish, we'd suggest about two pounds of steak for six people.

The halibut, incidentally, is the "kissin' cousin" of the European *turbot*.

CUCUMBER STUFFED HALIBUT STEAK SANDWICH WITH PEAS

4 tablespoons butter, melted
1 teaspoon paprika
2 halibut steaks, about 1½ pounds each
1 cucumber, peeled and shredded
¾ cup sour cream
2 tablespoons finely minced, fresh chives
1 tablespoon finely minced, fresh dill
   juice of 1 lemon
¼ teaspoon white pepper
1 pound fresh or frozen green peas,
   cooked

Preheat oven to 450°F.

Butter an oven-to-table baking pan with a pastry brush. Add the paprika to the rest of the butter and brush all four sides of the 2 steaks liberally with this mixture. Lay 1 steak in the pan. Mix the cucumber, sour cream, chives, and dill and spread it on the steak, then top with the other steak. (If filling oozes out, do not be concerned; it forms part of the sauce.) Sprinkle the top with lemon juice and pepper and pour any remaining butter on top. Bake in the preheated oven, allowing 9 to 10 minutes per inch of fish. Baste often. Serve with peas spooned around the edge of the dish.

Serves 6

SAUTEED HALIBUT STEAKS WITH DUXELLES AND TARRAGON CREAM

   Basic Duxelles (see Index)
   Tarragon Sauce (see Index)
2½ pounds halibut steaks, each ½ inch
   thick, cut into 6 pieces
1 tablespoon olive oil
2 tablespoons butter, melted

Prepare Basic Duxelles and Tarragon Sauce first and set aside.

Dry fish well.

Heat the oil and butter in a large, heavy skillet, or use 2 skillets for each 3 pieces of fish. Saute the fish for 3 to 4 minutes on each side and test with a skewer. Transfer to an oven-to-table baking pan and spread some Basic Duxelles on each piece of fish. Slip under the broiler for 2 minutes while warming the Tarragon Sauce. Do not allow the sauce to boil or it will curdle. Spoon the sauce over the fish and serve at once.

Serves 6

HALIBUT
SEVICHE

1 cup fresh lime juice (juice of 6 to 8 limes)
½ small onion, grated
1 clove garlic, finely minced
1 large tomato, peeled and chopped
¼ cup tomato juice
1 or 2 fresh hot peppers, seeded and finely chopped
½ cup minced, fresh Chinese parsley (cilantro)
¼ cup olive oil
1 teaspoon finely minced, fresh thyme or ½ teaspoon dried
2 pounds halibut, skinned, boned, and cut into 1-inch pieces
lettuce leaves
1 small red onion, thinly sliced
1 orange, peeled and thinly sliced

Place lime juice, onion, garlic, tomato, and tomato juice in a nonmetallic bowl.

Add peppers to the tomato-lime mixture. Then add the Chinese parsley, olive oil, and thyme. Toss the pieces of halibut in the marinade and refrigerate overnight or for 6 to 8 hours. Stir once while marinating. When ready to serve, make a bed of lettuce and surround it with alternate slices of red onion and orange slices. Heap the fish in the center and serve cold.

Serves 6

Tip: Pour boiling water over limes and let stand for 1 minute, then rinse under cold water. This procedure extracts more juice from the limes.

POACHED HALIBUT STEAK
WITH MINTED LEMON CREAM SAUCE

2 pounds halibut steak (whiting, grouper, or tilefish may be used)
Aromatic Milk Broth (see Index)
1 teaspoon grated lemon rind
1½ cups Basic *Creme Fraiche* (see Index) or sour cream
½ teaspoon white pepper
¼ teaspoon nutmeg
1 tablespoon lemon juice
1 teaspoon arrowroot, mixed with 1 tablespoon cold water
1 tablespoon finely minced, fresh mint

Poach the halibut steak in the Aromatic Milk Broth for only 2 minutes. Lift the steak out with a wide perforated spatula and drain. Discard liquid. Transfer fish to a heavy skillet.

Mix the lemon rind, Basic *Creme Fraiche*, pepper, and nutmeg and pour over and around the fish. Simmer on top of stove for about 8 to 10 minutes. Lift the steak out to a warm serving dish, add the lemon juice and the arrowroot to the sauce. Stir until thickened and then stir in the mint. Pour the sauce over the halibut steak.

Serves 6

Note: Halibut poached in milk and served hot can also be served with these sauces (see Index):

Hollandaise-Based Sauces
Mornay Sauce (with Gruyere Cheese)
Tomato Sauces
Veloute Sauces

It may also be chilled, flaked and served with: *Remoulade* Sauce (Pungent Mayonnaise Sauce) or other Mayonnaise-Based Sauces. (See Index.) When broiled, it may be served with any of the herbed butter sauces (see Index).

Vera Cruz Style, Baked Weakfish, Stuffed with Limes   For this recipe, see page 404

Sauteed Soft-Shell Crabs   For this recipe, see page 257

HALIBUT
CASSEROLE
WITH ASPARAGUS

1½ pounds halibut steak or fillets
1½ cups milk
 1 bay leaf
 4 tablespoons butter
 3 tablespoons whole wheat flour
¼ teaspoon black pepper
½ teaspoon paprika
 1 small onion, grated
½ pound cooked asparagus spears
⅔ cup fine, dry, whole grain bread
    crumbs
½ cup grated Parmesan cheese
 2 tablespoons butter, melted
 2 tablespoons lemon juice

Place fish in boiling milk with the bay leaf. Lower heat, cover, and simmer for 8 minutes or until fish turns opaque and will flake. Lift fish out and drain until cool to the touch. Remove bay leaf from milk and reserve. Remove the skin and bones, and break fish into small chunks. Then add the fish to a buttered casserole.

Preheat oven to 400°F.

Melt the butter in a saucepan and stir in the flour, pepper, and paprika. Add the reserved hot milk and stir with a whisk. Add the grated onion and simmer for 5 minutes. Pour sauce over fish in the casserole. Arrange the asparagus spears on top. Sprinkle with combined bread crumbs, Parmesan cheese, melted butter, and lemon juice. Bake for 10 minutes or until heated through and bubbling.

Serves 6

Baked Herring Fillets with Potatoes and Thyme
Grilled Fresh Herring
Cold, Spiced Herring with Carrots
and Onion Rings

The poor herring has been known as a "bread and butter" catch for commercial fishermen for centuries. This versatile fish has been overexploited in recent years by electronically equipped fleets that have swept whole areas clean, making it necessary for the fishermen to go further and further out to make their catch.

In addition, the herring is not only eaten by man, but birds and other fish consider it a most delicious morsel as well, making it a potential breakfast, lunch, and dinner for everything that walks, floats, flies, or swims. To make matters even worse, some types of herring, such as the *Pacific sea herring*, deposit as many as 20,000 eggs each during spawning season, but storms, sea gulls, and ducks decimate up to 80 percent!

In light of all this, it is remarkable that the annual catch of herring still runs to the millions of tons and it can be found around the world kippered, salted, smoked, or pickled.

In the United States, fresh herring is available in its healthier, natural, unbrined, unsmoked state and it can generally be purchased in weights averaging about one pound. These firm, fatty fish can be filleted or cooked whole and presented in many appetizing ways.

BAKED
HERRING FILLETS
WITH POTATOES AND THYME

6 herring, about 1 pound each, cut into
    fillets
4 tablespoons butter
3 medium-size potatoes, peeled and
    sliced paper thin
8 green scallions, finely chopped
¼ teaspoon black pepper
1 tablespoon grated lemon rind
    juice of 1 lemon
6 sprigs fresh thyme or ¾ teaspoon dried
¾ cup water or milk

Preheat oven to 350°F.

Butter a large, oven-to-table baking dish.
Layer the fillets on the bottom of the dish.
Dot with some of the butter, then add a
layer of the potatoes, and then the
scallions. Sprinkle with pepper, lemon rind
and juice, and the thyme. Add the water or
milk and dot with the remaining butter.
Bake until the potatoes are cooked through,
basting occasionally with the juices that
form in the pan.

Serves 6

GRILLED
FRESH HERRING

6 fresh herring, about 3 pounds, split in
    half lengthwise, with backbone
    removed
4 tablespoons butter, melted
¼ teaspoon black pepper
½ teaspoon paprika
2 small onions, thinly sliced and
    separated into rings
6 sprigs dill
    vinegar

Butter a baking pan and lay the split
herring on their backs. Brush well with
some of the melted butter. Sprinkle with
pepper and some of the paprika and place
the thin slices of onion rings over the
herring. Pour the remaining butter over the
onions and sprinkle with the rest of the
paprika.

Broil 4 inches from source of heat for about
5 minutes. Test with a skewer to see if the
fish flakes easily. Onions should be crisp,
but tender and slightly brown. When fish is
cooked, remove to serving dish and top
each fish with a sprig of dill. Pass a bottle
of vinegar to be sprinkled over the fish
before eating.

Serves 6

COLD, SPICED
HERRING
WITH CARROTS AND ONION RINGS

2 tablespoons butter
6 carrots—chop 4 and slice 2 paper thin
3 medium onions—chop 2 and slice 1
    into thin rings
1 clove garlic, minced
3 tablespoons minced, fresh parsley
1 bay leaf
  water
2 sprigs thyme or ¼ teaspoon dried
8 peppercorns
⅛ teaspoon allspice
2 cloves
12 small herring, about 3 pounds, cleaned
    and dressed, but left whole, or 6
    large herring
½ cup vinegar
2 tablespoons olive oil

Melt butter in large casserole, and cover the bottom with the chopped carrots, onions, garlic, parsley, and bay leaf. Add enough water just to cover the vegetables. Then add the thyme, peppercorns, allspice, and cloves. Bring to a boil, then lower heat and simmer for 15 minutes or until vegetables are tender.

Meanwhile, preheat oven to 350°F.

Place the fish over the vegetables and cover with the carrot slices and onion rings that remain. Pour vinegar over all and bake covered for 20 minutes.

Allow fish and vegetables to cool and then chill before serving. Pour olive oil over the cold fish at the table.

Serves 6

Note: When herring is not available, you can substitute any small, whole, firm-fleshed fish in this recipe.

**Baked Lingcod with Spinach
and Parmesan Cheese
Crunchy Crusted Baked Lingcod
Lingcod Sandwiches Stuffed with Shrimp
in Tomato Basil Sauce**

Of course, if *lake herring (cisco)* are not really *herring* and *sea trout* are really part of the *drum* family, it stands to reason that the *lingcod* would not be a *cod*—and with all the illogic of the fish world, this is quite true. The lingcod is not a true cod!

It is, however, a member of the *Greenling* family, a fish native to the West Coast and it is considered by many to be one of the finest eating fishes of the area. It is unfortunate, then, that much of the lingcod catch goes directly to the "fish and chips" industry and fast food outlets. The reason is because its firm flesh dresses easily as fingers and steaks, as well as fillets. The unusual and characteristic blue green color of its flesh turns into a delicate, white, tender flesh when it's cooked and it takes well to broiling, sauteing, baking, or poaching. Incidentally, the lingcod is very low in fat.

Lingcod

BAKED LINGCOD
WITH SPINACH
AND PARMESAN CHEESE

2 pounds lingcod fillets (whiting or hake may be used)

¼ teaspoon black pepper

10-ounce package frozen, chopped spinach

2 tablespoons butter

1 small onion, grated

1 tablespoon whole wheat pastry flour

¼ cup grated Parmesan cheese

¼ cup milk

¼ teaspoon mace

2 tablespoons lemon juice mixed with 5 tablespoons water

lemon wedges dipped in paprika for garnish

Preheat oven to 350°F.

Sprinkle fish with pepper and set aside.

Cook the spinach only until it is defrosted and press out all liquid. Dry on paper towel to remove all excess liquid.

Heat the butter in a medium-size skillet and add the onion. Stir and cook until onion is wilted. Add the flour and then the spinach and stir until slightly thickened. Add the Parmesan cheese, milk, and mace. Let cool and set aside.

Butter an oven-to-table baking pan and place the fish in it in a single layer. Pour the lemon-water mixture over the fish and bake and baste for 10 minutes. Remove from oven and spoon the spinach mixture on top of the fillets and continue to bake until spinach is heated through. Serve with paprika-dipped lemon wedges.

Serves 6

CRUNCHY CRUSTED BAKED LINGCOD

¾ cup stone-ground yellow cornmeal
¼ cup plus 2 tablespoons grated Parmesan cheese
1½ tablespoons toasted wheat germ
1½ tablespoons sesame seeds
1 teaspoon finely minced, fresh parsley
1 tablespoon finely minced, fresh thyme or 1½ teaspoons dried
¾ teaspoon dried sage
¾ teaspoon black pepper
1½ teaspoons finely minced garlic
3 pounds lingcod fillets, cut into serving portions
2 eggs, beaten
2 teaspoons light cream
1½ tablespoons corn oil
4½ tablespoons butter
lemon wedges dipped in minced parsley for garnish

Mix all dry ingredients listed before the fish in a plastic bag. Dip the fish in a mixture of beaten eggs and cream. Put a few pieces of fish at a time into the bag and shake to cover evenly.

Preheat oven to 450°F.

Use a 10 × 15-inch jelly roll pan. Put the oil and butter in the pan and place in the oven just until butter melts. Arrange pieces of coated fish in the pan, turning to coat evenly with the butter mixture. Bake in the oven for 7 to 10 minutes or until fish flakes easily when tested with a skewer. Turn pieces over once while baking. Serve on a warm platter with wedges of lemon dipped in parsley to be squeezed over fish at the table.

Serves 6

Note: When Mel was writing his last book, *Bread Winners* (Emmaus, Pa.: Rodale Press, 1979), he discovered a most unusual sesame seed and he began to top his sourdough breads with them. They're toasted Japanese sesame seeds called *Irigoma* and they make an unusual difference in your cooking. You might want to try them in this dish in place of the regular sesame seeds.

LINGCOD SANDWICHES STUFFED WITH SHRIMP
IN TOMATO BASIL SAUCE

6 lingcod fillets, each about ½ pound
¼ teaspoon white pepper
1 tablespoon Homemade Mayonnaise
    (see Index)
1 tablespoon dry mustard
2 tablespoons softened butter
½ pound small shrimp, shelled and
    deveined
3 large tomatoes, quartered
3 to 4 fresh basil leaves, finely minced, or
    1 teaspoon dried
½ cup whole grain bread crumbs
2 tablespoons butter
    fresh basil or parsley for garnish

Oil an oven-to-table baking pan, place half the fillets in the pan and sprinkle with half the pepper. Mix the Homemade Mayonnaise, mustard, and butter together and smear ½ over the fillets in the pan. Lay the shrimp in one direction on top of the fillets. Spread the mayonnaise-mustard butter on the remaining fillets and place them spread side down over the shrimp.

Preheat oven to 350°F.

Surround the fish with the quartered tomatoes and basil. Sprinkle the bread crumbs over the fish and tomatoes to absorb and thicken the liquids that form during cooking. Dot with butter. Cover the pan with buttered aluminum foil, butter side down. Bake for 20 minutes. Remove the foil and bake for 5 minutes more and test to see if fish is cooked through. Serve garnished with an additional bouquet of fresh basil or parsley if you wish.

Serves 6 to 8

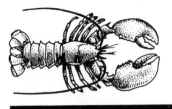

**Herb Batter Crepes Stuffed with Lobster
and *Duglere* Sauce
Lobster Salad with Tarragon
Lobster Souffle with Duxelles *Veloute*
Lobster Pie**

We remember most vividly an early trip to Maine, driving up and down the coastline, stopping at the little hotels that sat along the rugged shore, eating *lobster*—only lobster—for breakfast, lunch, dinner, and snacks. And what lobsters they were! At Bar Harbor, Ogunquit, Boothbay Harbor, we sat on the piers as the freshly caught crustaceas were plunged into boiling sea water that bubbled in huge barrels, and then devoured them, sitting at wooden tables, using our hands as utensils, the butter dripping down our chins. We do remember, though, that lobsters at that time were much more reasonably priced. At today's costs, we would soon become paupers if we ate lobster three or four times a day.

For us natives of the East Coast, the state of Maine is most closely associated with the lobster, and the harvest from that region (which includes Nova Scotia and Newfoundland, by the way) has always remained our favorite. However, lobsters in one form or another are found around the world and, though they only vaguely resemble the Maine variety, they are certainly as tasty when prepared properly. Next to the Maine lobster, the *spiny lobster* (or *rock lobster*) is probably the next most popular variety. They're found in Europe and off the coast of Florida, and they're the variety that is sold here as rock lobster tails from Australia and South Africa. These spiny creatures have superb and plentiful tail meat, but the claws are rather puny and are not of any importance to the gourmet.

There are tiny lobsters or lobsterettes, sometimes called *langostino*, sometimes Danish lobster or Dublin Bay prawns. These small crustacea are also the true bearers of the name of *scampi* in Italy, though as we have mentioned in the chapter on Shrimp, it is the giant shrimp that generally carry that designation on restaurant menus.

(continued on page 290)

Lobster

Two Lobstermen from Menemsha

They are part of a fast disappearing breed of men. They come from Menemsha, on Martha's Vineyard, where you are either a "Cricker" (or "Creeker") if you make your living from the water, or a Flatlander (a farmer or sheepherder). Robert Flanders and Donald Poole are, indeed, true Crickers. Both still make their own lobster traps and mend their own nets; both are steeped in the traditions of the sea.

Robert Flanders was a fisherman who turned carpenter and then came back to the sea when he could no longer stand being a Flatlander. Each lobsterman has his own individual marker for his traps—his own size, shape, and color, and no lobsterman would dare touch the trap of another. Robert collects the ones that have broken off and floated away, very much the way others of us collect stamps or coins.

Donald Poole is almost 80 years of age. Six years ago he went to the local jeweler to have two gold earrings put in his ears. Tradition has it that if you've sailed the Cape Of Good Hope or Cape Horn, you have the right to wear one earring and if you've been married to the same woman for 50 years, you are entitled to wear a second one. Donald says he wears them out of memory for the tradition of whaling and won't say whether he's sailed either Cape, though he has been married for at least that many years to Dorothy Cottle Poole (Dorothy is author of a delightful book of Vineyard history entitled *Vineyard Sampler* (Edgartown, Mass.: Dukes County Historical Society, 1978).

Those of us who come from the city wait with bated breath for the jewels that fall from the mouths of men like these, and Donald did not disappoint us: "There are only two things a fisherman chooses well—his boat and his women. . . ." to which his friend Susan Whitney added, "Don't think for one minute that they don't choose the boat first!"

How a Maine Lobster Is Caught

If you've traveled through New England, and especially Maine, you've seen the lobster traps sitting on the docks, waiting to be towed out to sea. The traps are a simple, but ingenious invention and they have been used for over a hundred years. The wooden slats contain the cage portion, while the opening is covered with a cord netting, allowing the lobster in, but not out.

The traps are taken out by the lobstermen, then dropped anywhere from 50 feet to several miles apart, each trap marked with a buoy to identify it. The depth varies from 5 to 50 fathoms. When the lobsters enter the trap to get to the bait, the flexible cord net keeps them from escaping until the traps are ready to be hauled in by the lobsterman. The lobsters are stored in tanks and then shipped live in iced barrels.

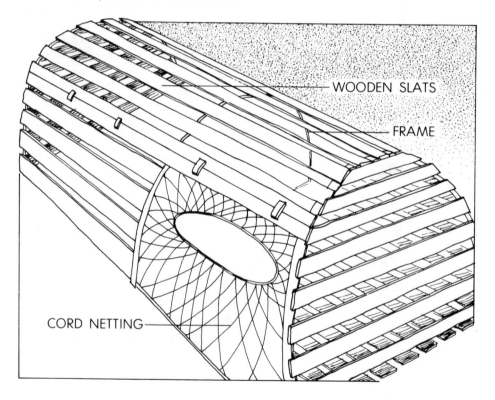

How to Choose Your Lobster

Possibly the best advice we can give is: buy lobsters live at your fishmonger. Certainly, if you're vacationing by the sea and you are lucky enough to purchase your lobster at dockside or in the holding shed on the same day the catch is brought in, it will no doubt be active, scrappy, and at its peak of perfection. On the other hand, if you buy lobster at your local store as most of us are forced to do, make certain that the lobster is fairly active. The longer a lobster is kept, the less it eats, and the flesh then has a tendency to shrivel and pull away from the shell. The claws, of course, will be banded and pegged, not only to keep the lobster from pinching you, but to prevent it from eating the *other* lobsters, for they are all cannibals.

There are times when you are in a hurry, when you don't want to go through the trouble of boiling or broiling your own lobster, and the temptation is to buy the lobster precooked. If you do plan to purchase the lobster this way, make certain that you either know and trust the fishmonger or that the lobster is chosen while it is alive and is cooked before you. If you can't do the latter, test the cooked lobster by pulling back on its tail to lay it straight out. If it was alive and fresh when cooked, the tail will snap back into a curled position against the body.

What Size to Buy

An easy method of choosing a lobster according to its size is to allow about one to one and one-quarter pounds per person, and the yield will be about three to four ounces of cooked lobster meat. A two-pound lobster will yield about one-half pound of meat.

Lobsters are graded according to weight:

Chicken—three-quarters to one pound
Quarter—one and one-quarter to one and one-half pounds
Large—one and one-half to two and one-half pounds
Jumbo—over two and one-half pounds

For years we've been hearing that the "chicken" lobster, being the smallest, is the tenderest. We have no idea where this notion came from but it is just not true. The larger lobsters are equally good, equally tender and, in fact, surpass the smaller ones in many respects.

Once, while visiting the docks at Montauk, New York, on Long Island, in a fit of abandon we purchased a *20-pound* behemoth. It was, to put it mildly, huge and threatening. The biggest problem after getting it to our rented cottage was to find a pot large enough in which to boil it. Our farmer neighbors across the road solved that one for us. They had kept their old galvanized washtub for these many years and, by placing the tub across all four burners of the stove, we came up with the perfect cooking utensil.

The second most difficult problem was to get the squirming giant into the pot once the water was boiling. After that was accomplished, the results were incredible! That lobster tasted better than any we had ever eaten before. The claws made huge steaks, and the other meat lasted for several days. We served lobster to guests for dinner, we had lobster salads for lunch, lobster steak as a snack, and we even gave some as a gift to the neighbor who had lent us the washtub. It seemed that it would never end, and we were sorry when it finally did end. There just never can be too much lobster in our family.

How to Cook a Lobster

The night before we began writing this chapter, the Great Lobster Controversy was finally settled at our island house. To boil—or to steam. We settled the question by plunging one chicken lobster into a large pot of boiling sea water, and placing the other on a rack in a steaming Dutch oven. The experiment was a huge success. *Both* were superb. There was no discernible difference in taste or texture, and the feast was consumed with gusto.

However, if taste and texture are not the considerations, you might want to think about another factor before deciding whether to boil or steam your lobster. Steaming takes less time, since you use much less water. Bringing a large pot of water to boil will take anywhere from 30 to 45 minutes on our stove, while boiling the water needed for steaming takes only about 10 minutes. Steaming also means handling a much lighter load, when you consider the weights of the two cooking utensils—one completely filled with water, the other only partly filled. Both methods are simple. Both are effective. The choice is yours.

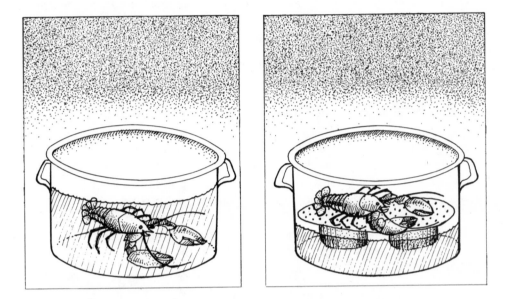

Boiling

We are lucky enough to live near the ocean, so we always use sea water for preparing our lobsters. This is not very practical in most other parts of the country, but ordinary tap water will do. Take a large pot and fill it with enough water to cover the lobsters completely while cooking. Cover and bring to a boil. When the water is boiling rapidly, grasp the lobster behind the claws and plunge it headfirst into the pot. (For the more squeamish among us, marine scientists assure us that the lobster is killed instantly and feels no pain.) When the lobster is plunged into the water, the boil will stop. Allow the water to come to a boil again—this will take from 3 to 5 minutes. *Begin your timing from this point.* For the average chicken lobster of one to one and one-quarter pounds, allow 12 minutes, keeping the pot covered. For each additional pound of lobster, add 3 minutes.

Steaming

Take a large pot or Dutch oven and put a rack on the bottom, raised about two to three inches from the floor of the vessel. We use crumpet rings under the rack. (Tuna or salmon cans, with tops, bottoms, and labels removed, will do just as well.) Fill the pot to just below the rack, cover and bring to a boil. When steam escapes from the cover, open and place the lobsters on the rack, then cover tightly again. As soon as you see steam escaping, begin to time. Allow 12 minutes for chicken lobsters (one to one and one-quarter pounds) and add 3 minutes for each additional pound.

Broiling

We prefer ours boiled or steamed, but when properly cooked and basted, a broiled lobster can be a delicious treat. Have your fishmonger split the lobster for broiling. If you prefer to do it yourself, put the lobster on its back and make a vertical cut from the top right down through the tail section. Remove the stomach and intestinal vein that is in the tail section close to the shell. Baste the lobster with butter and keep a small pot of melted butter handy so that the lobster can be basted constantly during the broiling process. Place the lobster under the broiler, flesh up, and broil—basting every few minutes—for about 12 minutes for the average chicken lobster. We would not recommend broiling the larger ones, since the longer required cooking time under the flame will dry out the meat.

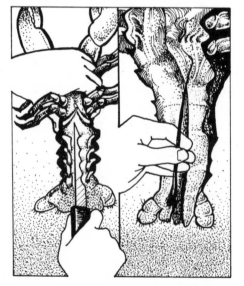
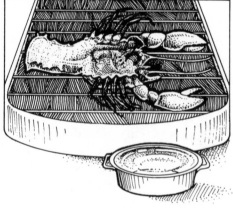

The Spiny Lobster

The spiny lobster (or rock lobster tail) can be boiled, broiled, or steamed just like its distant cousin, the American lobster. You can also remove the raw meat from the shell and use it for other dishes. If the tail is frozen, thaw it out under cold, running water and then prepare just as you would any lobster. For broiling, split the tail. For boiling or steaming, add 1 teaspoon of vinegar to the water and wait for the second boil before timing, just as you did for the American lobster. However, plan to use two tails for each person, and time them to cook for five minutes for each average tail weighing about four to five ounces, including the shell. Add one minute for each additional ounce.

The Accompanying Sauce

For each element of cuisine, there is a purity of design and method. For lobster it is butter—melted butter, laced with lemon—and nothing else. For whichever method you have chosen to cook your lobster, a small dish of the lemon butter is all you need provide for your guests. You can use a lobster fork to dip or you can use your fingers, as we do in our family. Just be sure to provide generous napkins or towels to each of the diners. In addition to this lemon butter, boiled or steamed lobster can be eaten with these other sauces (see Index):

Basic Clarified Butter
Herbed Butter Sauce *(Beurre Nantais)*
Mint Butter Sauce

If you have lobster left over or if you prefer to serve it cold as a summer salad, it can be served in the shell with any of this variety of different sauces (see Index):

Cresson Mayonnaise (Watercress Mayonnaise)
Remoulade Sauce (Pungent Mayonnaise Sauce)
Sorrel Mayonnaise
Cucumber Mayonnaise Sauce with Dill

How to Eat a Whole Lobster

When a lobster is eaten properly, there is very little waste. You can even use the left-over shells to make sauces or to add a special flavor to fish stews and soups such as lobster bisque. Incidentally, when you open the lobster, you'll find a green substance called "tomalley"—it's the liver and it's delicious. If the lobster is a female, you'll sometimes find the pinkish red roe (or lobster coral). This, too, is a nourishing treat and both the roe and the tomalley can be used in the preparation of elegant sauces as well.

The lobster is out of the pot, gloriously red and shining. The butter is drawn. On the table, each guest has a cracker such as you use to crack nuts, a small lobster fork, and a large napkin. It is time to dismantle the dinner.

1. Grasp the lobster firmly in one hand and twist off the claws right down to the body with the other hand. Place these aside on your plate. (Of course, they can be eaten first, but everyone we know saves this best part until last!)

2. Using a heavy, sharp-pointed knife, cut through the entire length of the lobster from the head to the tail. Grasp both sides with paper towels (the lobster will be hot) and break apart. Remove the intestinal vein and the craw. The tail meat will be exposed and can be easily removed for dipping and eating.

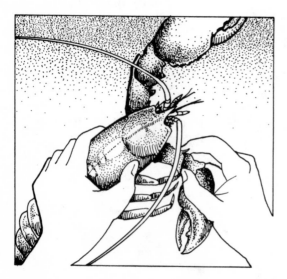

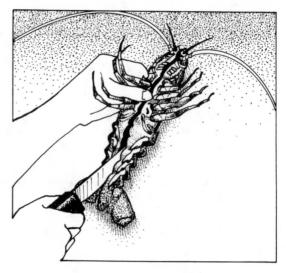

3. In the body cavity, you'll notice that the lobster is divided into small armored segments, with a leg coming from each one. Break into each segment, discarding the feathery material and you'll find small morsels of meat in each part. Then remove the legs one at a time, break them and suck the meat out like sipping through a straw.

4. Using the nutcracker or a mallet or small hammer, crack the shell around the claw sections, peel off with your fingers and remove the meat.

5. Relax and contemplate the superb dinner you've just devoured.

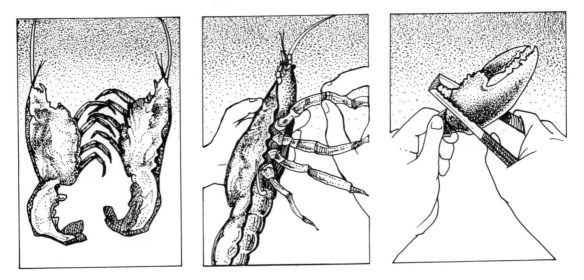

A Note about These Lobster Recipes

The price of whole lobster varies. In the early days of New England history, they sold as low as a penny apiece. Depending upon availability today, they range from moderately high to "out of sight" per pound. So, to serve six people, you'll need *six* lobsters, one-and-one-half pounds each, and the price may be exorbitant. For that reason, the recipes that follow have been designed to stretch the amount of fresh lobster that you'll need, while still allowing you to serve this elegant creature as a party centerpiece.

HERB BATTER CREPES STUFFED WITH LOBSTER
AND DUGLERE SAUCE

Prepare the sauce and crepes in advance.

Sauce

Prepare and set aside ½ recipe of *Duglere* Sauce (Cream and Tomato Sauce with Anise). (See Index.)

Herb Batter Crepes (about 12 crepes)

  1 cup whole wheat pastry flour
  2 eggs
1½ cups milk
 ¼ teaspoon black pepper
1½ tablespoons butter, melted
  1 tablespoon finely minced, fresh parsley
  1 tablespoon finely minced, fresh chives
  1 tablespoon finely minced, fresh tarragon or ¾ teaspoon dried

Place the flour in a mixing bowl, make a well in the center, and add the eggs. Start stirring with a wire whisk while gradually adding the milk to the eggs in the center, until the batter is the consistency of heavy cream. Continue to stir and beat until well blended. Strain the batter through a strainer into another bowl and add all the remaining ingredients. Using a seasoned, 7-inch crepe pan, heat to medium before ladling enough batter to cover the bottom of the pan thinly when the batter is swirled around.

Cook briefly and turn out on wax paper until cool. Lift carefully to fresh wax paper and place more wax paper between layers of crepes. Continue to make crepes until all batter is used. These crepes can be made a day before or frozen and defrosted before using.

Lobster Filling

  3 tablespoons butter
  1 large shallot, finely minced, or 2 scallions, white part only, finely minced
  6 tablespoons lemon juice
 ½ teaspoon cayenne pepper
  1 cup Basic Creme Fraiche (see Index)
  3 cups cooked, finely diced, fresh or frozen lobster

Melt butter and saute shallot until wilted. Add lemon juice and pepper and let it cook until most is evaporated. Stir in the Basic Creme Fraiche and lower heat. Simmer for a few minutes and add lobster. Stir to heat, and use to stuff herb crepes.

When ready to assemble, spoon lobster into crepes, fold in thirds, and spoon *Duglere* Sauce over all. Heat in hot oven for a few minutes before serving.

Serves 6

LOBSTER SALAD
WITH TARRAGON

4 cups cooked, cubed, fresh or frozen
    lobster
½ cup finely chopped red onion
½ cup finely chopped celery
⅓ cup finely chopped green pepper
3 tablespoons finely minced, fresh
    parsley
1 tablespoon chopped, fresh tarragon or
    ¾ teaspoon dried
1 cup Homemade Mayonnaise (see Index)
1 tablespoon lime juice
¼ teaspoon white pepper
    leaf lettuce

Place the lobster in a large bowl and add all the ingredients listed above lettuce. Blend well. Make a bed of lettuce on each of 6 individual, chilled salad plates. Spoon the lobster salad in the center. Serve cold.

Serves 6

Note: Add eye appeul to the salad by decorating the dish with hard-cooked eggs, quartered, cherry tomatoes, or quartered large tomatoes, and slim sticks of cucumber.

LOBSTER SOUFFLE
WITH DUXELLES VELOUTE

½ cup butter
1 cup whole wheat pastry flour
2 cups milk
8 eggs, separated
¼ teaspoon black pepper
⅛ teaspoon cayenne pepper
¾ pound finely diced, fresh or frozen
    lobster meat or lobster tail meat
2 tablespoons finely minced, fresh chives
1 recipe Duxelles *Veloute* (see Index)

Preheat oven to 350°F.

Boil a kettle of water and butter a 6-cup souffle dish. Melt the butter over low heat in a saucepan and add the flour. Stir with a wooden spoon. Do not brown. Slowly add milk and continue stirring. Add the egg yolks, black and cayenne pepper and stir. Remove from heat and add the lobster and chives. Let cool slightly.

Beat egg whites until stiff and gently fold into the mixture. Spoon all into the souffle dish and set in a larger pan. Pour 2 inches of the boiling water in the larger pan. Bake for 45 minutes. While baking, prepare the sauce. Serve at once in the souffle dish and pass the sauce separately to be spooned over the souffle.

Serves 6

LOBSTER
PIE

Pastry Crust

1½ cups whole wheat pastry flour
 ½ cup slightly softened butter
  1 tablespoon tamari soy sauce
     about 2 tablespoons ice water
  1 egg yolk, beaten

Place the flour in a bowl and make a well in the flour. Cut the butter into small pieces and place in the center. Use a pastry blender or 2 knives and cut the butter into the flour until it has the texture of coarse oatmeal. With a fork, add the soy sauce and then just enough ice water to make the dough hold its shape. Roll out on a floured cloth or board to fit into a buttered, 10-inch pie pan, turn and flute the edges, and then chill in the refrigerator while assembling the ingredients for the pie filling or prepare in advance and chill longer.

When ready to bake, preheat the oven to 400°F.

Brush some beaten egg yolk on the bottom of the crust and bake for 5 minutes. Remove and prick the crust all over with a fork. Place a piece of aluminum foil over the bottom of the crust and weight the foil down with a layer of dried beans or metal pastry weights. Return to the oven and bake for 10 to 15 minutes more, or until the crust is partially baked, and remove from the oven. Take out the beans and aluminum foil, lower the oven temperature to 375°F. Set crust aside, and prepare the filling.

Filling

  3 tablespoons butter
  3 tablespoons whole wheat pastry flour
  1 cup milk
 ½ cup grated Gruyere cheese
 ¼ teaspoon cayenne pepper
1½ pounds fresh or frozen lobster meat, uncooked

Using a double boiler, melt the butter and add the flour. Stir until smooth. Add the milk, cheese, and cayenne pepper and cook until cheese is melted and sauce is smooth and thick. Stir in lobster and set aside.

Spoon lobster mixture into pie crust. Place in oven and bake for about 20 minutes or until pastry is golden. Serve hot.

Serves 6

Lobster-Lobster-and More Lobster

It is amazing how many festivals and events are dedicated to fish, not only in North America, but all over the world. Possibly it's only an excuse to have a party—but festivals abound when the fleets leave port, when they come back again, when the catch is in season, and even when it's not. *Catfish* is celebrated, and so are *trout* and *whiting* and *salmon*. *Shrimp* festivals take place on the Gulf and on the west coast of Mexico. And *lobsters* are the stars in Rockland, Maine, every summer.

The town breaks out in red welcome signs, the parades announce the coming of the lobster, the queen is crowned just as queens are crowned all over the world, and the food is nonstop. The main course—lobster, of course!

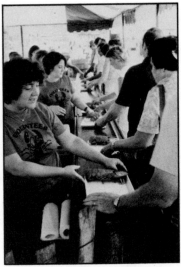

Broiled Kingfish Steaks with Fennel Butter
Mackerel in Coconut Cream (a Fijian *Seviche*)
Sauteed Mackerel with Garlic and Rosemary
Sauteed Mackerel Served Cold
with Fresh Coriander
***Seviche* of Kingfish, Tomato, and Avocado**

Though the family actually includes "big brother" *tuna*, the *mackerel* is really a fish quite unto its own, and a favorite among fishermen for its jolting and sudden strikes and fierce struggle when hooked. Mackerel is widely abundant, and there have been reports of *Atlantic mackerel* (also known as *Boston mackerel*) covering the water like a carpet. At other times, fishermen have searched in vain for schools that have all but disappeared. The most common and widely known mackerel, the *Spanish mackerel,* is known for its spectacular leaps out of the water after it's been hooked—sometimes as high as ten feet over the surface!

The most delicately flavored of the family is the Spanish mackerel and the *cero*. The texture is firm and fatty and it is generally marketed at two to four pounds—whole, in fillets, and as steaks.

Should you ever be fortunate enough to catch one of your own, make sure it's kept carefully on ice, for the mackerel loses its flavor quickly. In fact, mackerel was not fully fished commercially for many years because techniques for freezing and storing were not known, and the fish lost its flavor before reaching market. Recently, however, new technologies have been developed and storage life has been improved. As a result, frozen mackerel fillets are becoming more readily available.

Kingfish

The *Kingfish* is more accurately called *king mackerel*. However, most of our fishing friends in Florida call this fierce fighter just plain "king" or kingfish.

It's a relatively large mackerel, found primarily in the southern Gulf regions. Most kingfish spend the winter months around both coasts of Florida. Some have weighed in at 70 pounds or more, but the average market weight is about 15 to 30 pounds—still a rather large species.

Mackerel can be cooked using any of the methods described in this book, and it takes well to the following piquant sauces (see Index):

Mustard-Dill Sauce
Salsa Cruda (a Mexican Hot, Fresh, Tomato Sauce)
Shallot and Vinegar Sauce (also called "Escargot Butter")

If mackerel or kingfish are not available, you may use *butterfish* or *bluefish* in any of the recipes that follow.

BROILED
KINGFISH STEAKS
WITH FENNEL BUTTER

2½ pounds kingfish steaks
½ teaspoon black pepper
4 tablespoons softened sweet butter
2 teaspoons fennel seeds, pulverized in a blender or with mortar and pestle
1 teaspoon lemon juice

Garnish
3 sprigs parsley
3 lemons, cut in half

Oil a baking pan and place steaks on it in one layer.

Sprinkle the steaks with pepper. In a small bowl, mash the butter with the fennel seeds and lemon juice. Spread evenly on each steak and broil 3 inches from source of heat, basting occasionally. Turn once and test with a skewer after 8 to 10 minutes to see if fish flakes easily; if not, broil until it does.

Remove steaks carefully with a wide spatula and serve on warm platter. Decorate with sprigs of parsley and perhaps a few decorative lemon halves.

Serves 6

MACKEREL IN
COCONUT CREAM
(A FIJIAN SEVICHE)

2½ pounds filleted and skinned mackerel,
      cut into bite-size pieces about 1 inch
      square
  2 tablespoons tamari soy sauce
¾   cups fresh lemon juice (4 to 6 lemons)
  1 small carrot, finely shredded
  3 scallions, finely minced
¾   cup Coconut Cream (see Index)

Mix the fish with the soy sauce and add lemon juice to cover. Refrigerate overnight and stir occasionally.

The next day, prepare the Coconut Cream.

Drain and dry the fish, then add the carrot and scallions. Add the Coconut Cream and refrigerate the mixture for 30 minutes more, or until liquid is absorbed by the fish. Serve chilled.

Serves 6

SAUTEED MACKEREL
WITH GARLIC AND ROSEMARY

½   cup olive oil
  6 cloves garlic, crushed
  6 mackerel, about ¾ pound each,
      scaled, gutted, but with heads left
      on
  6 tiny sprigs rosemary or ½ teaspoon
      dried and crushed fine
½   teaspoon black pepper
      juice of 1 lemon
¼   cup water
      lemon wedges for garnish

Heat the oil over medium heat in a heavy skillet large enough to hold the mackerel in one layer placed end to end so they fit more easily. Add the garlic to the oil and saute until tan, about 2 to 3 minutes. Remove garlic with a slotted spoon and set aside. Add the fish, end to end, the rosemary, and pepper. Reduce the heat to medium and saute fish until brown on each side, turning carefully with a wide spatula so they do not break. When the fish has browned, add the lemon juice and water and return the garlic to the pan. Cover tightly, lower heat, and cook for 5 to 10 minutes more, or until fish flakes easily. Serve with lemon wedges.

Serves 6

SAUTEED MACKEREL
SERVED COLD
WITH FRESH CORIANDER

6 mackerel fillets, about 3 pounds,
    skinned
  juice of 1 lime
½ cup whole wheat flour
6 tablespoons butter
5 cloves garlic, finely minced
1 small onion, finely minced
1 carrot, shredded
½ green pepper, seeded and cut into thin
    strips
½ red sweet pepper, seeded and cut into
    thin strips
1 small, dried hot pepper
1 teaspoon finely minced, fresh thyme or
    ½ teaspoon dried
¼ cup vinegar
¾ cup water
3 tablespoons minced, fresh coriander
    leaves

Dip fillets in lime juice and let stand for 5 minutes. Lift out and dip in flour. Melt the butter and saute the fish over medium heat until they are brown, turning once. Lift out with a wide spatula and place in a flat dish with sides. Set aside.

In a saucepan, add all the remaining ingredients except the coriander leaves. Bring to a boil, lower heat, and simmer for 5 minutes.

Pour this hot liquid over the sauteed fillets. Let cool and then chill for 24 hours. Remove hot pepper and sprinkle with coriander leaves before serving.

Serves 6 to 8

Note: If you have a spare flower pot or a small garden, you can grow your own coriander (also known as *cilantro* in Spanish or as Chinese parsley). Just take some coriander seeds and plant them and you can use the leaves of the plant in your cooking. It's a lovely way to impress your guests.

SEVICHE OF KINGFISH, TOMATO, AND AVOCADO

2½ pounds kingfish fillets, boned and cut into 1-inch chunks (pompano or mackerel may be used)
1 cup fresh lime juice (juice of 6 to 8 limes)
2 medium-size tomatoes, peeled and cubed
3 roasted, green, hot chili peppers—*jalapeno* or *serrano*—peeled, seeded, and finely chopped
2 tablespoons coarsely chopped, fresh coriander or parsley leaves (reserve 1 teaspoon)
2 sprigs oregano, leaves only, or ½ teaspoon dried
¼ teaspoon black pepper
1 small onion, thinly sliced
1 ripe avocado, peeled, seed removed, and cut into ¾-inch cubes
⅓ cup olive oil

Place the fish and lime juice in a nonmetallic bowl and refrigerate about 5 hours, or until the fish loses its transparency and becomes opaque. Stir occasionally to "cook" evenly.

Mix everything else together and stir into the fish. Chill again for at least 1 more hour. Sprinkle with reserved teaspoon of coriander or parsley. Serve cold.

Serves 6 to 8

Tip: Pour boiling water over limes and let stand for 1 minute, then rinse under cold water. This procedure extracts more juice from the limes.

Baked Butterflied Mullet on a Bed of Herbs
Arabic Red Mullet with Walnut Stuffing
Cooked and Marinated Mullet
and Squid, Tuscan Style
Egyptian Fried Mullet Served
in Newspaper

The traditions of the countries in which we've traveled have always had a fascination for us. In the Philippines, the ears of the pig are served to the honored guest (and, yes, we ate them as duly honored guests—they taste like *hairy rubber*). In Turkey, the *mullet* is always served whole and the head is given to the head of the household as a choice morsel to symbolize his wisdom and leadership.

The Romans raised this ancient fish in ponds and held them in high esteem. The Egyptians also cultivated them in the deltas of the Nile and they're still farmed in the Hawaiian Islands and the Philippines.

Most of our mullet comes from Florida and because they are a jumping fish, night fishermen listen to the splashing of the water to locate the schools.

Of course, as is so common with fish, the name of the family does not always distinguish a true mullet. The mullet, in fact, is not always a mullet. The famous *red mullet* or *rouget de roche* of France is really a *goatfish*. However, there are over 100 varieties of true mullet scattered throughout the world, with the *striped* (or *black*) *mullet* and the *silver mullet* the most common.

Mullets are found in both salt water and fresh water and they're readily available from Florida and the Carolinas during the late fall and early winter months. They're a fat (polyunsaturated), firm, flaky fish, rich in minerals, with a mild, nutlike flavor. They're sold whole or pan dressed and come in a variety of sizes, readily adaptable to broiling, baking, deep fat frying, or oven frying.

Mullet

Incidentally, the larger, heavier mullets generally contain roe, which are a taste treat in themselves. Don't discard them if you're lucky enough to find them. See the chapter on Roe for suggestions on how to use them.

BAKED BUTTERFLIED MULLET
ON A BED OF HERBS

1 whole mullet, about 5 to 6 pounds, pan dressed and split open in butterflied fashion
1 large Bermuda onion, sliced into rings
1 tablespoon peanut oil
4 sprigs thyme
6 sprigs parsley
2 small sprigs rosemary
2 tablespoons minced, fresh parsley
3 tablespoons softened butter
½ teaspoon lemon juice
⅛ teaspoon cayenne pepper

Preheat oven to 425°F.

Wash and dry the mullet and set aside.

In a skillet, saute the onion rings until tender-crisp in the hot peanut oil. Do not brown onion.

Oil a large, oven-to-table baking dish. Place half the thyme, parsley, and rosemary on bottom of the baking dish, then lay the open fish over these herbs. Top with the rest of the herbs and the onion rings. Bake for about 10 to 12 minutes.

Meanwhile, mix the minced parsley with butter, lemon juice, and cayenne pepper and form into small balls. Test fish with skewer. Serve and top with the parsley-cayenne butter balls melting on top to form a sauce.

Serves 6

ARABIC
RED MULLET
WITH WALNUT STUFFING

Marinade
4 tablespoons olive oil
¼ teaspoon black pepper
1 clove garlic, crushed
   juice of 2 lemons
1 tablespoon tamari soy sauce

Mix all marinade ingredients in a large shallow dish (not metal).

The Fish
3 red mullets, about 2 pounds, gutted, washed, but with heads left on

Lay fish in marinade and refrigerate for 4 hours, turning several times.

Stuffing
1 tablespoon olive oil
1 onion, finely chopped
1 green pepper, seeded and cut into strips
⅔ cup chopped walnuts
2 tablespoons finely minced, fresh parsley
   juice of 1 lime
¼ teaspoon black pepper

1 lime sliced for garnish

Preheat oven to 400°F.

To make the stuffing, heat olive oil and fry onion until soft. Add green pepper and walnuts, stir and cook for 5 minutes. Remove from heat and add 1½ tablespoons of the parsley, the lime juice, and pepper.

Rest of Procedure
Drain fish and reserve marinade. Dry fish and fill the cavities with walnut stuffing. Secure the opening with skewers.

Oil a large baking dish and place fish in it. Bake for 25 minutes or 10 minutes per inch at thickest part of fish, basting occasionally with the marinade. Remove skewers. Sprinkle with remaining parsley and arrange slices of lime. Serve hot.

Serves 6

COOKED AND MARINATED
MULLET AND SQUID, TUSCAN STYLE

2 pounds mullet, whole and pan dressed
  water
1 tablespoon vinegar
2 small onions—1 left whole and stuck
    with 1 whole clove and 1 thinly
    sliced
1 pound squid, cleaned and cut into
    ¼-inch rings, with legs and
    tentacles left whole (see Index for
    directions on preparation)
2 tablespoons olive oil
2 cloves garlic
2 sprigs sage
2 bay leaves
2 sprigs rosemary
2 cups vinegar

Poach mullet for 15 minutes in water to cover with vinegar and the onion stuck with clove. (See Index for poaching directions.) Then for the last 3 minutes, add squid. Drain and discard onion and clove.

Heat the oil and saute garlic and sliced onion until golden. Add the herbs and the vinegar. Bring to a boil.

Pour this marinade mixture over the fish and refrigerate for 2 days before serving. Serve at room temperature.

Serves 6

EGYPTIAN FRIED MULLET
SERVED IN NEWSPAPER

These small fish are traditionally cooked and sold on the streets of Cairo by vendors. They are wrapped in the local newspaper, *El Aram,* and can be adapted easily and served this way outdoors, with no mess to clean up afterward.

3 tablespoons minced, fresh parsley
3 cloves garlic, crushed
1 teaspoon finely minced lemon rind
3 pounds very small red mullet, pan
    dressed and boned
½ cup stone-ground cornmeal
  corn oil for frying

Mix together the parsley, garlic, and lemon rind and rub inside and outside of the fish. Let stand for 20 minutes to absorb flavor. Then dip fish in cornmeal.

Heat oil to 370°F. and deep fry a few fish at a time until crisp and golden. Wrap fish in newspaper as they are cooked. The paper blots the excess oil from the fish; it acts as a serving "plate" and it even insulates the fish to help it stay warm until served!

Serves 6

Note: If you wish to avoid having the fish come in contact with the newsprint, lay a piece of paper toweling over the newspaper and put the hot fish on it, then wrap fish in both papers!

Lobster Salad with Tarragon   For this recipe, see page 299

Roe Baked in Seashells   For this recipe, see page 337

**Ocean Perch with Orange Sauce
Cucumbers Stuffed with a Mousse
of Ocean Perch
Ocean Perch Pie**

The National Fisheries Service (U.S. Department of Commerce) calls these tasty fish the "Cinderellas" of the commercial fishing industry. Before 1930 they were almost totally unexploited, until a clever fish cutter discovered that the fillet from the *ocean perch* closely resembled the small white fillet of the *freshwater perch* with a white, flaky texture and a most delicate taste. Since then, the once unloved and unused, abundant ocean perch has become a princess among fish. Almost the entire catch—nearly 200 million pounds a year—is filleted, frozen, packaged, and sold at frozen seafood counters across the country.

Ocean perch caught in the Atlantic by trawlers are also called *rosefish* and *red perch,* while on the Pacific Coast, they're called *rockfish* and, though the colors vary from species to species, they are all basically the same fish and can be prepared in the same way.

This is a versatile fish, easy to cook and it can be broiled, steamed, sauteed, fried, or poached. However, if you poach or broil the ocean perch, leave the skin on the fillet so that it retains its shape while cooking. For the other methods, you can remove the skin.

When broiling ocean perch, try any of the following sauces (see Index):

   White Butter Sauce with Vinegar *(Beurre Blanc)*
   Maitre d'Hotel Butter
   Chivry Butter

When poaching or steaming ocean perch, try these sauces (see Index):

   Sauce Maltaise (Orange Hollandaise)
   Gazpacho Sauce (a Tomato and Raw Vegetable Sauce)
   Sweet and Sour Pineapple and Vegetable Sauce

Ocean Perch

Ocean perch is excellent when poached, chilled and then served cold in a salad, using any of these sauces (see Index):

Spinach and Chive Sauce
Cucumber Mayonnaise Sauce with Dill
Remoulade Sauce (Pungent Mayonnaise Sauce)

OCEAN PERCH
WITH ORANGE SAUCE

2 pounds ocean perch fillets
3 tablespoons olive oil
1 clove garlic, minced
1 tablespoon lemon juice
  juice of 1 whole orange
  rind of 1 orange, finely minced
½ teaspoon peeled and grated, fresh
    ginger root or ½ teaspoon ground
    ginger
1 cup Fish Stock (see Index)
2 teaspoons cornstarch
2 teaspoons cold water

Coat the fish fillets on both sides with 1 tablespoon of the oil and place in a broiling pan. Broil 4 inches from source of heat, turning once until fish flakes easily, about 3 to 4 minutes on each side. When fish is cooked, place on a serving platter and keep warm while preparing the sauce.

Heat the remaining 2 tablespoons of oil and add the garlic. Over low heat cook the garlic slowly until it is soft but not brown. Add the lemon juice, orange juice, orange rind, ginger, and Fish Stock to the garlic and cook for 5 minutes. Mix the cornstarch with cold water and add to the sauce to thicken. Cook for a few minutes until thickened and pour over fish.

Serves 6

CUCUMBERS STUFFED WITH A MOUSSE OF OCEAN PERCH

1½ pounds ocean perch fillets, skinned and cut into small pieces
2 eggs
4 tablespoons Basic *Creme Fraiche* (see Index)
¼ teaspoon white pepper
1 teaspoon minced, fresh dill
6 thick cucumbers, each about 8 inches long, peeled and cut in half to produce 12 equal 4-inch pieces
Court Bouillon (see Index)
6 tomatoes, peeled and chopped
2 scallions, finely chopped
¼ teaspoon black pepper
1 tablespoon olive oil
1 teaspoon minced, fresh parsley
¼ cup grated cheese (Parmesan, cheddar or Swiss)
several sprigs dill for garnish

Using a food processor or a blender, place the fish in the bowl and process briefly. Add the eggs and Basic Creme Fraiche and process until smooth. Add the white pepper and dill. Chill in the refrigerator for 30 minutes.

Use a long handled spoon or a melon ball scoop to scrape out the center seed parts of the cucumber pieces. Fill the cucumber pieces with the chilled fish mousse. Place 3 pieces of stuffed cucumber in a line and wrap together in cheesecloth. Tie each end. Make 4 of these rolls.

In a large, deep skillet, heat 6 cups of the Court Bouillon to boiling. Lower heat and add the stuffed cucumber packages side by side. Do not let liquid boil. Cover and simmer for 10 to 15 minutes, then remove the rolls from the Court Bouillon and drain and refrigerate in the cheesecloth wrapping.

Meanwhile, place the tomatoes in a food processor or blender with the scallions, black pepper, olive oil, and parsley and process for about 30 seconds or until there is a smooth puree. Pour puree into a skillet and cook over low heat for 2 to 3 minutes to evaporate the liquid that has accumulated and to thicken the sauce. Cool the sauce to room temperature.

To serve, make a bed of the sauce, unwrap the stuffed cucumbers and cut each piece into 3 sections, then place upright so the fish mousse shows in the center. Sprinkle with your favorite cheese and scatter the sprigs of dill over the cucumbers.

Serves 6

OCEAN PERCH PIE

¼ cup plus 3 tablespoons butter
¼ cup whole grain flour
¼ teaspoon white pepper
¼ teaspoon mace
1¼ cups milk
1 bay leaf
1 small onion, grated
2 pounds ocean perch fillets, cut in chunks
½ pound small, whole mushrooms
1 teaspoon lemon juice
1 cup fresh or frozen green peas, cooked
2 hard-boiled eggs, coarsely chopped
2 cups mashed potatoes
¼ teaspoon cayenne pepper
1 tablespoon minced, fresh chives

In a saucepan, melt ¼ cup of butter and stir in flour, white pepper, and mace with a wooden spoon. Cook over low heat until smooth but not brown. Gradually add the milk and beat with a wire whisk. Add the bay leaf and onion and cook and stir until thickened. Remove bay leaf.

Preheat oven to 400°F.

Butter a 10 × 6 × 2-inch baking dish, and spoon the sauce into the bottom of the dish. Add the fish to the sauce.

In a small skillet, melt 2 tablespoons of butter and stir the mushrooms to coat. Sprinkle with lemon juice and then add to the sauce and the fish. Add the cooked green peas and the chopped eggs. Spoon or pipe the mashed potatoes on the top and sprinkle with cayenne. Dot with remaining butter. Bake for 25 to 30 minutes or until top is lightly browned. Sprinkle with minced chives before serving.

Serves 6

Baked Pike with Crab Meat Stuffing
Mousse of Pickerel in a Fish Mold
Pike and Shrimp Quenelles
Poached Pike or Muskellunge with Fresh Dill

The members of the family:

> muskellunge
> pike
> pickerel

As children, we went to the country every summer and on the way passed a new resort built around an artificial lake, still showing half-submerged tree stumps poking out of the water. A large billboard heralded the new utopia and, on the sign, as the main attraction, was a lunging, fierce-looking, long, coiled fish—the *muskellunge*. The unwritten promise was, of course, that everyone who built a house on this new lake could have muskellunge on their fishing doorstep. In actuality, it is probably the most difficult fish to catch—moody, temperamental, unpredictable, tricky. There are fishermen who have been after them for years and have yet to get their first strike. I've often wondered how many people living at that lake have actually caught one.

The "musky," as fishermen like to call them, is actually a member of a larger group of fish in the *pike* family. Many varieties of the fish are not commercially marketed, but are caught mostly by sport fishermen, who promptly pan fry them, thus losing the exquisite potential of these tasty fish.

The pike is a long fish with a pointed, duck-bill-shaped nose and a set of double canine teeth that give evidence of the fact that it is a voracious eater. In fact, besides eating smaller fish, it has been known to dine on small water birds, ducks, and frogs.

Occasionally, you will come across *little pickerel* in the market, either called *walleye* or *yellow pike*. In fact, these are actually members of the *perch* family and are not true pike or pickerel at all. The true *chain pickerel* has a softer flesh than the pike, though it still retains the long shape and needlelike nose, and it's generally found only as a sport fish.

The fierce muskellunge that we saw on the billboard as children is the largest of the pike family, and they're still caught by the Chautauqua Indians in the Upper Ohio Valley.

All the members of the family are speedy, marvelous game fish and they're a delight to eat. Even Izaak Walton mentioned a recipe for it in his 17th century masterpiece, *The Compleat Angler,* using the pike liver, sauteed in herbs, as a stuffing.

This freshwater delicacy is a special treat around the world, and it is superb when baked or poached. It particularly lends itself to the light, airy quenelles and fish mousse that are famous throughout France and the Scandinavian countries, and yellow pike or little pickerel (even though they are truly perch) are one of the fish traditionally used in the preparation of Jewish Gefilte Fish (see Index).

Cleaning and Preparing Pike, Pickerel, and Muskellunge

Put the fish in the sink and pour a large quantity of boiling water over it to scald and loosen the scales. This will also help to get rid of the slimy coat. Since this is a long fish and there is not much meat in the head, cut off the head and use it for fish stock. Besides, a ten-pound fish in this family can be as much as *38 inches long.* Our oven measures 24 inches square, so we'd have trouble baking it whole.

If you like, you can pan dress the fish and use the widest center cut section for stuffing. If the fish is large enough, it can be cut into steaks. Filleting these fish is a little more complicated because of their bone structure, quite similar to the *shad,* though the skeleton is longer and narrower.

How to Fillet the Pike Family

1. After pouring boiling water on the fish to loosen the scales and remove the slime, place the fish belly down on a board or flat surface. Hold the head in your left hand and with a sharp knife make a horizontal slit behind the head until you touch the backbone with the blade. Run the knife along the backbone until you get to the dorsal fin. This will be your first boneless fillet. Place it aside until you have completely filleted the fish.

2. Lay the fish on its side, spine toward you, and with the point of the knife make a lateral cut above the center bones, from head down to the dorsal fin.

3. Make a vertical cut behind the head at right angles to the length of the fish, then do the same at the dorsal fin.

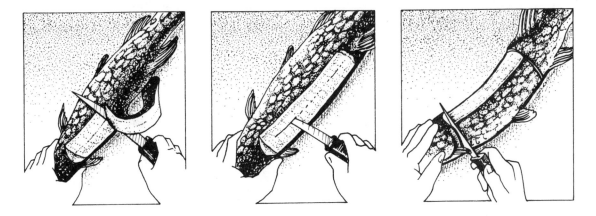

4. Then, just as filleting *bass* or *bluefish*, begin to cut the flesh away from the bones, lifting as you do so, until the side fillet is free of the bones. Cut bottom of fillet to release it from the fish and put aside with the first fillet that you cut from the back.

5. Turn fish over and repeat on other side. Then, cut the small tail fillets from the bone by sliding the knife along the spine from the dorsal fin to the tail.

6. Skin the fillets as you would any other fish. (See the chapter on Readying Your Fish for the Fire.)

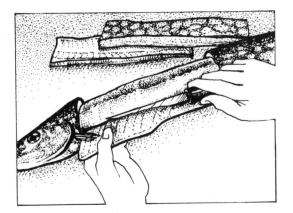

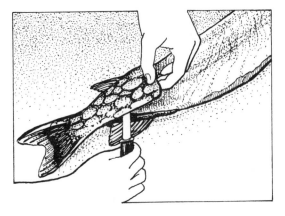

BAKED PIKE
WITH CRAB MEAT STUFFING

Crab Meat Stuffing (see Index)
1 center cut pike, about 5 to 6 pounds,
    pan dressed, filleted, and cut in half
    with skin left on
juice of 1 lemon
½ cup butter, melted

Garnish
    sprigs parsley
    lemon wedges

Prepare Crab Meat Stuffing first.

Preheat oven to 350°F.

Butter a large, oven-to-table baking dish. Lay the fish in it, skin side down, and sprinkle with lemon juice. Spread cool Crab Meat Stuffing in a layer on one side of the fillet. Top with the other side, like a sandwich. Tie fish neatly with string to keep the filling in place. Pour butter over all and bake, basting with the butter, for about 30 minutes before testing to see if it flakes easily. If not, bake until it does. If the butter starts to brown, add ½ cup of boiling water to the bottom of the pan for more sauce.

Untie string after fish has cooled for 5 minutes. Cut into serving slices and garnish with sprigs of parsley and lemon wedges.

Serves 6

MOUSSE OF PICKEREL IN A FISH MOLD

1   tablespoon butter
1   tablespoon minced shallots (young spring onions may be used)
2   tablespoons water
1½ pounds pickerel (yellow pike), cut into 1-inch cubes and chilled (flounder, sole, halibut, red snapper, or salmon may be used)
2   egg yolks, beaten
2   cups very cold heavy cream
¼   teaspoon cayenne pepper
¼   teaspoon white pepper
3   egg whites, beaten until stiff
1   tablespoon softened butter
1   recipe for any one of the following sauces: *Duglere* Sauce (Cream and Tomato Sauce with Anise), Mornay Sauce (with Gruyere Cheese), Shrimp Sauce, Crab Meat Sauce, or Lobster Sauce (Sauce Cardinal). (See Index.)

In a small saucepan, melt butter and saute shallots until soft. Add the water and bring to a boil. Lower heat and simmer until shallots are lightly browned. Set aside to cool. Butter a 1-quart, fish-shaped mold.

Preheat oven to 350°F. and boil a kettle of water.

Using a food processor or blender, puree the fish until smooth. Add the shallot mixture and puree again. Add the egg yolks and puree a few seconds. With the machine running, gradually pour the cold cream into the machine. Add the cayenne pepper and white pepper. Remove fish puree from bowl and gradually fold into the beaten egg whites. Spoon into the mold. (If there is any extra mousse, prepare small decorative molds and use as a garnish.) Place the mold in a larger pan. Butter a piece of wax paper, cut to fit fish mold on one side, and place butter side down over the mousse. Pour boiling water around the mold in the larger pan. Bake for 30 to 35 minutes. Prepare sauce while fish is baking.

When top of mousse is firm and sides have shrunk away from the mold, remove from oven. Unwrap wax paper. Let stand for 10 minutes before inverting over a warmed serving plate. Serve with the sauce.

Serves 6 to 8

PIKE AND SHRIMP QUENELLES

These lighter than air, gossamer creations used to be, to our way of thinking, a tedious, complex, and time-consuming chore, a dish worthy of the most sublime French chef—and created only by the cook with expertise and time—then the food processor was invented. Now these clouds of fish can be made by any devoted home cook with an interest in presenting a special, ethereal taste treat.

1 recipe for any one of the following sauces: *Duglere* Sauce (Cream and Tomato Sauce with Anise), Mushroom Cream Sauce, or Seafood Shell Sauce (see Index)
1 pound pike fillets, cut into 1-inch pieces (reserve bones and skin for poaching liquid)*
6 cups water
½ pound raw shrimp, shelled and deveined
½ teaspoon white pepper
⅛ teaspoon cayenne pepper
⅛ teaspoon grated nutmeg
1 egg yolk
1½ cups heavy cream
4 tablespoons softened butter

Prepare the sauce first and set aside.

Use a 6-quart saucepan and put bones and skin covered with 6 cups water to boil. Cover and boil for 20 minutes and strain liquid and discard bones. This is the poaching liquid for the quenelles.

Keep all ingredients cold, except the egg yolk. Using a food processor, prepare mixture in 2 batches, if necessary.

Place the shrimp and fish in the container, and blend briefly. Add the white pepper, cayenne, nutmeg, and the egg yolk and blend again, adding some cream if mixture is too thick to blend. With processor on, gradually add the cold cream. Chill mixture while preparing the pan.

Use 1 tablespoon of the butter to grease an oval, stove-top baking pan, large enough to accommodate the quenelles. (There should be about 18.) Cut a piece of wax paper into the shape of the pan and butter it lavishly on one side with the remaining butter.

Prepare a bowl of boiling hot water. Also heat the poaching liquid to boiling.

Use 2 oval tablespoons. Dip 1 spoon at a time into the bowl of hot water and scoop up a heaping spoonful of the quenelle mixture. Dip the second spoon into the hot water and run it around under the mixture in the first spoon. Start on top and turn the

(continued on following page)

second hot spoon inside the first spoon to produce a smooth oval-shaped quenelle. As they are shaped, carefully transfer them to the buttered, oval baking pan. Place the wax paper, buttered side down, over the quenelles. Gently ladle the boiling poaching liquid over the wax paper so that it flows gradually into the baking pan. Continue until the quenelles are barely covered.

Bring to a boil on top of the stove, then lower heat to the barest simmer at once. Simmer gently about 10 minutes or until they are heated through. The tops should be firm, not pasty. Do not overcook. Remove as quickly as possible with a slotted spoon to drain on paper towels. Serve hot with the sauce.

Yield: about 18 pieces

*Quenelles can be made with other fish as well, such as whiting, flounder, fluke, trout, salmon, red mullet, or carp, but they will all have their own individual fish taste and texture. Pike is the lightest in texture.

POACHED PIKE OR MUSKELLUNGE
WITH FRESH DILL

1 recipe Court Bouillon (see Index)
1 small bunch fresh dill
1 whole pike, about 5½ pounds, or 4 pounds muskellunge steak, gutted and pan dressed
2 recipes Basic *Veloute* Sauce (see Index)

Bring the Court Bouillon to a boil and add ½ of the bunch of dill, tied with a string. Mince the leaves of the rest of the dill and reserve to add to the Basic *Veloute* Sauce.

Wrap the fish in cheesecloth (see Index for poaching methods), and lower fish into the liquid. Bring to a boil again and lower heat immediately to a slow simmer. Cover and cook about 20 to 25 minutes until the fish is opaque. Lift out with cheesecloth and unwrap carefully. The Court Bouillon can be frozen again, or some of it used in the Basic *Veloute* Sauce.

Heat the Basic *Veloute* Sauce and add the minced dill. Pour the hot sauce over the fish before serving.

Serves 6

**Baked Pompano Fillets Stuffed
with Nuts, Fish, and Spices
Pompano *en Papillote* with Three Variations**

We remember an automobile trip to Florida in the 1950s. It was summer, cars were not yet air-conditioned, motels were few and far between, and three days in the heat were exhausting and enervating. Upon our return to New York, not one question from our friends even touched on the difficulties of traveling to Florida during the month of August, but almost *all* of them asked: "Did you eat the *pompano?*"

The Florida pompano is very well known, and with good reason. It's excellent for broiling, baking, and planking, and a great many northern gourmet restaurants have featured Pompano *en Papillote* (see page 326) for years. It's a most distinctive fish, with its deeply forked caudal and dorsal fins, but because the demand usually exceeds the supply, it can be a fairly expensive delicacy at your local fishmonger. However, pompano has a great potential for fish farming and though the research is still in the experimental stage, we may soon see the day when the supply increases, along with a decrease in the cost.

The pompano, incidentally, is the most popular member of the *jackfish* family, most of whom are noted more as game fish than they are for dining purposes. A cousin of the pompano, the *yellowtail,* is known, however, as a popular part of the Japanese raw fish dish, *sashimi*. The entire family, including the *blue runner, amberjack,* and the beautiful *rainbow runner,* all have dark meat and the distinctive tail that also makes the pompano so recognizable.

With today's modern transportation systems, there's no need to wait for a trip to Florida, as we did in the 1950s, to try this delicious fish. Just as with Florida's *red snapper,* the pompano is now shipped all over the country.

BAKED POMPANO FILLETS
STUFFED WITH NUTS, FISH, AND SPICES

2 tablespoons walnut oil
2 medium-size onions, finely minced
1 cup ground walnuts
½ cup ground hazelnuts
¼ cup seedless raisins
¼ teaspoon ground allspice
¼ teaspoon cinnamon
⅛ teaspoon nutmeg
1 pinch ground cloves
¼ teaspoon black pepper
½ pound raw fish fillets, such as flounder or monkfish, finely chopped
2 tablespoons finely minced, fresh dill
3 tablespoons finely minced, fresh parsley
6 pompano fillets or 3 whole fish, about 1½ pounds each
orange slices for garnish

Prepare stuffing by heating oil and sauteing onions until wilted. Add the ground nuts, raisins, allspice, cinnamon, nutmeg, cloves, and pepper. Mix well and add the chopped raw fish fillets. Cook and stir for 3 minutes. Then add the dill and parsley. Set aside.

Preheat the oven to 425°F.

Oil a baking pan. Lay 3 of the fillets on the pan. Place some stuffing on each half and top the stuffing with the other 3 pompano fillets. Tie with string to keep in shape or skewer and lace the halves together to keep the filling intact. (If stuffing a whole fish, see Index for directions for stuffing a whole fish.) Oil the tops of the fish and bake for 25 to 30 minutes. Test to see if fish flakes easily. After 10 minutes of baking, pour some water in bottom of pan and use to baste fish occasionally. More water can be added if needed during baking time to keep fish moist. Serve garnished with orange slices.

Serves 6

POMPANO
EN PAPILLOTE
WITH THREE VARIATIONS

6 pompano fillets, or 3 whole fish, about
    1½ pounds each
6 large mushrooms, finely chopped
2 scallions, minced
¼ teaspoon black pepper
6 teaspoons finely minced, fresh parsley
6 tablespoons butter
6 lemon slices

Preheat oven to 450°F.

Tear off 6 large pieces of parchment paper. Place 1 fillet on ½ of each piece of paper. Fold the other half over fish and cut heart shapes leaving a 2-inch border around the fillet. Mix the mushrooms and scallions together and mix well and divide into 6 portions. Then unfold and in each package place portion of mushroom mixture, some pepper, 1 teaspoon of parsley, 1 tablespoon of butter and 1 slice of lemon over each fillet. Fold the paper over in half again. Seal edges by slashing with a scissors about ½ inch all around to allow for easy folding. Fold edges tightly and clip with paper clips if necessary. Allow for steam expansion while baking so don't wrap the fish too tightly. Place on a buttered baking sheet and bake 10 minutes per inch of thickness of fish. Open 1 package to test after 10 minutes to see if it flakes easily with a skewer. Serve 1 package per person to be slashed with an X at the table.

Serves 6

VARIATIONS

I. Substitute 1 slice of onion, 1 slice of tomato, and 1 green pepper ring instead of the mushrooms.

II. Flavor with ½ teaspoon finely minced, fresh tarragon or ⅛ teaspoon dried, and use 2 to 3 slices of lemon on the fillet instead of the mushrooms.

III. Top each fillet with 1 tablespoon crab meat and chopped dill instead of the mushrooms.

Escabeche of Porgy
Porgy with Saffron, Lemons, and Mint,
Moroccan Style

Though the fish is found around the world by whatever name it's called, the *porgy* (or *scup*) is strictly an American name. These fish are members of a vast family from tiny perchlike fish to the huge *tunas* and *marlins,* and about one-quarter of the annual catch is taken by sports fishermen who love these lively fighters for their spirit and their fine eating quality. They're generally small, but fun to catch and they taste equally good whether pan fried, sauteed, or baked.

The porgy has been increasing in popularity around the country and we have found them readily available almost everywhere, usually whole dressed. Because of their unusual shape, they're easily recognized on their beds of ice at the fishmongers.

ESCABECHE
OF PORGY

2 porgies, about 2 pounds each, pan
    dressed and cleaned
½ teaspoon black pepper
½ cup whole wheat pastry flour
1 cup olive oil
8 to 10 cloves garlic, unpeeled and
    smashed
¾ cup thinly sliced carrot rounds
1 small onion, thinly sliced
⅓ cup white wine vinegar
3 tablespoons water
1 teaspoon finely minced, fresh thyme or
    ½ teaspoon dried
2 small, dried, hot red pepper pods
1 bay leaf
6 parsley sprigs
2 tablespoons minced, fresh parsley

Score both sides of fish with a sharp knife making checkerboard slashes almost to the bone and sprinkle the fish inside and out with the pepper.

Put the flour in a bag, add the fish and shake until fish is well covered with the flour.

Heat the oil and, when very hot (370°F.), add the fish. Cook about 4 to 5 minutes on each side, turning once until fish is golden in color. Lift out with a slotted spoon and place in a deep dish.

Strain the remaining oil in which the fish was cooked, and put into a saucepan with a cover. Add the garlic, carrots, and onion slices and cook over high heat for about 2 minutes, stirring until onion is wilted. Then add vinegar, water, thyme, hot pepper pods, bay leaf, and parsley sprigs. Cover pot, lower heat, and simmer for 10 minutes. Pour this mixture over the fish. Cool. Cover all tightly with plastic wrap and let marinate in the refrigerator for about 24 hours. Lift out of marinade when ready to serve and allow to come to room temperature. Sprinkle with minced parsley when served.

Serves 6

PORGY WITH SAFFRON, LEMONS, AND MINT, MOROCCAN STYLE

½ teaspoon crushed saffron strands
1 cup water
¼ cup peanut oil
2 cloves garlic, finely minced
2 porgies, about 2 pounds each, pan dressed and cut across into 1-inch steaks
3 lemons, peeled and cut into thin slices
1 tablespoon finely chopped, fresh mint

Mix saffron with ¼ cup of the water and let stand for 15 minutes. In a skillet combine oil with the remaining ¾ cup water, the saffron water, and garlic. Arrange pieces of fish over all and cover the top of the fish with the lemon slices. Bring to a boil, lower heat at once, and cover. Simmer for 10 to 15 minutes. Test with a skewer to see if fish flakes easily. Remove with a slotted spatula to a warm serving dish; with tongs pick out lemon slices to decorate fish and then sprinkle with mint.

Serves 6

Note: There's no doubt that saffron is one of the world's most expensive spices. No wonder. It takes over 200,000 stigmata of a special kind of crocus to make 1 pound of saffron. And each one has to be picked by hand! Luckily, though, you don't need much else to season this dish. If a friend of yours happens to be leaving for Spain and asks what he or she can bring back as a gift for you, just whisper the word, "saffron." It's much much cheaper there, but no bargain at best.

**Florida Red Snapper Steaks with Lime
and Black Butter Sauce
Baked Red Snapper, Spanish Style
Stuffed Red Snapper, Armenian Style**

Red Snapper

We were filming down on the Gulf Coast last year and during the hours when the weather played havoc with our schedule, we'd wander down to the docks and the shoreline to watch the fishermen try their luck at catching a variety of Gulf prizes. During an idle conversation we had with a local fisherman, he made the statement that the *red snapper* was the stupidest fish around—almost any kind of line with any kind of bait would bring one in if a school happened to be swimming through the deeper waters.

Considering that our mothers told us that fish were "brain food," we wondered about how the red snapper could fill the bill if it were really as stupid as the fisherman said? Nevertheless, the IQ of the red snapper aside (and we wonder how you prove it), it is, without a doubt, one of the most delectable fish in the sea.

Its colorful eye appeal and its lean, delicate flavor make it particularly attractive and dramatic to serve whole—baked and stuffed or poached, its elegant red is beautiful when surrounded with anything green. We remember vividly and fondly a lunch we had in Mexico many years ago, at which the whole red snapper was wrapped in banana leaves and baked between hot rocks.

The red snapper can weigh as much as 30 pounds, but the smaller 4- to 6-pound fish are the ones that are generally marketed whole. The larger ones are cut into fillets or steaks. However you serve it, this is, indeed, a tasty and beautiful fish.

FLORIDA RED SNAPPER STEAKS
WITH LIME AND BLACK BUTTER SAUCE

6 red snapper steaks, about ½ pound
    each
1 tablespoon tamari soy sauce
¼ teaspoon Dried Hot Pepper Sauce (see
    Index)
    juice of 3 limes
    Black Butter Sauce (see Index)
    lime wedges for garnish

Place steaks in a glass baking dish or ceramic dish (do not use metal). Mix the soy sauce and Dried Hot Pepper Sauce with the lime juice and pour over the fish. Refrigerate for 1 hour, turning fish once.

Prepare Black Butter Sauce and set aside.

Oil a broiler plate. Place the drained fish in broiler pan and reserve marinade. Broil, basting occasionally with the tamari-lime juice. Turn fish carefully with a wide spatula after 5 minutes. Broil 5 minutes more or until fish flakes easily with a skewer.

Serve hot Black Butter Sauce in a sauce boat to be passed at the table. Garnish fish with lime wedges.

Serves 6

BAKED
RED SNAPPER,
SPANISH STYLE

½ cup lime juice
½ teaspoon black pepper
1 red snapper, about 5 pounds, gutted and cleaned, preferably with head left on (2 red snappers, about 2½ pounds each, placed head to tail, may be used)
½ cup olive oil
1 large onion, thinly sliced
1 teaspoon finely minced, fresh thyme or ½ teaspoon dried
1 teaspoon finely minced, fresh oregano or ½ teaspoon dried
1 bay leaf, crushed
1 medium onion, finely chopped
2 cloves garlic, finely minced
1 fresh, hot, red or green chili pepper, seeded and finely chopped
1 tablespoon finely minced, fresh parsley
½ cup toasted almonds, ground
1½ cups Fish Stock (see Index)

In a flat dish (not metal) with sides, mix the lime juice and pepper and pour it inside and over the fish. Set fish aside to marinate for 15 minutes.

Meanwhile, pour 6 tablespoons of the olive oil into a large, oven-to-table baking dish and preheat the oven to 400°F. Arrange the sliced onion in the baking pan and sprinkle with thyme, oregano, and bay leaf.

Heat the remaining olive oil in a separate skillet and add the chopped onion and garlic. Saute slowly, stirring occasionally until wilted but not brown. Add the hot pepper, parsley, almonds, and ½ cup of the Fish Stock.

Lift the fish out of the marinade and place it over the sliced onion-herb mixture and pour the marinade over the onion and fish along with the 1 cup of remaining Fish Stock. Spread the chopped onion-almond mixture over the top and sides of the fish. Bake for 40 to 45 minutes. Test with skewer after 40 minutes to see if fish flakes easily.

Serves 6

STUFFED
RED SNAPPER,
ARMENIAN STYLE

1 whole red snapper, about 5 to 5½
    pounds, or 2 red snappers, about
    2½ pounds each
½ cup olive oil
2 large onions, finely chopped
¼ cup pine nuts, toasted (sunflower seeds
    may be used)
1 cup whole grain bread cubes, cut into
    ½-inch squares and dry toasted
½ teaspoon black pepper
¼ teaspoon ground allspice
¼ cup dried currants
¼ cup minced, fresh parsley
¼ cup minced, fresh dill or 4 teaspoons
    dried
¼ cup lemon juice

Garnish
    sprigs parsley
    lemon wedges

Remove backbone from fish to be able to stuff it more easily, but leave the head on and make sure fish is scaled. Heat 2 tablespoons of the olive oil in large skillet until hot. Add the onions and saute over low heat for 5 minutes, stirring occasionally. Add the pine nuts and stir and cook until they turn golden. Add the bread cubes, pepper, and allspice and stir until the cubes of bread are well coated. Remove from heat and add the currants, parsley, and dill. Stir to mix and let cool for 15 minutes before stuffing the fish. Use the remaining olive oil to coat the large, oven-to-table baking pan and to rub over the fish.

Preheat the oven to 350°F.

Spoon the filling into the fish and use a large needle and heavy white thread to sew up the opening—or skewer the opening across the fish and lace with white string like a boot. Pour the lemon juice over the fish. Bake for 40 to 45 minutes and test with a skewer to see if fish flakes easily. If not, continue to bake until it does flake. Before serving, remove the thread and garnish the serving dish with parsley sprigs and lemon wedges.

Serves 6

Note: If there is any filling left over after stuffing the fish, wrap it in aluminum foil and place it in the same baking dish. When served, additional stuffing can be used as a side dish.

Mouth-Watering Poached Roe Recipes
Broiled Shad Roe in Herbed Sauce
Carp Roe and Potato Pancakes
Roe Baked in Seashells

Roe is another of those foods whose potential as a flavorful dish rich in vitamins and minerals has been sadly neglected. Somehow, it is not surprising to learn that the American Indians knew the value of roe and fed it to weaning babies as an especially nourishing food.

Roe are the two ovarian sacs containing the eggs of the female fish and these are encased in a delicate membrane pouch. Roe should be eaten in the prespawning stage, when they're at their best—the sacs are clear, well formed and smooth, and filled tightly with the translucent egg mass.

Caviar, which is the processed roe of the *sturgeon,* is a luxurious, costly, and salty delicacy which is coveted by gourmets—but should be avoided by those who have high blood pressure. The demand for sturgeon roe has seriously depleted the supply, hence the high cost.

But the roe of *other* fish are equally delectable and nourishing and do not contain the large amounts of salt used in caviar preparation.

The best known roe—and the herald of springtime—is the *shad* roe. But others are excellent too, though not as well known: *flounder, carp, pike, cod, salmon, whitefish, mullet, tuna, alewife, herring, mackerel, sea trout, lumpfish,* and *haddock.* Only the roe of the freshwater *gar* and the saltwater *puffer* or *blowfish* contain toxic substances and should *not* be eaten.

Try some of the following recipes and you'll soon know that a roe by any other name smells and tastes as sweet (pun intended).

Roe

When You Cook Roe

Roe are only moderately fatty, except for the roe of salmon, turbot, and sturgeon, which are very rich in polyunsaturated fats. Just like eggs, roe are toughened by overcooking. Blanching or poaching gently in simmering liquid, just until they lose their transparent color and turn opaque, will float away some of the fatty substances and allow them to be handled more easily. Roe are rich and filling and they can be served nicely with a piquant or tart sauce.

To poach or blanch, lower the roe into boiling liquid, consisting of four cups water mixed with one tablespoon lemon juice. Lower the heat immediately and simmer *only until the color turns opaque*. Lift out with a slotted spoon and plunge into a bowl of ice water. Drain on paper towels and use in all of the recipes that follow. Allow about four to six ounces per person. One pair of shad roe equals about three-quarters of a pound. To serve six, use two or three pairs, depending upon their size and the eaters' capacity. Roe can also be used in soups as a garnish or pureed and used to enrich sauces.

MOUTH-WATERING POACHED ROE RECIPES

1. Serve poached roe with a dipping sauce made of 2 tablespoons tamari soy sauce, 1 tablespoon rice wine vinegar, 3 drops Dried Hot Pepper Sauce (see Index) and 1 teaspoon toasted sesame seeds.

2. Marinate poached roe for several hours in a Piquant Sauce (see Index), and chill.

Place on a bed of lettuce with cucumber and tomato slices, and serve as a salad.

. . . and for Blanched Roe

3. Dip blanched roe in Lemon Batter (see Index) and deep fry. Serve hot with a few grindings of fresh, black pepper.

Tip: Any kind of simply prepared roe can be served with these sauces (see Index):

Cold Walnut and Garlic Mayonnaise (Turkish *Tarator* Sauce)
Butter Sauces (Hot)
Basic Hollandaise Sauce

BROILED SHAD ROE
IN HERBED SAUCE

6 tablespoons butter, melted
2 to 3 pairs shad roe, about ¾ pound
    each
½ clove garlic, finely minced
2 tablespoons lemon juice
¼ teaspoon black pepper
1 tablespoon finely minced, fresh chives
1 tablespoon finely minced, fresh parsley

Butter a baking pan with 2 tablespoons of the melted butter. Blanch the roe for 1 minute (see page 335). Dry roe and place in the buttered pan. Pierce with a skewer in several places so they won't burst under high heat.

Mix the rest of the butter with garlic, lemon juice, and pepper and pour over roe.

Broil for 5 minutes on each side and baste periodically. Sprinkle with chives and parsley.

Serves 6

Note: If the membrane that encases the roe is not pierced before broiling to allow built-up steam to escape, it will burst when cooked this way and mess up your oven. In other recipes, keep membrane intact, unless otherwise instructed.

CARP ROE
AND POTATO PANCAKES

1 pound carp roe
2 tablespoons finely minced scallions
1 tablespoon finely minced, fresh
    parsley
½ teaspoon black pepper
1 egg, lightly beaten
1½ cups mashed potatoes
1 cup whole grain bread crumbs
4 tablespoons butter, melted
¼ teaspoon paprika

Butter a baking dish large enough to hold pancakes in one layer.

Remove outer membrane of roe and put roe in a mixing bowl. Add the scallions, parsley, pepper, egg, and mashed potatoes. Combine gently and form mixture into 3-inch patties with hands, and flatten slightly. Dip patties in bread crumbs and place in buttered baking pan. Drizzle butter over the cakes and sprinkle with paprika. Broil 6 inches from heat source for about 2 minutes on each side. Turn once.

Serve with applesauce or sour cream.

Serves 6

ROE
BAKED IN
SEASHELLS

1½ pounds roe
2 cups Court Bouillon (see Index)
4 tablespoons butter
2 shallots, finely minced (young spring onions may be used)
½ teaspoon white pepper
½ cup heavy cream
2 egg yolks, lightly beaten
1 teaspoon lemon juice
12 small, fresh mushrooms, sliced (optional)
¾ cup whole grain bread crumbs
¼ cup grated Gruyere cheese

Poach roe in Court Bouillon. (See Index for poaching directions.)

After the roe have been poached, boil the liquid down to 1 cup and reserve. Cut roe into small pieces and drain on paper towels. Set aside.

Melt 2 tablespoons of the butter in a saucepan and cook the shallots until wilted. Add the reserved liquid, pepper, and cream. Bring to a boil, lower heat, and simmer for 15 minutes. Raise heat under the sauce to medium. Add the egg yolks and beat with a whisk, cooking until sauce thickens. Remove from heat and add lemon juice and roe. If mushrooms are being used, add them here.

Preheat oven to 400°F.

Butter 6 large scallop shells and spoon mixture equally into each. Mix the remaining 2 tablespoons of butter with the bread crumbs and distribute evenly on top of the shells. Sprinkle the cheese evenly on top of each and bake for 8 to 10 minutes, until brown and bubbly. Serve hot allowing 1 shell per person.

Serves 6

**Japanese Salmon Scallops with Sesame Seeds
Baked, Spiced Salmon Fillet
Salmon Cucumber Salad
Marinated and Broiled Salmon Steaks
in Three-Citrus Sauce
Salmon and Potato Balls
Whole, Baked Salmon Fillet with Sour Cream
and Dill Sauce
Salmon Mousse in a Fish Mold with Dill,
Cucumber Sour Cream Sauce
Scandinavian Salmon and Potato Casserole
Salmon and Broccoli with Pine Nuts
Sweet and Sour Salmon with Raisins
and Almonds
Simple Salmon**

Not too long ago, a talented young performer opened at New York's Performing Garage, Off-Off-Broadway, with an unusual title for a play. It was called *The Salmon Show* and through it all, Bob Carroll, in the tradition of ancient storytellers, relived the life cycle of a most unusual and exciting fish—the *salmon*. From the ocean, through its long and exhausting trip upstream to the spawning ground, through fertilization, birth, and finally death, Mr. Carroll captured audiences and reviewers alike. Only the salmon could have been the heroine of such a tale.

For the story of the salmon is not just another fish story. It is, indeed, one more of the unsolved mysterious sagas of the deep, fraught with drama and trauma, triumph, and death. In fact, we might even say that the story of the salmon reads like a Shakespearean tragedy.

Salmon, at specific times in the life cycle, are both saltwater and freshwater fish. They hatch in fresh water and the young fish (called "fingerlings") live for about two years in the fresh water of the rivers and streams. When they're two years old and about six inches long, their names change to "parr."

By the third year (when they're called "grilse"), they are mature enough to take to the open saltwater seas of the Pacific Ocean and parts of the Atlantic. They spend at least a year at sea where they mature into the beautiful aristocrats that they are. Only then do we finally call them salmon.

The Long Trip Home

At sea, the curtain rises and the awesome, spectacular drama begins as the salmon sets out on its mating trek. (In Bob Carroll's one-man show, he also begins at this point with a chant that repeats, "To the spawning ground. . . .") The salmon will migrate about 2,000 miles to spawn, going back to the fresh waters where they were born. The swim is made against great odds and man-made obstacles. Navigating by the sun and by a radarlike sense of smell, they battle against the turbulent rapids and leap over powerful waterfalls. The breeding urge that constantly goads them onward to their trysting grounds has them covering as much as 65 miles in one day!

The females become leaden, torpid, and engorged with eggs. Their outer coloring fades and changes from the bright, startling blue and silver of the ocean into their freshwater guise—greenish heads with dark, red orange, mottled bodies.

The males, their reproductive glands swelling and pressing against their digestive tracts, are prevented from eating by the constant pressure. As they fast, the salmon begin to use up their own body energy. The inner flesh, which is naturally pink or red, fades to a pale shade, making them inferior in food value and flavor. This is the main reason that the prime salmon are those taken in the ocean just before they enter the freshwater streams.

At the spawning grounds, the eggs are laid by the female, who lingers briefly and then dies. The eggs are fertilized by the male and the dull gray mass, known as kelt, soon gives up its fingerlings, most of whom die after spawning or are eaten on their way back to the sea.

Salmon and the Seattle Aquarium

One of the most fascinating exhibits that we've ever seen is at the aquarium in Seattle, Washington. The scientists have raised salmon right on the premises, so that the cycle will begin there—and when the salmon go to sea and then come back to spawn, the completion of the drama will take place right before the eyes of the visiting public. We spent hours standing under the glass dome over our heads watching the salmon swim in a constant circle and noting the date the scientists expected the spawning fish to return.

On that historic day, the Seattle Aquarium awaited its first salmon—the only ones to be spawned in captivity. They would be the first to return to the aquarium as the place of their birth. The overhead pool was empty, ready for its first return visitor, and the Rodale Press photographer was ready with his camera. Suddenly, there was a shout, "Here comes the first fish! Here it comes!" Quickly, they pulled our photographer toward the overhead dome. He raised his camera for the critical shot—and the fish, frightened by all the commotion, swept back out the sluice to sea. The aquarium officials are now awaiting the second coming. We strongly recommend this exhibition as one of the most exciting in the world!

The Kinds of Salmon

There are two basic kinds of salmon:

Atlantic salmon is found in fresh water as well as salt water from Maine and Cape Cod to the St. Lawrence River. Its regional names are many: *New England salmon, man salmon, Kennebec salmon,* and *silver salmon.* They differ from their Pacific Coast relatives in that they may survive two or three spawning sessions, whereas the Pacific salmon die after only one spawning.

Pacific salmon thrives primarily because of special conservation programs. There are five different kinds of Pacific salmon, also known under their regional names: *Chinook salmon, coho* (or *silver*) *salmon, chum* (or *dog*) *salmon, pink* (or *humpback*) *salmon,* and *red* (or *sockeye*) *salmon.*

Whatever they're called, wherever they're found, fishermen and gourmets alike never doubt the description of Izaak Walton, author of *The Compleat Angler,* who dubbed the salmon "king of fish." Americans and Europeans agree that this delicate, flavorful, colorful sporting fish well deserves its exalted rank and title.

Special Tips for Cooking Salmon

Things to remember when buying salmon for a specific recipe:

1. For poaching and baking, try to get center cut steaks from the body.

2. For broiling, the cut nearest the head is the fattiest and best.

3. The tail end is perfect for scallops or fillets and is good for both poaching and baking.

4. Allow four to six ounces per serving, depending on appetite—two pounds of steaks for six people will do nicely. (One-half-inch steaks take about 3 minutes of broiling time on each side; one-inch steaks, 8 to 10 minutes. Allow about 11 minutes per pound at 400°F. when baking a whole salmon that is about two and one-quarter inches thick.)

American salmon is best cooked simply, but takes well to many sauces. Some of the best are listed in this section. Recipes for all are contained in this book. See the Index. To skin salmon, wait until it is cool to the touch.

JAPANESE SALMON SCALLOPS
WITH SESAME SEEDS

12 slices salmon, about 2 to 3 ounces for each piece, cut from the tail (no skin or bones)
½ cup tamari soy sauce
1 hot chili pepper, seeded and finely minced
1 teaspoon honey
1 teaspoon vinegar
2 tablespoons sesame oil
3 tablespoons sesame seeds, toasted
2 scallions, green part only, thinly sliced

Place salmon in marinade made by mixing soy sauce, hot pepper, honey, vinegar, and 1 tablespoon sesame oil and allow to marinate for 2 hours. Lift fish from marinade, and dry well on paper towels.

Heat remaining sesame oil in skillet. Add salmon scallops and saute quickly, turning once—about 2 minutes on each side. Sprinkle with sesame seeds and scallions.

Serves 6

BAKED, SPICED
SALMON FILLET

1 large onion, thinly sliced
2 teaspoons mixed pickling spice
1 small clove garlic, thinly sliced
2 pounds tail cut of salmon fillet, in one
    piece, with skin left on
3 tablespoons lemon juice

Garnish
1 lemon, sliced
   sprigs parsley

Preheat oven to 350°F.

Oil a baking-serving dish. Make a bed of sliced onion, pickling spice, and garlic. On top of this lay the fillet, skin side up. Sprinkle with lemon juice. Cover pan with aluminum foil and bake about 20 minutes or more according to thickness of salmon.

Test with skewer. Let salmon stand until slightly cool. Remove skin. Cover top with slices of lemon and a few sprigs of parsley. Serve warm or chill and serve cold.

Serves 6

SALMON CUCUMBER
SALAD

3 large cucumbers, peeled and coarsely
   chopped
½ teaspoon white pepper
2 tablespoons sweet red pepper,
   coarsely chopped
1 tablespoon sweet green pepper,
   coarsely chopped
1½ cups left-over, cooked, flaked salmon
1 tablespoon finely minced, fresh dill
2 tablespoons finely sliced scallions
1 cup sour cream
¼ cup Homemade Mayonnaise (see
   Index)
1 tablespoon lemon juice
½ teaspoon celery seed
  lettuce
  parsley
  cherry tomatoes
3 hard-cooked eggs, cut in half

Using a large bowl, add cucumbers, all peppers, salmon, dill, and scallions.

Mix sour cream with Homemade Mayonnaise, lemon juice, and celery seed. Add to bowl and mix in carefully.

Line a glass plate with lettuce leaves and mound salad in center. Ring with a garland of parsley and cherry tomatoes, and tuck in halves of hard-cooked eggs.

Serves 6

MARINATED AND BROILED SALMON STEAKS
IN THREE-CITRUS SAUCE

2 pounds salmon steaks, ¾ inch thick
   juice of 1 small orange and 1 teaspoon grated rind
   juice of 1 lemon and 1 teaspoon grated rind
   juice of 1 lime and 1 teaspoon grated rind
1 small onion, grated
1 teaspoon light, mild honey
1 small, fresh hot pepper, seeded and minced
2 tablespoons butter, melted

Garnish
   lime slices

Place salmon steaks in a single layer in a pan that is not made of metal. Mix orange, lemon, and lime juice and rinds, onion, honey, and hot pepper together. Pour over salmon. Marinate in the refrigerator for 3 hours. Occasionally baste the fish with the marinade so the liquid covers all areas of the fish.

Brush a perforated, broiling rack (that fits over another pan containing boiling water) with melted butter. Lift the salmon steaks out of the marinade and brush tops with butter. Broil for about 6 minutes, and test with a skewer. Continue broiling until fish flakes. Heat marinade and pour over fish before serving.

Serve with slices of lime and sprigs of watercress as a garnish.

Serves 6

Broiled Spanish Shrimp with Saffron   For this recipe, see page 366

Salmon Mousse in a Fish Mold with Dill, Cucumber Sour Cream Sauce   For this recipe, see page 348

SALMON AND
POTATO BALLS

1 tablespoon butter
2 tablespoons grated onion
2 tablespoons finely minced celery
1½ cups left-over, cooked, flaked salmon
½ cup mashed potatoes
⅛ teaspoon white pepper
1 teaspoon lemon juice
½ teaspoon dried dill
1 teaspoon tamari soy sauce
1 egg, beaten
1 cup fine, dry, whole grain bread crumbs
corn oil for frying

Heat butter in skillet and saute onion and celery until wilted. Mix with salmon, potatoes, pepper, lemon juice, dill, soy sauce, and egg. Shape into walnut-size balls and roll in bread crumbs. (Mixture may seem to be too moist, but will work when rolled in bread crumbs.)

Heat oil to 370°F. for deep fat frying. Using a slotted spoon, lower a few balls at a time into the oil and fry until brown.

Drain on paper towels and serve speared on toothpicks as an appetizer.

Yield: 2 dozen 1-inch balls

WHOLE,
BAKED SALMON FILLET
WITH SOUR CREAM AND DILL SAUCE

2 pounds tail cut or filleted salmon in one piece, with skin left on
2 tablespoons softened butter
1 tablespoon lemon juice
1 tablespoon grated onion
1 cup sour cream
1 egg yolk
1 tablespoon minced, fresh dill
¼ teaspoon white pepper
1 teaspoon grated lemon rind
lemon slices for garnish

Preheat oven to 400°F.

Place salmon, skin side down, in buttered, oven-to-table pan and spread some butter on top of salmon. Mix lemon juice with onion and smear on top of fish also. Bake about 20 minutes (or according to thickness).

While salmon is baking, mix sour cream with the egg yolk, dill, and pepper. Spread mixture on fish for the last 5 minutes of baking. Sprinkle fish with grated lemon rind before serving. Serve with lemon slices.

Serves 6

SALMON MOUSSE
IN A
FISH MOLD
WITH DILL, CUCUMBER
SOUR CREAM SAUCE

½   envelope unflavored gelatin
⅛   cup cold water
¼   cup boiling water or Fish Stock (see Index)
¼   cup sour cream
¼   cup Homemade Mayonnaise (see Index)
 1   tablespoon lemon juice
½   large onion, grated
¼   teaspoon Dried Hot Pepper Sauce (see Index)
⅛   teaspoon paprika
⅛   teaspoon nutmeg
1½   teaspoons finely minced, fresh dill
1½   teaspoons finely minced, fresh tarragon or ½ teaspoon dried
 1   cup left-over cooked salmon
⅓   cup heavy cream, stiffly whipped

Garnish
   watercress
   cooked asparagus tips
   deviled eggs
   red pepper
   lemon slices, cut in half

Soften gelatin in cold water. Then add boiling water or Fish Stock, stir and cool slightly.

Mix all other ingredients together, except whipped cream, using a food processor or a blender. Add the gelatin mixture and blend again for a few seconds. Chill in refrigerator for 30 minutes.

Brush a 6-cup, decorative fish mold lightly with oil. Fold the whipped cream into the salmon mixture with a rubber spatula. Spoon it into the mold, cover tightly with plastic wrap, and chill for 24 hours.

To serve, unmold and surround platter with watercress, cooked asparagus tips, and deviled eggs. Decorate molded fish with small circle of red pepper for eye and half pieces of thinly sliced, overlapping lemon on body. Serve with Dill, Cucumber Sour Cream Sauce (see Index).

Serves 6

Note: We suggest using safflower oil to grease the mold, since it is very light and virtually tasteless.

SCANDINAVIAN SALMON AND POTATO CASSEROLE

½ cup fine, whole grain rye bread crumbs
1 pound potatoes, peeled and sliced paper thin
2 large onions, peeled and sliced paper thin
1½ pounds sliced salmon, cut into thin slices
½ teaspoon black pepper
3 tablespoons minced, fresh dill
3 eggs, well beaten
2 cups milk
½ cup butter, melted

Preheat oven to 350°F.

Generously butter an oven-to-table casserole that has deep sides and sprinkle with bread crumbs. Alternate layers of potato, onion, and slices of salmon. Sprinkle each layer with pepper and dill. Continue until all layering ingredients are used, ending with a layer of potatoes. Cover with combined eggs and milk. Bake for 35 minutes or until potatoes are tender.

Serve hot with the melted butter to be spooned over each serving.

Serves 6

SALMON AND BROCCOLI
WITH PINE NUTS

1 large bunch broccoli, trimmed and separated into spears
1 tablespoon lemon juice
3 tablespoons butter
3 tablespoons whole wheat flour
3 cups milk, scalded
½ cup grated Parmesan cheese
½ teaspoon cayenne pepper
⅛ teaspoon nutmeg
1 teaspoon dry mustard
2 cups left-over cooked salmon
4 tablespoons pine nuts, toasted (sunflower seeds may be used)

Steam broccoli for 5 minutes until tender-crisp. Drain and put in bottom of buttered, oven-to-table baking dish. Sprinkle with lemon juice and set aside.

Preheat oven to 450°F.

In a saucepan, melt the butter and add the flour. Stirring with a wire whisk, gradually add the milk. Cook over low heat, stirring constantly until mixture has thickened. Add the Parmesan cheese, cayenne pepper, nutmeg, and dry mustard. Let cook for 1 minute and add the salmon. Pour this mixture over the broccoli and bake for 15 minutes. Sprinkle with pine nuts and bake 5 minutes more.

Serves 6

SWEET AND SOUR SALMON
WITH RAISINS AND ALMONDS

This is an excellent dinner for hot summer days. It is prepared at least 2 days before eating to mellow the flavors. It can be kept refrigerated for at least a week.

2½ cups water
¾ cup cider vinegar
 2 bay leaves
 2 large onions, sliced and cut in half
 2 teaspoons mixed pickling spice
½ teaspoon peppercorns
½ teaspoon ground ginger
 2 pounds salmon steaks, about 4 to 6
    ounces each, cut 1 inch thick
½ cup dark, seedless raisins
¼ cup slivered almonds
¼ cup mild, light honey
½ cup lemon juice

Pour water into a fish poacher and add the vinegar, bay leaves, onions, pickling spice, peppercorns, and ginger. Bring to a boil, lower salmon steaks into broth and simmer for about 15 minutes, or until the fish flake easily. Remove rack with fish and let cool.

Add the raisins to the liquid and bring back to a boil. Cook uncovered until the liquid is reduced to 2 cups. Add the almonds, honey, and lemon juice. Taste the broth to adjust to your own personal taste of more sweet or more sour.

Return the salmon to the liquid when the liquid has cooled slightly, and refrigerate for at least 2 days. Remove bay leaves and serve cold or at room temperature.

Serves 6

SIMPLE SALMON

With simply broiled, baked, or poached salmon, use any of these sauces (see Index):

Heavy Cream (or *Creme Fraiche*) Sauces
Butter Sauces (Hot)
Hollandaise-Based Sauces

For cold, poached salmon, use any of these sauces (see Index):

Mayonnaise-Based Sauces
Sour Cream Sauces
Sour Cream-and-Mayonnaise-Based Sauces

Left-over, cooked salmon can be used in any of these dishes (see Index):

Mousses   Loaves
Souffles   Croquettes
Salads   Soups

**Baked Roe-Stuffed Shad
in a Vegetable Cream
Shad and Shad Roe Sauteed in a Chive Cream**

The *American white shad* is a very special and seasonal delicacy found on the Atlantic Coast from Newfoundland to the waters of Florida, although it's been transplanted recently to the Pacific Coast as well.

In the spring, the shad travels from its home, the sea, into the coastal rivers and streams to spawn above tidewater—somewhat like the West Coast *salmon.* Also, just like the salmon, it is a herald of spring.

For some, this flavorful fish is a favorite, while others shy away from the shad because of its unusual bony structure. However, shad can be expertly filleted when you buy it. If you catch your own shad and *you* have to fillet it, follow the step-by-step drawings that follow. You may not do a perfect job at first, since it does take some practice, but don't be discouraged—even surgeons must practice!

Keep in mind that a freshly caught shad must be well iced for two to three days to firm it up enough for deboning. If you try to fillet a shad immediately after you catch it, you are apt to tear the soft flesh to ribbons.

Instructions for Boning Shad

1. Remove fillets from both sides of the scaled shad using the filleting method for round fish (see page 25).

2. Place the fillets, skin side down, on a cutting board and locate, with your finger, the three rows of bone points running nearly parallel from head to tail end of the fillet.

3. Starting with the row of bones closest to the back side of the fillet (thickest side), slide a sharp knife blade from head to tail end along the outside plane of the bone line. Angle the cut down and out following the lay of the bones. Keeping the blade close to the plane of bones, peel the strip of flesh away from the bones until the blade reaches the skin and end of the bones. Do not cut completely through the strip of flesh. It should remain connected to the skin.

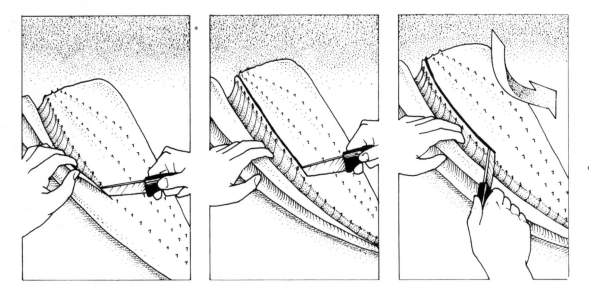

4. Starting from the head end, slide the blade behind the same bones at the same angle until the bones spread into upside down Y's, halfway down the fillet. Then adjust the blade angle down and in, to separate the line of upside down Y bones from the flesh. Prying the strip of bones loose with the point of your knife, peel it from the length of the fillet with your fingers or grip the bones at the head end with the blade and thumb, and peel the strip from the fillet.

5. The same procedure may be followed for the row of bones closest to the belly side. Remove that strip of bones.

6. The center line of bones are upside down Y's from head to tail end. Angle the blade down and out on both sides of the bones for the length of the fillet. Strip the bones from the fillet with the help of the knife point.

7. The finished fillet, with three bone rows removed, leaves four separate strips of flesh just slightly connected to the skin. The fillet is usually wrapped in a parchment paper to retain its original shape.

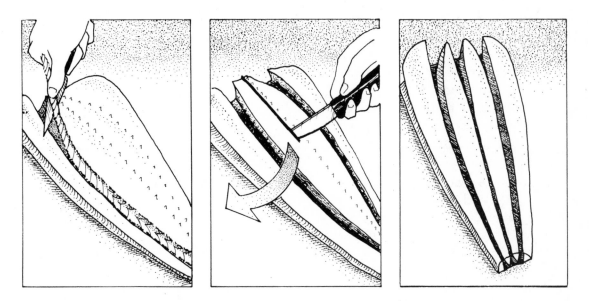

Cooking Shad

Shad can be stuffed and baked or it can be broiled beautifully. For six people, allow a three-pound boned fillet or one whole four- to five-pound drawn fish. Shad ranges in size from about one-and-one-half pounds to eight pounds.

Salmon, halibut, buffalo fish and *gar* can be interchanged in any of the recipes that follow—but do try the original if shad is available, for it's the equivalent of the sight of the first daffodil of spring and the season for this fish is as fleeting as the glimpse of a rainbow.

BAKED ROE-STUFFED SHAD
IN A VEGETABLE CREAM

Stuffing

- 6 ounces shad roe
- 1 cup soft, whole grain bread crumbs
- ¾ cup milk
- 1 tablespoon lemon juice
- 1 tablespoon finely chopped, fresh parsley
- 2 tablespoons finely minced, fresh chives
- 1 basil leaf, minced
- 1 teaspoon finely minced, fresh tarragon or ¼ teaspoon dried

Parboil the roe. (See chapter on Roe.) Soak the bread in the milk, mixed with the lemon juice. Squeeze liquid out of the bread but keep it slightly mushy. Break and discard the membrane of the roe. Add the roe to the bread mixture with all the herbs and mix well. Use for stuffing the shad.

The Fish

- 2 large whole shad fillets, about ¾ to 1 pound each, with skin intact
- 3 to 4 large leaves Swiss chard
- 3 leeks, white part only, finely chopped
- ½ teaspoon white pepper
- 3 tablespoons butter
- 1 cup heavy cream, scalded
- ⅛ teaspoon cayenne pepper

Clean and trim the shad fillets. Remove white center stem from the Swiss chard leaves and cut thinly. Keep the leaves whole.

Preheat the oven to 375°F.

Butter an oven-to-table baking dish large enough to accommodate the fish. Lay the chard leaves on a flat surface, overlapping them. Place one side of the fillet on the bottom half (the other half will be folded over to encase the whole fish when the stuffing is complete).

Spread roe stuffing evenly over one fillet and top with the other fillet, skin side up. Fold over the chard blanket and tie it with a white cord, making a neat package.

Make a bed of leeks, season with pepper and half the butter. Lay the fish over this bed and pour the cream around the sides of the leeks. Sprinkle the cream with

(continued on following page)

cayenne pepper. Dot the top of the fish with the remaining butter and bake for 40 minutes. Test, and if the fish does not flake easily, allow another 5 to 8 minutes. Baste the fish occasionally with the cream.

When ready to serve, remove the fish and let stand for 5 minutes before cutting the strings. Pour the liquid into a saucepan and boil for 10 minutes to reduce. Strain, pressing the solids against the sides of the pan. Slice the fish crosswise and lay it flat on the center of a warm plate. Spoon the sauce around the sides of the plate.

Serves 6

SHAD AND SHAD ROE SAUTEED IN A CHIVE CREAM

 2 shad fillets, weighing a total of about 1½ to 2 pounds, cut in half lengthwise
¼ teaspoon white pepper
 5 tablespoons butter
 2 pairs shad roe
 2 tablespoons finely chopped shallots (young spring onions may be used)
1½ cups heavy cream
   juice of ½ lemon
 3 tablespoons finely minced, fresh chives

Sprinkle fillets with pepper. Using 2 skillets, divide the butter in half and melt an equal amount in each skillet over medium heat. Place 1 shad fillet and 1 roe alongside it in each skillet. Divide the shallots in half and sprinkle them in the center of the pans, between the fillet and the roe. Add ½ cup of the heavy cream to each skillet, cover and bring to a boil, cooking over moderate heat for 10 to 15 minutes.

With a slotted spatula remove the fish to a warm serving dish. Split the roe in half and top each portion of the fish with a piece of roe. Add the remaining cream to the skillet and bring to a boil. Strain the sauce into a clean saucepan, pressing the shallots against the sides of the skillet. Bring to a boil again and simmer for a few minutes. Pour sauce and sprinkle lemon juice and chives over the fish and roe.

Serves 6

Dilled Shrimp Mold
Broiled Spanish Shrimp with Saffron
Fried Butterflied Shrimp, Chinese Style
Indian Shrimp with Yogurt and Coriander
Salad of the Sea with Squid,
Shrimp, and Avocado
Scampi, Italian Style
Shrimp Creole with Eggplant
and Brown Garlic Rice
Shrimp Salad with Six Variations
Shrimp Stuffed with Shrimp and Mushrooms

One of the members of our film crews, Herbert Raditschnig, comes from Austria and he practically commutes between Salzburg and New York in order to film our motion pictures. As soon as he arrives, he orders a meal that always begins with shrimp cocktail. At every lunch and every dinner, Herbert eats shrimp and, over a period of more than 12 years, we have never known him to vary. If breakfast menus had "Shrimp Omelette" or "Shrimp Cereal" listed, he might well order them too. Of course, he is not alone. Shrimp is a beloved seafood, and almost *600 million* pounds are harvested and imported for United States consumers. No wonder we see shrimp on virtually every menu we pick up.

The largest supply of shrimp comes from the Carolinas, Florida, and the Gulf of Mexico. They're also found in great quantities along the Pacific Coast from Mexico to Alaska. On one of our film trips at Puerto Penasco in Mexico, we watched the fleet being prepared for weeks and then, on one sunny, breathtaking day, the official beginning of the shrimp season, we saw the colorful little boats sail out of the harbor into the Gulf of Cortez in search of the delicate shellfish. The entire town of Puerto Penasco exists because of shrimp, very much as many New England coastal towns grew because of their own fishing fleets.

Shrimp

A Guide to Shrimp for Travelers

They are, of course, found everywhere! All over the world, the *shrimp* is the most popular shellfish in the sea. The name derives from the British word, *shrimpe,* meaning "puny," and the Swedish *skrympa,* meaning "to shrink." If you travel the world, as we do, you need never go hungry if you know the local name for shrimp. Here is a brief guide for the gourmet:

Italian - *gamberi* or *scampi*
Spanish - *camerones*
Greek - *natantia*
French - *crevettes*
German - *garneelen*
Danish - *rajer*
Chinese - *har*
Norwegian - *standreker*

The designation of prawns or scampi on a menu usually indicates that the shrimp are large. And, if you keep seeing the dish "Shrimp Scampi" on United States menus, as we often do, you are merely ordering "Shrimp Shrimp," a delicious redundancy.

From June through January, shrimp are generally available as truly fresh delicacies, but the flash frozen shrimp are probably just as good, since we never know just how long it takes to get the "fresh" shrimp to market, while the flash frozen catch is generally prepared right on the fishing vessel as soon as the nets are pulled in.

Shrimp are an excellent source of high-quality protein, vitamins, and minerals. They're low in calories and fat and they're easily digested. The edible part of the shrimp is, of course, the tail section, and no matter what the variety of shrimp, they are quite interchangeable in recipes. The raw colors vary, though all cooked shrimp turn pink white. Basically, though, the most popular shrimp imported or caught and marketed in the United States are:

Pink: Shrimp fishermen call these "pink gold."

Pinkish brown: Sometimes these are called "grooved" or Brazilian shrimp.

Grayish white with green tinges: This is the most common color and shrimpers call them "white" shrimp.

How to Buy Shrimp

If you don't catch your own (see page 362), and most people (including the authors) do not, you will find shrimp marketed fresh, frozen, dried, canned, smoked, breaded, and as paste. We will deal only with the first two forms, fresh and frozen shrimp.

Use your nose and use your hands when you buy shrimp. Fresh shrimp smells fresh and briny and the flesh feels firm to the touch. Shrimp are high in iodine, as well as in vitamins and minerals, but they should *not* smell of iodine. This iodine smell (and thus the taste) may be a natural outgrowth of the shrimp's diet at sea, or it may result from the use of sodium bisulfite, a preservative that gives the shrimp an even more pronounced iodine smell. The United States has banned the chemical preservative from this country, but we are still very wary of its possible presence when we buy shrimp and, frankly, we just don't like the iodine taste. Incidentally, the shrimp that smell that way are not actually spoiled, just unappetizing to our sensitive noses.

What Size Shrimp Should You Buy?

They vary in size from very tiny to the "shrimp shrimp" we mentioned earlier in our menu listings. Frequently, the heads are removed from the tails and discarded out at sea when the shrimp are netted, thus helping the ecology by returning food to feed the other ocean creatures.

When you buy, keep these tips in mind: There is a 25 percent loss due to shrinkage when cooking shrimp. There is another 25 percent loss in shelling and cleaning. Two pounds of uncooked shrimp in the shell will equal *one pound* cleaned and cooked.

At the New York Fulton Fish Market, one of the largest wholesale markets in the world (see Index), shrimp are sold by count:

Tiny: Up to 160 per pound (These are the tiny Alaskan shrimp.)

Small: 31 to 35 per pound

Medium: 25 to 30 per pound

Large: 16 to 20 per pound

Jumbo or *Extra Large:* 10 to 15 per pound

Colossal: Under 10 per pound

When we took the photographs of Captain Richie's shrimp boat down in Corpus Christi (see page 361), we began to develop an appetite for the jumbo shrimp we saw him sell right at dockside—they were running 12 to the pound. That night, we hungrily descended on the best seafood restaurant in Corpus Christi and ordered the "Giant Shrimp" listed on the menu. The hot platters arrived and the film crew was near tears as 5 small shrimp masquerading as giants presented themselves curled up and overcooked. Where were the jumbos we had seen just that very afternoon? Shipped out of Corpus Christi to New York! Just as California's best vegetables are shipped east. So much for giant shrimp!

The Shrimp Boats Are Coming

Whenever we work on the Gulf Coast, we like to go down to the docks late in the afternoon to watch the shrimp boats return with their catch. There are over 5,000 shrimp boats that trawl the Gulf of Mexico from Louisiana down the coast of Texas, with an annual catch of over 75 million pounds a year, about one-fifth of the total haul of shrimp taken in the United States.

We took these photographs late one afternoon in Corpus Christi, Texas, as Captain Frank Richie's "Miss Mariner" came into port. His catch, as all the others, comes up from the bottom in a large cone of nylon netting called an otter trawl that is dragged along the bottom, sweeping the shrimp into the mouth of the net.

The catch is mixed, all sizes of shrimp, plus small fish and *blue claw crabs*. The larger boats of the fleet flash freeze their catch at once, but Frank Richie puts his on ice until he reaches port, where the shrimp are sized and sold fresh at dockside to wholesalers and restaurant owners.

Frank Richie has been a shrimp boat captain for over 20 years and he told us he never tires of eating them. Judging from the availability and popularity in restaurants all over North America, most of us feel the same.

Can You Catch Your Own?

Yes, there are places where fishermen go out to catch their own shrimp, fresh and delicate. If you are ever in south Florida, you'll probably see the shrimp dippers at night as they scoop up their catch from sea walls, boats, and on the docks.

Armed with lanterns and long scoop nets, they wait until the shrimp are attracted to the light and then haul them up by the netful. The best way to join in is to ask questions and then try to borrow a net at first, just to get the hang of it. If you get the shrimp home quickly, you'll find that they have an incredibly fresh, sweet flavor, quite unlike any shrimp you've tasted before. Possibly, though, it's just your imagination at work, since you caught them yourself and nothing ever tastes as good as a meal of seafood you know is fresh from the sea.

In the Carolinas the fishermen use a more difficult method of catching their own shrimp, for it requires a trip into the backwater marshes where the streams empty into the sea. At the change of tide, as the water rushes out, the shrimp are caught in nets strung across the flow of water. It requires standing waist high in a lot of black mud, but just think of what the shrimp will taste like when you get them home! Again, we strongly suggest asking for advice and help from the local natives before attempting it.

How to Clean and Prepare Shrimp

1. Peel off the outer crusty shell of the raw or cooked shrimp. You'll find a narrow strip on the back of the shrimp that pulls off like a "zipper," revealing the dark line that is the vein or intestinal tract.

2. With the tip of a small knife, remove this part—this is called "deveining" the shrimp. Do not throw away the crusty shells, because they're filled with flavor. Rinse them under cold water and cook them in boiling water for ten minutes. Strain the liquid and use it to boil the shelled shrimp. Or, if you like, cook the shrimp right in their shells and then peel and clean them afterward. The shells can also be ground up in a food processor and made into a butter, as in Lobster Butter (see Index).

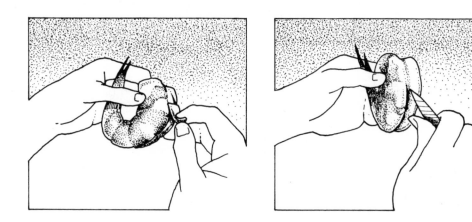

Cooking Shrimp

Butterfly Shrimp

For butterfly shrimp, use any size larger than "medium."

1. Insert the tip of a sharp knife at the top part of the shrimp, and cut through the outer shell.

2. Cut down toward the tail without cutting all the way through the shrimp.

3. Gently pull off the outer shell, leaving the tail fan attached to the shrimp.

4. Open the shrimp and lay it flat for stuffing, baking, or broiling.

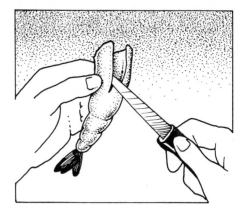
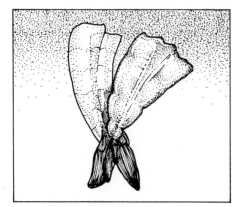

Using Frozen Shrimp

Shrimp that are peeled, deveined, and flash frozen are excellent to use if you remember only one thing: *Do not thaw them before cooking!*

If you use them in a sauce, cook them frozen right in the sauce just to the point where they turn color, but are not yet opaque. Remember, too much cooking makes shrimp tough and rubbery.

How to Cook Shrimp in Their Shells

The biggest crime against "Shrimpdom" is overcooking! To insure your having tender, juicy, crisp, delicate shrimp, follow this simple method:

1. Place the shrimp with their shells on in a pot with enough water to cover. Use a tight fitting cover, but leave it slightly ajar to prevent the water from boiling over.

2. Bring the water to a rolling boil and, when steam starts to puff from the small opening of the lid, immediately cover the pot tightly and turn off the heat.

3. Using pot holders, slide open the lid very slightly, just enough to pour off the water into the sink. Quickly clamp down on the lid again and let the shrimp sit in the pot for 10 to 15 minutes in their own steam. *Do not lift the lid to peek!*

4. After the allotted time, peel and devein the shrimp when they're cool enough to handle. They can also be served hot in their shells with any of the butter sauces given in this book (see Index). If you prefer the latter method, the shells can be peeled right at the table by your dinner guests. It's slightly messy, but it's luscious and it's simple. There is no better feast that can be prepared as quickly, with practically no work for the cook, and there's practically no dinner that will get you as many compliments on your culinary abilities.

Sauces for Shrimp

Shrimp go well with a large variety of sauces (see Index):

For Hot Shrimp:
    Basic Clarified Butter
    Tarragon-Lemon Butter Sauce
    Mint Butter Sauce
    Orange Butter and Chive Sauce
    White Butter Sauce with Vinegar *(Beurre Blanc)*
    Mornay Sauce (with Gruyere Cheese)

Spanish Saffron *Veloute* Sauce
Duxelles *Veloute* (a Mushroom Sauce)
Crab Meat Sauce
Lobster Sauce (Sauce Cardinal)
Sweet and Sour Pineapple and Vegetable Sauce
Basil, Eggplant, and Tomato Sauce
Sauce *Provencale* (a Tomato-Garlic Sauce)

For Cold Shrimp:
Cucumber Mayonnaise Sauce with Dill
Spinach and Chive Sauce
Gazpacho Sauce (a Tomato and Raw Vegetable Sauce)
Remoulade Sauce (Pungent Mayonnaise Sauce)
Almond Ginger Sauce
Yogurt and Horseradish Sauce with Mustard Seed

DILLED SHRIMP MOLD

¾ cup tomato juice
1 envelope unflavored gelatin
2 teaspoons minced, fresh dill
1 tablespoon lemon juice
2 teaspoons minced, fresh chives
⅛ teaspoon cayenne pepper
1 cup sour cream
2 to 3 drops Dried Hot Pepper Sauce (see Index)
½ pound cooked shrimp, peeled, deveined, and coarsely chopped
1 small cucumber, peeled and finely minced

Garnish
lettuce
watercress

Put tomato juice in a saucepan, sprinkle with the gelatin and let stand for 5 minutes. Heat over medium burner, stirring until the gelatin is completely dissolved. Remove from heat and cool slightly. Then add the dill, lemon juice, chives, pepper, sour cream, and Dried Hot Pepper Sauce. Stir until smooth. Let sit in the refrigerator until slightly gelled. Add the shrimp to the gelatin along with the cucumber. Mix with a wooden spoon until all ingredients are well blended. Pour into a 3-cup mold, cover and refrigerate for at least 4 hours, or until completely set. To serve, unmold onto a cold serving plate and surround with lettuce and watercress.

Serves 6

BROILED
SPANISH SHRIMP
WITH SAFFRON

30 large shrimp, about 2 pounds, peeled
    and deveined, but with tails left on
 1 teaspoon crushed saffron strands
 1 large shallot, chopped, or 2 green
    onions, white part only, chopped
 2 small cloves garlic, finely minced
½ teaspoon minced, fresh thyme or ¼
    teaspoon dried
 3 tablespoons olive oil
   juice of 2 lemons
½ cup butter
 1 tablespoon finely chopped, fresh
    parsley

Dry shrimp well on paper towels.

Prepare a marinade with saffron, shallot, garlic, thyme, olive oil, and lemon juice. Add the shrimp and toss. Refrigerate and marinate for 1½ hours, turning the shrimp once or twice.

Melt the butter in a small saucepan and set aside.

Lift out shrimp from marinade. Do not dry. Place on rack of a broiling pan. Pour marinade into melted butter and heat just to the boiling point and reserve as a sauce.

Broil shrimp, turning once. Allow 2 to 3 minutes for each side, until shrimp turn pink and opaque. Arrange on a warm platter and sprinkle with parsley. Serve hot butter-marinade sauce separately in a sauce boat to spoon over the shrimp at the table.

Serves 6

FRIED BUTTERFLIED SHRIMP, CHINESE STYLE

Chinese Sweet and Sour Sauce (see Index)
1½ pounds raw shrimp, about 15 to 20 per pound, in their shells
2 cloves garlic, finely minced
¼ teaspoon black pepper
juice of 1 lemon
1 tablespoon tamari soy sauce
½ recipe Lemon Batter (see Index)
corn oil for frying

Prepare Chinese Sweet and Sour Sauce first and set aside.

Peel each shrimp to the tail leaving the tail shell attached to the shrimp to act as a handle. Devein and wash the shrimp and split each shrimp almost completely through along the inside curve. Open shrimp and lay flat, pressing with the palm of the hand.

Combine garlic, pepper, lemon juice, and soy sauce and lay the shrimp flat in this marinade. Refrigerate for 30 minutes while making the Lemon Batter.

Using a wok or deep fryer, heat the oil to 370°F. Dip the shrimp into the batter carefully and deep fry 1 to 2 minutes on each side until golden brown and puffed. Drain on paper towels and serve with warm Chinese Sweet and Sour Sauce.

Serves 6

INDIAN SHRIMP
WITH YOGURT AND CORIANDER

50 medium-size fresh shrimp, about
    2 pounds, peeled and deveined
½ teaspoon crushed, dried mint
¼ teaspoon dried, red hot pepper flakes
2¼ teaspoons turmeric
½ teaspoon ground coriander
1 teaspoon peeled and grated fresh
    ginger root or ½ teaspoon ground
    ginger
2 cloves garlic, finely minced
½ teaspoon ground cumin
4 tablespoons butter
1 medium-size onion, grated
1 cup yogurt, whipped lightly with a
    whisk
1 teaspoon mild, light honey
2 tablespoons minced Chinese parsley
    (cilantro)
  juice of ½ lemon
  hot, cooked brown rice

Place the shrimp in a bowl and add the mint, hot pepper, turmeric, coriander, ginger, garlic, and cumin. Mix well until shrimp are coated and let stand at room temperature for 1 hour.

Then heat 3 tablespoons of the butter in a deep, heavy skillet and add the onion, stirring and cooking until the onion is fairly dry, but not brown. Stir often to prevent onion from sticking to the skillet. Add the remaining butter and the shrimp mixture. Cook, stirring and turning the shrimp gently, until they start to turn color all over, then lower heat. Stir the yogurt and honey together, add to the cooked ingredients, and simmer, covered, for 3 minutes. Uncover skillet and cook for 3 minutes more. Add the Chinese parsley and lemon juice. This dish should be served spooned over hot, cooked brown rice to absorb the sauce.

Serves 6

SALAD
OF THE SEA
WITH SQUID, SHRIMP, AND AVOCADO

3 tablespoons olive oil
1 large clove garlic, crushed
1 sprig rosemary or ¼ teaspoon dried
1 small, hot red pepper
1 pound baby squid, cleaned and cut into
    ½-inch pieces (see Index)
1 pound very small shrimp, peeled and
    deveined
½ teaspoon black pepper
½ cup lemon juice
1 cup finely sliced celery
1 tablespoon minced, fresh parsley
1 avocado, peeled, seed removed, and
    diced
    leaf lettuce

Heat the oil in a large skillet and add the garlic, rosemary, and hot pepper. Saute until the garlic and pepper are tan. Add the squid, shrimp, and pepper. Stir and cook for 3 to 5 minutes or until the seafood becomes opaque. Be careful not to overcook, or the squid will become tough. Add the lemon juice and remove mixture from heat to let cool. Remove garlic clove, hot pepper pod, and rosemary. Add the celery, parsley, and avocado cubes, and adjust the seasoning. Serve cold on bed of leaf lettuce.

Serves 6

Note: If not served on the same day this salad is made, sprinkle with 2 tablespoons fresh lemon juice before serving.

SCAMPI,
ITALIAN STYLE

½ cup Basic Clarified Butter
¼ cup olive oil
4 to 6 cloves garlic, minced
¼ cup minced, fresh parsley
2 tablespoons lemon juice
½ teaspoon dry mustard
½ teaspoon black pepper
36 jumbo shrimp, about 10 to 15 per
    pound, cleaned, with shell left on
    and split to tail

Melt the butter in a saucepan. Add the oil, garlic, parsley, lemon juice, mustard, and pepper. Mix well and simmer over low heat until garlic is soft.

Over medium heat, quickly saute the shrimp, a few at a time, tossing them in the butter. Serve immediately.

Serves 6

SHRIMP CREOLE
WITH EGGPLANT
AND BROWN
GARLIC RICE

½ cup butter
2 cups coarsely chopped onion
1 cup chopped green pepper
1 cup coarsely chopped celery
2 cloves garlic, finely minced
4 large tomatoes, peeled and chopped
½ cup Basic Tomato Sauce (see Index)
½ teaspoon black pepper
3 slices fresh lemon rind, shredded
3 whole cloves
1 bay leaf
3 sprigs thyme or ½ teaspoon dried
½ teaspoon mild, light honey
¼ cup olive oil
1 small eggplant, skin left on and diced
36 medium-size fresh shrimp, about
1½ pounds, peeled and deveined
3 tablespoons finely minced, fresh
parsley

Melt 3 tablespoons of the butter in a large, oven-to-table casserole. Add the onion, green pepper, and celery and cook, stirring until wilted. Then add the garlic and tomatoes. Bring to a boil, then lower heat and add the Basic Tomato Sauce, pepper, lemon rind, cloves, bay leaf, thyme, and honey. Simmer for 15 to 20 minutes, stirring frequently.

At this point, prepare the rice (see recipe below).

Heat the oil in a separate skillet and saute the eggplant cubes until lightly browned. Add to the casserole and cook for 5 minutes. Then add the shrimp to the sauce and cook 10 to 12 minutes or until the shrimp are opaque and pink. Stir in the remaining butter and sprinkle with the parsley. Serve with the hot rice.

Serves 6

BROWN
GARLIC RICE

2 tablespoons butter
1 tablespoon finely minced onion
1 large clove garlic, finely minced
1 cup brown rice
¼ teaspoon cayenne pepper
2¼ cups boiling chicken stock

Melt the butter in a saucepan and saute the onion and garlic until wilted. Stir and do not allow to brown. Add the rice and pepper and stir constantly to coat the rice for about 2 minutes. Add the chicken stock and cover the pot. Simmer for 20 to 25 minutes or until rice is tender. Drain off any extra liquid.

SHRIMP SALAD
WITH SIX
VARIATIONS

1 pound cooked shrimp, peeled, deveined and coarsely chopped (or use small, whole shrimp)
¼ teaspoon black pepper
½ cup finely minced celery
½ cup Homemade Mayonnaise (see Index)
1 teaspoon lemon juice

Mix all together and then add any of the following ingredients for variations:

1 tablespoon minced, fresh parsley and 1 tablespoon minced, fresh chives

1 tablespoon minced green pepper and 1 tablespoon minced red pepper

1 hard-cooked egg, coarsely chopped, and ½ cup chopped scallions

1 tablespoon minced, fresh dill and 1 small cucumber, peeled and chopped

2 teaspoons curry powder and 1 tablespoon slivered almonds

1 teaspoon grated onion and 2 teaspoons finely minced, fresh tarragon or ½ teaspoon dried

Serve any of these salads on beds of lettuce, stuffed into avocado halves, or in scooped out whole tomatoes. Garnish with hard-boiled egg quarters, watercress, cucumber sticks, steamed broccoli florets, cold asparagus spears, or artichoke hearts.

Serves 6

SHRIMP
STUFFED WITH
SHRIMP AND
MUSHROOMS

27 large shrimp—allow 3 per serving, the
    remaining shrimp for stuffing
 6 tablespoons butter
¾ cup finely chopped onion
¾ cup finely chopped celery
 1 large clove garlic, finely minced
 4 large mushrooms, about ¼ pound,
    coarsely chopped
¼ teaspoon black pepper
 1 tablespoon lemon juice
 1 cup fresh whole grain bread crumbs
    plus 2 tablespoons extra
¼ cup finely minced, fresh parsley
 1 egg, lightly beaten
 2 tablespoons grated Gruyere cheese

Set aside 18 of the shrimp and "butterfly" (see page 363).

Peel and devein the remaining shrimp and chop coarsely. There should be about ¾ cup. Set aside.

Heat 2 tablespoons of the butter in a skillet and add the onion, celery, and garlic. Cook, stirring until wilted. Add the mushrooms, pepper, and lemon juice. Stir and cook for 3 minutes. Remove from heat and add the chopped shrimp, 1 cup bread crumbs, parsley, and egg. Stir to blend. Spoon equal portions of this mixture on top of each butterflied shrimp in a mound.

Butter a baking dish large enough to hold the shrimp in one layer and arrange them in the dish. Sprinkle the tops with the remaining 2 tablespoons of bread crumbs and grated cheese, and dot with the remaining butter. Place the shrimp under the broiler about 5 inches from the source of heat and broil for 5 to 7 minutes, or until shrimp are heated through and the stuffing has browned. Baste once with the pan juices that will form.

Serves 6

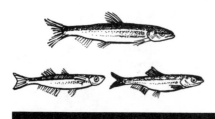

**Sweet and Spicy Fish, Italian Style
Baked Fresh Sardines Greek Style,
with Lemon and Marjoram
Fried Algerian Sardines with Cumin,
Garlic, and Oranges
Fried Whitebait with Sesame Seeds
Pan Fried Lemon Smelts
Portuguese Marinated Smelts**

They are tiny and sometimes ignored. When compared to the *swordfish* and the *striper* and the *tilefish,* they fade into insignificance. And yet it is the tiny, iridescent *sunfish* that we remember most from childhood fishing experiences, sitting dockside at the summer lake, too old for toys and too young to see any merit in the opposite sex. However bony those tiny fish were, they were *ours;* we had caught them and they tasted just delicious when pan fried for a very few minutes.

It is difficult to categorize *all* the "small" fish, for some species can be so labeled at certain times and in certain places, then going to three to four pounds on a later occasion. The very popular sunfish, the *bluegill,* is one good example, with an average size of about one-half pound and a top weight almost eight times that size. For the purchaser of small fish—or for the vacation fisherman who catches some down at the lake or bay—the best thing to do is to pan fry them or saute them quickly. This holds true for almost all species—*sardines, smelts, cisco, snook,* or the smaller sunfish such as *crappies* or *pumpkin seed.* So, if in doubt, pan fry or saute. In fact, we have mentioned in the chapter on Bluefish (see Index) the small *snappers* (tiny blues) that come into the bay in late summer. We need anywhere from 15 to 20 to make one portion per person and we actually fillet them with one sweep of the knife on each side and then pan fry them for seconds to make a superb dinner. So, even the giant blues can be considered "small fish" when they're babies.

We'd like to add a word about *whitebait,* an all-inclusive name for the tiny fried fish devoured by gourmets in Europe by the bucketful. It was in England, in fact, where we first tasted this combination of small fish. Generally, the Europeans include *smelts, sardines, sticklebacks,* and *pipefish* in the mixture. In North America, you will probably find *sardines, silversides, herring,* and *Pacific surf smelts* marketed under the name of *whitebait,* and though we also add the readily available *sand eels* to our mixture, these latter fish are not easily found commercially.

If you visit a friend at the seashore, or if you spend part of your vacation near a bay or salt pond, you'll see millions of silverside minnows swimming in the waters near the shoreline or the docks. It takes a net and two poles to scoop them up and the young people of our village wade into the water to catch them by the thousands. Unfortunately, the major part of the catch is used only for bait, and so these small fish remain one of our most underutilized resources. Since they deteriorate rapidly, they must go from bay to frying pan as quickly as possible. As soon as you get them home, place them on ice if you don't plan to use them immediately. And don't keep them in water, since they become soggy and tasteless almost at once. Try the whitebait recipe that we've included. We think you're in for a taste treat.

SWEET AND SPICY FISH, ITALIAN STYLE

4½ pounds small fish with heads left on and gutted, or pan dressed
1 cup whole wheat flour
¼ teaspoon black pepper
½ cup olive oil, or more, if needed for frying
1 sprig rosemary or ¼ teaspoon dried
1 cup water
2 tablespoons honey
juice of 3 lemons
6 tablespoons raisins
4 tablespoons pine nuts, toasted lightly (sunflower seeds may be used)
1 clove garlic, finely minced
1 tablespoon finely chopped, fresh mint with additional sprigs for garnish

Dip fish in flour and pepper.

Heat oil and add the rosemary to scent the oil. Fry the fish at 370°F. turning once to brown. Remove fish and drain on paper towels.

In a saucepan mix water, honey, lemon juice, raisins, pine nuts, and garlic together and bring to a boil. Place fish in a deep skillet and pour the liquid over the fish. Simmer uncovered for 5 minutes. Sprinkle with mint before serving. Garnish with additonal sprigs of mint.

Serves 6

BAKED FRESH SARDINES
GREEK STYLE,
WITH LEMON AND MARJORAM

2½ pounds fresh sardines, cleaned, with heads left on or pan dressed (other small fish may be used)*
juice of 2 lemons
½ cup olive oil
2 tablespoons fresh marjoram or 3 teaspoons dried

Preheat oven to 350°F.

Arrange sardines in a large, oven-to-table baking dish.

Beat the lemon and oil together with a wire whisk. Add the marjoram and pour mixture over the fish. Bake for 10 to 15 minutes or just until tender. Baste occasionally, so the fish keep moist. Serve hot in same baking dish. This dish is also delicious served cold the following day.

Serves 6

*To fillet a sardine, break off head with fingers. Slash underside of fish and cut so fish can lie flat but is still joined. Using fingers, remove the backbone, like a zipper, and rinse fish, folding it in half to retain its fish shape.

FRIED
ALGERIAN SARDINES
WITH CUMIN, GARLIC, AND ORANGES

2½ pounds fresh sardines—remove heads, split open, and remove backbones*
4 teaspoons ground cumin
2 cloves garlic, crushed
½ teaspoon cayenne pepper
2 eggs, beaten
1 cup fine, dry, whole grain bread crumbs
corn oil for frying
orange wedges for garnish

Spread fish open, and dip the inner side of ½ of the fish into a mixture of the cumin, garlic, and cayenne pepper. Press the open sides of 2 fish (one plain, the other seasoned) together to enclose the seasonings so they do not burn, and fasten with toothpicks. Dip the fish into the eggs and then into the bread crumbs.

Heat the oil to 370°F. and deep fry fish, one at a time. Lift out with slotted spatula, remove toothpicks, and serve hot with orange wedges.

Serves 6 to 8

*To fillet a sardine, break off head with fingers. Slash underside of fish and cut so fish can lie flat but is still joined. Using fingers, remove the backbone, like a zipper, and rinse fish, folding it in half to retain its fish shape.

FRIED
WHITEBAIT
WITH SESAME SEEDS

These are the tiniest (no more than 2 inches long) of edible fish. Their convenient size makes them disappear at the table much like popcorn at the movies. Several kinds of these sweet and nutlike fish are known throughout the country and are marketed under such names as *infant herring,* *silversides,* or *sand eels.* These fish can be netted at any seashore bay area on both coasts. Since they are so tiny, they are cooked, eaten whole and ungutted. They are a sensational "finger food" and much more nourishing than "processed supermarket nibbles."

Prepare the Dipping Sauce first.

Dipping Sauce
   6 tablespoons tamari soy sauce
   2 teaspoons vinegar
   ⅛ teaspoon Dried Hot Pepper Sauce (see Index)
   ¼ teaspoon honey

Mix ingredients together and set aside.

The Fish
   1½ pounds whole sand eels, silversides, or any other whitebait fish no more than 2 inches long
   ½ cup milk
   2 teaspoons tamari soy sauce
   1 egg, beaten lightly
   1 cup whole wheat pastry flour
   ¼ cup sesame seeds
      corn oil for frying
      lemon or lime wedges for garnish

Wash fish well in several changes of cold water until water is clear.

Mix the milk, soy sauce, and egg together. Add the fish, stir gently, and let marinate for 30 minutes.

Place the flour and sesame seeds in a plastic bag. Remove fish from marinade. Drain fish on paper towels and place a few at a time in the flour mixture to coat evenly. Place them on a sheet of wax paper to dry in the refrigerator for 5 minutes while you heat the oil.

(continued on following page)

Use a heavy iron skillet with deep sides and fill it with 2½ inches of oil. Heat to 370°F. Add the fish, a few at a time to keep the temperature constant. When golden, just after 1 to 2 minutes of cooking, skim them out and drain on paper towels. Keep warm until all are cooked in several batches. Serve with the spicy dipping sauce. Garnish with lemon or lime wedges.

Serves 6

PAN FRIED
LEMON SMELTS

2 pounds smelts, pan dressed
  juice of 2 lemons
2 cups white cornmeal
2 eggs, beaten
¼ cup milk
½ teaspoon black pepper
4 tablespoons corn oil or enough to cover
    pan to ¼-inch depth

Garnish
    lemon wedges
    sprigs parsley

Marinate fish at room temperature in a flat, glass pan with the lemon juice for 15 minutes.

Place the cornmeal on a piece of aluminum foil.

In a glass pie pan, beat eggs, milk, and pepper together. Dip fish first in cornmeal, then into egg-milk mixture, then in cornmeal again.

Heat the oil in a heavy skillet. Brown fish on both sides, using medium-low heat. Drain fish on paper towels, transfer to warm platter and serve with lemon wedges and parsley sprigs for decoration. Pass a bottle of malt vinegar to sprinkle on the top (but sparingly).

Serves 6

PORTUGUESE MARINATED SMELTS

2½ pounds small fish, pan dressed, or
  fillets (or small whole fish, such as
  smelts, whitebait and surfperch)
4 tablespoons olive oil
2 tablespoons lemon juice
½ clove garlic, crushed
¼ teaspoon black pepper
⅛ teaspoon nutmeg
1 bay leaf, crushed
2 eggs, beaten
1 cup fine, dry, whole grain bread
  crumbs
  oil for frying
1 cup apple cider
2 teaspoons minced, fresh parsley
2 tablespoons grated onion

Wash and dry fish on paper towels.

Prepare marinade of oil, lemon juice, garlic, pepper, nutmeg, and bay leaf and place fish in this marinade for 3 to 4 hours in refrigerator, turning occasionally. When ready to cook, remove fish and dry well on paper towels. Reserve marinade in a saucepan and set aside.

Dip fish in eggs, then in bread crumbs.

Heat 1 inch of oil to 370°F. in a heavy skillet and saute fish turning once, until golden, about 3 to 4 minutes depending on size of fish. Remove, drain on paper towels, and place in a bowl.

Add the apple cider, parsley, and onion to the marinade in the saucepan and bring to a boil. Pour over fish and let cool. Refrigerate overnight and serve on a platter the following day at room temperature.

Serves 6

Sweet and Spicy Fish, Italian Style   For this recipe, see page 374

Sashimi of Tuna For this recipe, see page 398

Striped Bass with Fresh Fennel and Garlic
Ecuadorian *Seviche* **of Striped Bass**
Moroccan Style Baked Striped Bass
Striped Bass with Dried Fruit and Walnuts

Though they are taken in large quantities by commercial fishermen in the Atlantic Ocean and are available at the fishmonger as fillets, steaks, chunks, or whole dressed, they are by far the favorite game fish of the surf fisherman all along the coastline. In fact, as this chapter is being written, autumn is fast approaching and fishermen on our island (including the authors) are busily checking lines, lures, and the roll of the ocean in anticipation of an encounter with these remarkable and unpredictable fish. Soon the *striped bass* will be feeding on baitfish offshore and, as an early dusk falls, possibly one will be waiting for us just over the sandbar, within casting distance. They are called *"stripers"* (or *"rockfish"*) and they are the prizes of our ocean surf, an unmatched combination of exciting game fish and superb eating.

Striped bass are relatively large fish and it is not unusual for a surf fisherman to take one that weighs about 30 to 45 pounds. However, they seldom go over 75 pounds, and though the largest recorded catch was over six feet in length and weighed 125 pounds, the average commercial catch runs about 1 pound up to about 6 to 10 pounds in size.

Striped bass has a high quality, white flaky flesh. It's nutritious, versatile, and deservedly popular, a delicate fish that adapts well to broiling, baking, pan frying, oven frying, planking, or poaching. It has a large cavity which can be stuffed nicely and it can be eaten hot or cold with a variety of sauces. If you can't get striped bass at your fishmonger, you can substitute *red snapper* in any of the recipes that follow.

For cold striped bass try this sauce (see Index):
   Mustard-Dill Sauce

For hot, poached striped bass try these sauces (see Index):
   Hollandaise-Based Sauces
   Sauce Bearnaise

For baked striped bass try these stuffings (see Index):
   Crab Meat Stuffing
   Arabic and Pine Nut Stuffing

STRIPED BASS
WITH FRESH FENNEL
AND GARLIC

¾ cup butter
3 tablespoons olive oil
4 to 5 cloves garlic, finely minced
1 striped bass, about 5 to 6 pounds, or 2
      striped bass, about 2½ pounds
      each, with head left on but gills
      removed
½ teaspoon black pepper
1 whole bulb fennel with the leaves

Preheat oven to 375°F.

In a large, oven-to-table baking dish, heat the butter, oil, and garlic slowly on top of the stove. Do not let garlic burn. Let cool briefly and add the fish, turning to coat all sides with this mixture. Sprinkle with pepper. Cut the fennel bulb coarsely, and lightly stuff it into the cavities of the fish. Snip the leaf tops of the fennel, pull off, and discard the tough outer leaves. Cut stalks into pieces and arrange around the fish. Bake for about 45 to 50 minutes basting both the fish and fennel frequently with the butter-garlic mixture. Serve in same pan.

Serves 6

ECUADORIAN SEVICHE OF STRIPED BASS

2 pounds striped bass fillets, skinned and cut into 1-inch pieces*
1½ cups lime juice
1 cup orange juice
¾ cup olive oil
1 fresh, hot, red chili pepper, seeded and finely minced
1 clove garlic, finely minced
¼ teaspoon black pepper
1 sprig Chinese parsley (cilantro), finely minced

Place the fish in a glass or pottery bowl. Mix all other ingredients together, and pour over the fish. Toss all gently and refrigerate for minimum of 4 hours or more.

Serves 6

*In Ecuador the fish used is called *corvina*. The striped bass is very similar and a fine substitute.

MOROCCAN STYLE BAKED STRIPED BASS

1 striped bass, about 5 to 6 pounds
½ cup olive oil or corn oil
3 tablespoons ground cumin
1 tablespoon paprika
1 clove garlic, finely minced
½ cup finely minced, fresh parsley
¼ teaspoon black pepper
lemon slices for garnish

Preheat oven to 350°F.

Lay the fish on a large sheet of heavy-duty aluminum foil.

Combine the oil, cumin, paprika, garlic, parsley, and pepper. Rub the fish inside and out with above mixture. Wrap tightly to enclose. Place on a pan and bake for 1 hour. Open foil, baste fish with juices, and continue to bake uncovered until browned and fish flakes easily with a skewer. Garnish with lemon slices and serve with foil rolled back on a serving platter.

Serves 6

STRIPED BASS
WITH DRIED FRUIT
AND WALNUTS

6 tablespoons olive oil
2 large onions, cut in half and thinly
    sliced
¾ cup dried currants
5 dried apricots, coarsely chopped or
    snipped with scissors (if apricots are
    extremely dry, soak them in hot
    water for 10 minutes)
½ cup lemon juice
¾ cup coarsely chopped walnuts
¼ teaspoon black pepper
¾ teaspoon cinnamon
¾ teaspoon allspice
6 tablespoons finely minced, fresh
    parsley
3 lemons, thinly sliced
1 striped bass, about 5 pounds, or 2
    striped bass, about 2½ pounds
    each, cleaned and with bones
    removed, but not cut down the back
½ cup Basic Tomato Sauce (see Index)

Heat 4 tablespoons of the oil in a heavy skillet and saute the onions until translucent, but not brown.

In a small bowl, soak the currants and apricots in the lemon juice for 15 minutes. Then drain and reserve both fruit and lemon juice and set aside.

Add the walnuts to the fruit and then the pepper, cinnamon, allspice, and parsley. Add this mixture to the sauteed onions and cook, stirring constantly for 2 to 3 minutes. Remove from heat and stir in half of the reserved lemon juice.

Preheat the oven to 350°F.

Oil an oven-to-table baking dish with remaining oil. Make a layer of the lemon slices on the bottom of the dish. Put the onion-fruit mixture inside the fish cavity and fasten with skewers. Mix the remaining lemon juice with the Basic Tomato Sauce and pour over fish. Place a row of overlapping lemon slices along the top of the fish. Bake for about 45 to 50 minutes or until fish flakes easily with a skewer. Serve the fish at room temperature. It would go well with a cold, brown rice salad.

Serves 6

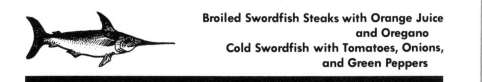

**Broiled Swordfish Steaks with Orange Juice
and Oregano
Cold Swordfish with Tomatoes, Onions,
and Green Peppers**

Few of us who fish for leisure will ever catch a *swordfish*. It takes a dedicated, determined, affluent fisherman to get even close to these deep-sea monsters, no less to catch one, an impression also expressed by Zane Grey in *Tales of Swordfish and Tuna*. So most of us will have to remain content just reading of boats attacked by swordfish and wrecks washed up on shore with a broken sword still embedded in the planking, and of the 1,100-pound giant caught off the coast of Chile. We will leave the catch to commercial fishermen who harpoon them in tropical waters around the world.

However caught—or however bought—the swordfish is delicious prepared as a steak. Firm fleshed and nonoily, it takes well to sauces and marinades. It's gaining in popularity around North America and demand still exceeds the supply, leading many cooks and dealers to substitute *mako* when the swordfish steaks are scarce. The taste and texture, incidentally, are quite similar, and mako can easily be substituted for swordfish in any of these recipes.

BROILED SWORDFISH STEAKS
WITH ORANGE JUICE AND OREGANO

6 swordfish steaks, about 2½ to 3 pounds, cut about 1 inch thick
¾ cup orange juice
rind of ½ orange, finely grated
¼ cup finely minced, fresh parsley
¼ cup Basic Tomato Sauce (see Index)
juice of 1 lemon
1 tablespoon finely minced, fresh oregano or 1½ teaspoons dried
1 teaspoon black pepper
2 large cloves garlic, finely minced
2 tablespoons olive oil

Place a plastic bag in a bowl and put the steaks into the bag. Mix all other ingredients together and pour into the bag over the fish. Secure the bag and marinate contents for 2 hours in the refrigerator, turning the bag occasionally.

Oil a broiling pan and lift out steaks from the marinade and place on pan. Broil 2 inches from source of heat for about 4 minutes basting occasionally with the sauce. Turn with 2 wide spatulas and broil on the other side about 5 to 6 minutes more, or until fish flakes easily with a skewer. Baste to keep fish moist.

Serves 6

COLD SWORDFISH
WITH TOMATOES, ONIONS, AND GREEN PEPPERS

4 tablespoons olive oil
2½ pounds swordfish steak with bones removed, cut into 1½-inch cubes
2 large, sweet, yellow onions, thinly sliced
2 green peppers, cut in rings
2 cloves garlic, finely minced
3 large tomatoes, peeled and sliced
4 tablespoons finely minced, fresh parsley
1 tablespoon Tomato Paste (see Index)
¼ cup water
¼ teaspoon cayenne pepper
1 sprig rosemary or ¼ teaspoon dried

Heat the oil in a large heavy skillet and fry the fish until it becomes opaque. Remove with a slotted spatula and reserve.

In the same skillet, add the onions. Saute until slightly golden and then add the peppers. Cook until tender but still slightly crisp. Add the garlic and cook, stirring for 1 minute more. Add the tomatoes, parsley, and Tomato Paste diluted with water. Season with cayenne and rosemary. Bring to a boil, lower heat, and simmer for 10 minutes. Carefully lay the fish cubes over the sauce and simmer, basting with the sauce frequently, for 10 minutes more. Let cool, then refrigerate and serve cold.

Serves 6

A Good Old-Fashioned Fish Fry

We came upon it by accident while driving through the South. It was the first old-fashioned church fish fry we'd ever seen. It took place in Bath, the oldest town in North Carolina, and throughout the two days over 500 people came by to sample the freshly fried trout.

We met Reuben, who is a painting contractor in Bath for the other 363 days a year, but on these 2 days he is the fillet-er extraordinary. Once a year he donates his time and 250 trout to the Church of God Fish Fry. We watched in awe as he filleted a fish with one swoop of the knife, turned the fish over and took the second fillet off with another swoop. Unfortunately, we only had time to taste one of the glowing examples of a real old-time fish fry, for we were on our way to another appointment for dinner!

The Sweetwater Fishing Expeditions

We met George and Paula Hunker through two other western friends of ours, Haven and Margaret Holsapple, who conduct mountain climbing trips in Alaska and who graciously wrote the chapter on high altitude bread baking in Mel's book *Bread Winners* (Emmaus, Pa.: Rodale Press, 1979). If you like fishing for *trout* and know the incomparable flavor of trout that goes right from the stream to the pan, you will envy the life the Hunkers lead. They run Sweetwater Fishing Expeditions out of Crowheart, Wyoming, in the Rocky Mountains and in New Zealand.

Since it's their business, they catch thousands of trout in a year. But because they could never eat all they catch, they and their guests thoroughly enjoy the *catching* of the fish—using barbless hooks and gentle handling—and then they return most of them to the streams. In a letter that George and Paula sent to us, they clearly and delightfully described the experience of fishing for *cutthroats, brook trout, rainbows, and golden trout:*

"The joy of fly-fishing is the fact that it's complicated, with consistent activity, and always changing. Actually, fly casting is an aesthetic process, a real art form. Deceiving trout into taking one's imitation fly as though it were a natural one, is a process that places the angler in an area still wild and free, with the hypnotic effect of running water always at hand. Playing and landing trout on a fly rod always brings excitement. . . ."

As for the eating, George and Paula prefer their trout simply prepared, fresh out of the cold mountain waters, rolled in cornmeal, and fried in high quality oil until the flesh falls off the bone.

Baked Trout with Bay Leaves
Broiled, Marinated Trout
with Raisin Sauce
Chilled, Poached Trout with Horseradish
Sour Cream and Dill Sauce
Pan Fried Trout
Trout with Sauce
Sauteed Trout with Sliced Brazil Nuts
Trout *au Bleu*

Early in April, the long awaited *trout* season begins and the passionate trout fisherman performs a ritual as mysterious as the lemmings' return to the sea. He has gotten through the winter by taking frequent trips to the fishing supply house or by browsing through mail-order catalogs for the beautiful and colorful "flies" that mimic the appearance of the small, aquatic insects that form the largest part of the trout diet. But not just any fly will do—the artificial lure must match the size, the color, and the weight of the real insect preferred by the fish at that particular time of the year. And so, those of us who fish for trout in spring spend a great part of the winter trying to *think* like a trout.

In early spring when the streams are icy, the chest-high waders are taken from their storage place in high anticipation. Then, when the season finally opens, the ardent trout fisherman begins a treacherous ballet, performed on slimy rocks amidst swiftly racing currents. Evaluating the depth, the swiftness of the current, watching for clues as to where the trout might be swimming, guessing at the type of fly to use, the line snaps out with a realistic meal tied to the end of a hook to tempt the fish.

It is an intensely consuming, somewhat dangerous, totally involving and challenging pursuit. It takes skill, it takes patience—and all of us find it relaxing. For the trout fisherman are die-hard anglers who prefer this sport to all others. In fact, there are many who fish only to catch the noble trout—and then throw it back into the stream.

Trout are most delicate in flavor—moist but not fatty, and they're quite tender. The skeleton is quite simple, so the backbone and rib cage lift out in one movement after the fish is cooked. The most popular of these fine fish are the *rainbow trout,* the *brook trout,* and the *brown trout.*

Cooking the Trout

Assuming you have caught some trout or you've received a gift from a fisherman as a result of his "relaxing," the fish are easy to dress. They have a small body cavity and they can be gutted in one motion by cutting the throat loose, extending the forefinger into the opening and then pulling the entrails out, gills and all.

If you buy your trout, you'll find them marketed fresh and whole, at which point the fishmonger can gut them for you if you like, or you'll find them frozen, gutted or boneless. One of our favorite fish stores has them swimming in a window tank for all the passersby to watch.

Tip: The size of the trout will determine how it should be cooked. Whole, small fish between 6 and 10 inches should be cooked quickly. Larger trout, about 12 to 14 inches, are tastier when poached, baked, or broiled. A really large trout (weighing over four pounds or about 20 inches long) can be elegantly stuffed and baked as well.

Tip: Since trout have very tiny scales, it is not really necessary to scale or skin them. As we mentioned, they are easily boned before or after cooking when the entire skeleton can be lifted out intact.

Note: If trout is not available in your part of the world, these fish can be used in any of the following recipes:

Bass
Pike
Crevalle
Salmon
Ocean perch

BAKED TROUT
WITH BAY LEAVES

1 clove garlic, crushed
2 teaspoons finely minced, fresh thyme or
    1 teaspoon dried
¼ teaspoon black pepper
6 whole trout, about ¾ pound each, pan
    dressed
6 bay leaves
4 tablespoons butter, melted
    juice of 2 lemons
¼ cup finely minced, fresh parsley

Preheat oven to 400°F.

Mix the garlic, thyme, and black pepper. Blend together and spread on top of trout with a small spatula. Insert 1 whole bay leaf into the interior of each fish. Oil an oven-to-table baking dish, large enough to hold the fish in a single layer. Pour the melted butter over the fish and bake for 10 to 12 minutes, basting once or twice with the butter. Sprinkle with lemon juice and parsley before serving.

Serves 6

BROILED,
MARINATED TROUT
WITH RAISIN SAUCE

6 whole trout, about ¾ pound each, split
    and boned
½ cup olive oil
¼ cup lemon juice
1 large clove garlic, thinly sliced
¼ teaspoon black pepper
½ cup raisins

Use a glass dish and place trout side by side in one layer. Mix oil, lemon juice, garlic, and pepper together and pour over trout. Let marinate for 30 minutes, turning fish over after 15 minutes.

Lift fish out of marinade. Do not dry the fish. Save the marinade.

Place the fish on perforated rack over a pan of water and broil about 2 to 3 inches from source of heat, turning the fish carefully once to brown the other side. While the fish is broiling, pour the marinade into a saucepan, add the raisins and bring to a boil.

Serve fish on warm platter with raisin sauce poured over.

Serves 6

CHILLED, POACHED TROUT
WITH HORSERADISH SOUR CREAM AND DILL SAUCE

Poaching Liquid
- 6 cups water
- 1 cup tarragon vinegar
  juice of 1 lemon
- 4 sprigs parsley
- 1 bay leaf
- 2 sprigs fresh thyme or ½ teaspoon dried
- 8 peppercorns
- 1 carrot, cut in half
- 1 stalk celery

The Fish
- 6 whole trout, about ¾ pound each, dressed, with or without head

Sauce
- ¼ cup freshly grated horseradish root (or drained, if bottled)
- 1 cup sour cream
  few drops lemon juice
- 2 sprigs dill, minced

Garnish
- 1 bunch watercress
- 1 cucumber, peeled and sliced

Prepare poaching liquid with water, vinegar, lemon juice, parsley, bay leaf, thyme, peppercorns, and vegetables and cook over medium heat for 25 minutes. Strain liquid, return it to the pot and bring to a boil. Add the trout, follow Basic Poaching Procedure (see Index), lower the heat to simmer and cook for 5 minutes. Turn off heat and allow fish to cool in liquid for 10 minutes more. Lift fish out carefully and when cool to the touch, remove the skin.

To prepare the sauce, simply mix all the ingredients together and pour into a sauce boat to be passed at the table.

Serve trout chilled on bed of watercress garnished with peeled cucumber disks.

Serves 6

PAN FRIED
TROUT

6 fresh, whole trout, about ¾ pound
    each, pan dressed
1 cup milk
⅔ cup stone-ground, yellow cornmeal,
    mixed with part rye flour
1 teaspoon black pepper
1 teaspoon paprika
¼ cup corn oil
2 large lemons, peeled, white pith and
    seeds removed, and pulp cut into
    tiny pieces
4 tablespoons butter
1 tablespoon minced, fresh parsley

Arrange the trout in a pan with sides and pour the milk over the fish. Let stand for 30 minutes, turning fish once. Drain the fish, but do not dry them. In a shallow plate, spread cornmeal and rye flour mixture, pepper, and paprika on the bottom. Roll each fish into this mixture to coat evenly. Let dry for 10 minutes in the refrigerator on wax paper in a single layer. Heat the oil in a skillet. When very hot, add the trout in a single layer. Saute over medium heat until golden on bottom. Carefully turn with wide spatula and cook the other side. Transfer to warm serving platter and keep warm. Clean the skillet with paper towels. Scatter the tiny pieces of lemon over the fish while melting the butter until golden brown. Pour the butter over all and sprinkle with parsley.

Serves 6

TROUT
WITH
SAUCE

Trout may also be poached, deep fried, sauteed, baked, or simply broiled, and enriched by serving with any of the following sauces (see Index):

Basic Hollandaise Sauce
Sorrel and Egg Sauce
Any Butter Sauces (Hot)
Sauce Bearnaise

SAUTEED TROUT
WITH SLICED BRAZIL NUTS

6 fresh, whole trout, about ¾ pound
    each, pan dressed
1 cup milk
1 teaspoon freshly ground black pepper
⅔ cup whole wheat pastry flour
½ cup corn oil, or enough to cover pan to
    ¼-inch depth
4 tablespoons butter
4 tablespoons sliced Brazil nuts

Garnish
    sprigs parsley
    lemon wedges

Arrange the trout in a dish with sides and pour the milk over them to cover. Let stand for 30 minutes. Remove the fish but do not dry them.

Mix the pepper with the flour in a strong plastic bag, and put the fish in the bag, one at a time, to coat with the flour mixture.

Add the oil to a large skillet. When hot but not smoking, add the trout in a single layer. Cook until golden brown over medium heat on one side and carefully turn to cook the other side until brown. Lift out and transfer to a warm serving platter and keep warm.

Quickly pour off the remaining oil from the skillet and wipe it clean with paper towels. Add the butter to the same skillet and cook until the butter is slightly tan. Add the Brazil nuts and stir, making sure they do not burn. Immediately pour the butter and nuts over the fish and garnish with parsley sprigs and lemon wedges.

Serves 6

TROUT
AU BLEU

Trout *au Bleu* definitely has a blue color! What causes the trout to turn blue when poached, particularly since it starts off as a rainbow trout, golden trout, or brown trout? It is simply this: a fresh, really fresh, trout is coated with a slippery film when pulled from a stream. This film gives the trout its blue cast. When killed, gutted, but *not* washed (so that this film remains intact), it is poached immediately. One way to be sure that the trout you are served in a restaurant is completely fresh—ask to have it prepared *au bleu*. If you wish to cook it this way at home, try this recipe for exquisite simplicity.

```
 8  cups water
    juice of 1 lemon
 2  stalks celery with leaves, cut in half
 1  large carrot, cut in half
 1  medium onion, cut in half
 4  sprigs parsley
 2  sprigs tarragon or ¼ teaspoon dried
 2  bay leaves
10  peppercorns
 1  cup tarragon vinegar
 6  fresh, whole trout, about ¾ pound
        each, gutted*
½  cup butter, melted
```

Garnish
    watercress
    lemon wedges

Put all but the last 5 ingredients into a large pot. Bring to a boil and then lower heat to medium. Let cook for 25 minutes, then pour through a strainer pressing the vegetables against the sides to extract their juices. Return this liquid to the pot and add the vinegar.

Bring the liquid to a boil and with tongs, lower the trout into the liquid, one by one. When all the fish are in the pot and the liquid comes to a boil again, remove pot from the heat. Cover the pot and let stand for 10 to 15 minutes.

Remove the fish carefully with a wide spatula and place on a platter lined with a folded cloth napkin to absorb excess liquid. Serve with melted butter or a hollandaise sauce (see Index) to be spooned over the trout at the table. Decorate the platter with nosegays of watercress and lemon wedges.

Serves 6

*The fins from the back and sides of the trout should be cut off leaving the head and tail intact. The freshly killed trout will curl naturally when poached, through muscle and nerve reaction to the boiling liquid. If you must keep the fish for a while until it is poached, simply run a large, threaded trussing needle through the head of the trout and then into the tail, and tie the head and tail together to form the curve.

Baked Fresh Tuna in Tomato Puree
***Sashimi* of Tuna (and Other Suggested Fish)
with Two Dipping Sauces**

We find the *tuna* mentioned in the history and the writings of the ancients all over the world. The Greeks not only hunted tuna, but their poetry and their art also reflected their intense admiration for this well-known fish. The Incas fished for them from reed boats off the coast of Peru and the Japanese have utilized them for *sashimi* for centuries. Today, the tuna is the number one seafood in the United States, with most of it going to the canning industry. Most tuna are caught by seining, with the fish immediately dropped into refrigerated holds and flash frozen, guaranteeing that the fish will remain fresh until they reach the canning or processing plants.

Though most North Americans are great consumers of the canned tuna—with over a billion cans sold in the United States each year—*fresh* tuna is also available, a delicious, rich source of protein, vitamins, and minerals. We include two recipes for you to try.

BAKED
FRESH TUNA
IN TOMATO PUREE

6 slices fresh tuna, about 4 ounces each
¼ teaspoon black pepper
⅛ teaspoon freshly grated nutmeg
1½ cups Fish Stock (see Index)
1 teaspoon softened butter
¼ cup Basic Tomato Sauce (see Index)
½ teaspoon finely minced, fresh oregano
    or ¼ teaspoon dried
    juice of 1 lemon
2 tablespoons finely minced, fresh
    parsley

Sprinkle the tuna slices with pepper and nutmeg.

Preheat oven to 350°F.

Place the tuna slices in a pan with sides. Pour Fish Stock over the tuna. Butter a piece of aluminum foil to fit the baking dish and place it, butter side down, over the fish. Bake for 15 minutes, lifting the foil and basting occasionally. When fish flakes on testing with a skewer, remove with a slotted spoon to a warm serving dish.

Transfer the pan liquid to a saucepan and boil down to ¾ cup. Add Basic Tomato Sauce and oregano, and simmer until hot. Add the lemon juice and pour sauce over fish. Sprinkle top with parsley.

Serves 6

SASHIMI OF TUNA
(AND OTHER SUGGESTED FISH)
WITH TWO DIPPING SAUCES

Raw, very fresh tuna is most delicate in flavor and texture. When it is cooked, the flavor is stronger and the texture firmer.

Prepare 2 Dipping Sauces First:

WASABI SAUCE

2 teaspoons wasabi powder*
   cold water
⅓ cup tamari soy sauce
2 teaspoons cold water

Mix the powder with enough cold water to make a paste, cover with plastic wrap and set aside to develop flavor. After 10 minutes, mix the soy sauce, cold water, and ¼ teaspoon of the paste together.

GINGER SESAME SAUCE

½ cup tamari soy sauce
¼ cup cold water
1 tablespoon sesame seeds, toasted
1 thin slice peeled and grated, fresh
   ginger root
1 tablespoon mild honey
2 tablespoons finely sliced scallions
1 teaspoon lime juice

Mix all ingredients together and let stand to develop flavor while slicing the fish.

THE FISH PLATE

2-pound piece fresh, raw tuna fillet, cut
   into a slab 6 × 2 × 3 inches
   (see note on following page)
¼ head of green cabbage, very finely
   shredded
¼ head of red cabbage, very finely
   shredded
4 strips lemon rind, cut into very fine
   shreds

Garnish
1 bunch watercress
1 large carrot, sliced paper thin

Place fish in the freezer compartment for 15 minutes to firm up so that it can be cut more easily. Slice with a razor-sharp knife into any of the traditional shapes. Place the cabbage on a chilled plate; red on one half and green on the other half. Arrange the pieces of raw tuna in the center over the two colored cabbages. Sprinkle the fish with finely shredded lemon rind. Tuck sprigs of watercress and carrot slices around the edge of the platter in a decorative design. Serve with the 2 dipping sauces.

Serves 6

*Wasabi is a green horseradish. It is a fiery condiment that is traditionally served with *sashimi* (raw fish). It may be purchased in 1-ounce cans, in powdered form, at Japanese specialty food shops.

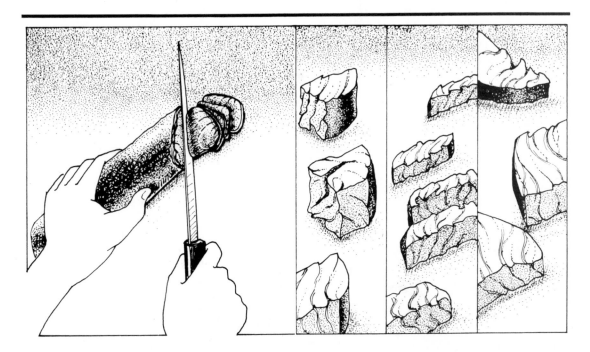

Note: If you wish to add other raw fish to your tuna *sashimi*—use 2 pounds total of any of the following fish fillets:

striped bass	flounder
red snapper	salmon
porgy	bluefish
mackerel	squid
tilefish	

Note: The presentation is all in the slicing and decoration. Here are three more traditional cutting methods that you can use:

1. *Cubes:* ½ × ½ inch (used for tuna; also may be used for tilefish)
2. *Threads:* ¼-inch-thick slices, then cut lengthwise into ¼-inch strips, and piled into a mound (good for squid or porgy)
3. *Flat Cut:* cut straight down on a fillet ¼ inch thick × ¾ inch wide (good for any other fish fillet such as striped bass, red snapper, or mackerel)
4. *Paper Thin Slices:* fish fillet sliced at an angle; slices are almost transparent (good for flounder or other tender, flat fish). These slices can be spread out in a circle like a flower or a fan.

The Artists of Sashimi

In the past ten years Japanese restaurants have sprung up all over the country and though we Westerners like to try our hands at making *sashimi,* raw fish, Japanese style (see page 398), we will, alas, never equal the artistry and the exquisite deftness of chefs who were trained in their homeland. We asked an old acquaintance, Toshio Marimoto, if we might photograph his chefs at work at the Kitcho ("Good Omen") Restaurant in New York. The result was better than a Broadway show. Each chef has an individual responsibility in preparing the dishes that come out of the kitchen—sashimi, sushi (balls of vinegared rice wrapped in seaweed, with raw fish), and the superb shrimp cooked on hot rocks.

After the demonstration by chef Norio Yada and after the stars had lined up to have their photographs taken, we, of course, ate the display.

Baked Weakfish with a Ground Almond Crust
Baked Weakfish with Garlic and Hot Pepper
Broiled Weakfish with Saffron Butter
and Pearl Onions
Vera Cruz Style, Baked Weakfish,
Stuffed with Limes

There are the many heralds of spring—for some it is the robin, for others the shad, for still others the crocus. For those of us who fish on our island, spring is the arrival of the *weakfish* in May. They're possibly one of the greatest game fish in our waters and the only thing weak about them is their mouth, which has a tendency to break easily when the fish is hooked, leading to much frustration among the fishermen who go out early to catch them.

They're known by different names, most common of which is *sea trout* and, for a long time during our trips to South America, we fell in love with *corvina* only to discover eventually that it, too, is weakfish. It's a member of the *drum* family and it's closely related to the *striped bass* and the *white perch*. The average size weakfish is about 5 to 6 pounds, but these last few years we've been catching them in a range of 9 to 11 pounds. Whatever their size, however, we love them.

There is one unusual thing about the weakfish that rapidly became evident to us. Whereas most fish taste better fresh from the water, the delicate, moist flesh of the weakfish *improves* and firms up with freezing! So, even after we catch them in the bay or in the ocean, we freeze them for at least two days and the difference in texture is remarkable.

Weakfish is generally best when baked or broiled, and it combines well with herbs. If you saute it, turn it carefully, since it has a tendency to break easily. It can also be stuffed with Arabic Rice and Pine Nut Stuffing (see Index), and baked. The fish is well complemented by the following sauces (see Index):

Tomato and Oregano Butter
Green Peppercorn Butter
Mustard-Cheese Sauce

Weakfish (or Sea Trout)

BAKED WEAKFISH
WITH A GROUND ALMOND CRUST

6 tablespoons butter, melted
2½ pounds weakfish fillets, skinned or
    unskinned
1 tablespoon lemon juice
½ teaspoon black pepper
½ cup ground almonds
1 tablespoon minced, fresh parsley

Preheat oven to 450°F.

Brush a shallow, oven-to-table baking pan with 1 tablespoon of the butter, place fish in pan, and sprinkle fish with lemon juice and pepper.

Heat the remaining butter in a small skillet and add the ground almonds. Stir and cook for only 1 or 2 minutes, watching carefully so the mixture doesn't burn. Spread this butter-almond mixture over the fish with a spatula and bake in the upper part of the oven for about 15 to 20 minutes. Test with a skewer after 10 minutes to see if fish flakes easily. Sprinkle with parsley.

Serves 6

BAKED WEAKFISH
WITH GARLIC AND HOT PEPPER

2½ pounds weakfish fillets, cut into 6
    serving pieces
1 tablespoon olive oil
2 cloves garlic, finely minced
¼ teaspoon black pepper
½ teaspoon dried, red hot pepper flakes
2 tablespoons butter
¼ cup tamari soy sauce
    juice of 1 lemon

Oil a shallow, oven-to-table baking dish with the oil and arrange the fish fillets in one layer.

Preheat oven to 375°F.

Mix the garlic, black pepper, and pepper flakes together and smear evenly on fish. Dot with the butter. Bake the fish for 5 minutes.

Combine the soy sauce and lemon juice and pour over the fish. Baste frequently and bake for 10 minutes more. Test with a skewer and continue baking and basting until fish flakes easily. Serve hot in same baking dish.

Serves 6

BROILED WEAKFISH
WITH SAFFRON BUTTER
AND PEARL ONIONS

12 tiny pearl onions
6 tablespoons softened butter
½ tablespoon boiling water
¼ teaspoon crushed saffron strands
1 tablespoon lemon juice
2½ pounds weakfish fillets, cut into 6 portions
¼ teaspoon black pepper
lemon wedges for garnish

Boil the onions for 5 minutes. Let cool and slip off skins. Put onions aside.

In a food processor or blender, cream the butter until light and fluffy.

In a separate cup, pour the boiling water over the saffron strands and let steep for 5 minutes. Add the lemon juice to the saffron and add this mixture, a few drops at a time, to the creamed butter.

Line a baking pan with foil. Smear some of the saffron-lemon butter on the foil and arrange the fish on it. Smear more saffron butter on top of the fish and then scatter the pearl onions around the fish. Sprinkle with pepper and broil 2 to 3 inches from source of heat until fish turns opaque and the top has browned. Baste frequently, and test with a skewer after 8 minutes.

Transfer to a warm serving dish and pour any remaining sauce over the fish and onions. Garnish with wedges of lemon.

Serves 6

Note: *Drum, croaker, corbina,* and *striped bass* are all similar to weakfish and can be substituted in any weakfish recipe.

VERA CRUZ STYLE, BAKED WEAKFISH, STUFFED WITH LIMES

4- to 5-pound weakfish, cleaned, scaled, and gills removed, but with head left on
juice and rinds of 2 limes
¼ teaspoon black pepper
2 tablespoons olive oil
1 large onion, thinly sliced
1 tablespoon minced garlic
8 Italian plum tomatoes, peeled and diced
2 green *jalapeno* peppers (or any other fresh, hot peppers), seeded and coarsely chopped
1 teaspoon finely minced, fresh oregano or ½ teaspoon dried
½ bay leaf

Garnish
lime wedges
coriander sprigs

Use a nonmetallic, shallow, oven-to-table dish, large enough to accommodate the whole fish. Prick both sides of the fish with a fork several times. Squeeze the juice of the limes over the fish and then stuff the cavity of the fish with the lime rinds. Allow to marinate for 3 to 4 hours.

Preheat the oven to 375°F.

Sprinkle the fish with the pepper. In a skillet, heat the oil and add the onions and garlic and cook until wilted. Add the tomatoes, *jalapeno* peppers, oregano, and bay leaf and simmer about 10 minutes.

Spread this sauce around and over the fish in the dish. Bake uncovered for 50 to 60 minutes or 10 minutes per inch, measured at the thickest part. Weakfish requires longer cooking than most other fish to flake easily, and needs the extra baking time when covered with a sauce. Garnish with lime wedges and sprigs of coriander.

Serves 6

The Charter Boats

They leave from every port in the United States—on the Atlantic and the Pacific and the Gulf of Mexico. On weekends they are crowded right to the gunwales (pronounced "gunnels," we landlubbers were told). They fish for *weakfish (sea trout), flounder, tuna, salmon, drum, sailfish,* and *striped bass.* On their return to port, they are followed by flocks of shrieking gulls as the fish are cleaned and the leavings thrown overboard.

Out in Westport, Washington, Ellie and Walt Blanchard run a charter fleet devoted mostly to tuna and salmon. Westport is known as the Salmon Capital of the World and it's just two-and-one-half hours south of Seattle. The boats leave early and the limit is just three salmon per person, meaning that the charter boat might be out only an hour when it "limits out," or it may take all day before the count is made. The day ends when the fishermen get to the cannery at Aberdeen and can the catch themselves.

**Poached Whitefish with Baked Cucumbers,
Basil, and Parsley
Baked Whitefish with *Tahini* Sauce
Broiled Whitefish with Fennel and Egg Sauce**

Though the members of the *whitefish* family are called by many names, the *lake whitefish* being the most popular, one of the members of this northern delicacy provided us with a fascinating story some years ago.

There has always been a rumor afoot that some (if not all) fishermen are slightly crazy. (You can prove it again in the chapter on The Cod Family.) To those of us in the northern part of the United States, trying desperately to cope with the winter cold, the *cisco* fishermen out in Utah and Idaho certainly appear to be the most daft. Either that, or they know something we don't know.

The *cisco* is the smallest, freshwater member of the whitefish family and it's at its very best during the winter months. Every year, out in Utah and Idaho, a ritual takes place that lasts only ten days and brings as many as 20,000 fishermen into the freezing waters of the inland lakes to net the tiny, delicious two-ounce *bonneville cisco*. At Bear Lake in Utah, the cisco come to shore along a stretch of beach about one mile long (naturally known now as Cisco Beach) and a busy Saturday can bring as many as 3,000 people to line the shore, dressed in waders, wearing rubber gloves and wielding dip nets at the end of ten-foot poles in order to take the limit of only 50 fish a day. The yearly catch from this lake alone is somewhere around 200,000 fish!

Other whitefish are fished commercially as well as by sport fishermen and they range in weight from the tiny bonneville cisco up to 30 pounds for the *inconnu* and as much as 20 pounds for the lake whitefish. However, the average market weight of most whitefish is about 4 pounds. They're found from New England through the northern part of the Midwest and up through Canada. The cisco are generally marketed under the name of *chub* (or *tullibee* in Canada) and, if you live in an area where they're caught, you can buy them fresh. Otherwise, you'll probably find them as a smoked fish.

Though our fisher friends out in Utah recommend that we deep fry whitefish, and especially the small cisco, we find that the delicate flavor of the fish makes it perfect for poaching. You can also broil, bake, or oven fry whitefish.

Incidentally, almost all the salmon and trout recipes that we've included in their own chapters, as well as the sauces that go well with them, can also be used in preparing whitefish.

POACHED WHITEFISH
WITH BAKED CUCUMBERS, BASIL, AND PARSLEY

3 whole whitefish, about 2 pounds each, or 6 fish about 1 pound each, poached and cooked (see Index for poaching directions)
2 tablespoons rice wine vinegar
1 tablespoon tamari soy sauce
1 teaspoon honey
6 cucumbers, peeled, cut in half lengthwise, with large seeds scooped out
6 tablespoons butter, melted
4 fresh basil leaves, finely minced, or 1 tablespoon dried basil
4 scallions, finely chopped
¼ teaspoon white pepper
2 tablespoons minced, fresh parsley

Place poached fish aside in a large serving dish and refrigerate. Mix a marinade of vinegar, soy sauce, and honey, and marinate the cucumbers for at least 1 hour, tossing frequently to coat with marinade. Then drain and dry on paper towels.

Preheat oven to 375°F.

Pour the butter into a baking dish and add the cucumbers, basil, scallions, and pepper and toss until well coated. Bake for 30 minutes, then add the poached, whole fish arranged in a decorative pattern. Spoon some of the accumulated liquid over and continue baking until fish is warm and cucumbers are crisp-tender. Sprinkle the dish with minced parsley.

Serves 6 to 8

BAKED WHITEFISH WITH TAHINI SAUCE

TAHINI SAUCE

1 cup Tahini Paste*
2 cloves garlic, pressed
  juice of 2 lemons
1 teaspoon tamari soy sauce
⅛ teaspoon cayenne pepper

First prepare the sauce by mixing together the Tahini Paste, garlic, lemon juice, soy sauce and cayenne pepper. Put into blender and process at high speed until mixture becomes smooth. Set aside.

6 to 8 small whitefish, about ½ pound each, whole, cleaned, and gutted
¼ teaspoon black pepper
2 tablespoons olive oil
3 large onions, thinly sliced
3 tablespoons minced, fresh parsley lemon wedges for garnish

Preheat oven to 375°F.

Sprinkle the fish with the pepper. Heat the oil and fry fish 1 minute on each side and place in an oiled baking dish. Fry the onions in the same pan until wilted and slightly browned and then distribute evenly over the fish. Spoon the sauce over the fish and onions and bake for 10 to 15 minutes or until fish flakes easily and the sauce is golden. Sprinkle with parsley and serve with lemon wedges.

Serves 6 to 8

*Tahini paste or sesame paste, served over fish, is a Middle Eastern specialty that is enjoyed in Mediterranean, Jewish, and Arabic households as well. It is available in natural foods stores and specialty shops that sell Middle Eastern foods.

BROILED WHITEFISH WITH FENNEL AND EGG SAUCE

1 lemon, sliced
¼ cup olive oil
½ cup coarsely chopped fennel bulb or
    stalk, or ¼ teaspoon crushed fennel
    seed
2 whole whitefish, about 3 pounds each,
    cleaned and scaled
    feathery stalks of the fennel
½ cup butter, melted
    juice of 1 lemon
1 teaspoon paprika
2 hard-cooked eggs, finely chopped

Prepare a marinade of the lemon, oil, and chopped fennel. Lay the whitefish in a nonmetallic, shallow dish. Stuff some of this mixture inside the fish as well as outside and marinate for 2 hours at room temperature. Remove from marinade. Place a sheet of parchment paper or foil in a broiler pan and line it with the feathery stalks of the fennel, making a bed for the fish. Place some fennel stalks inside the body cavity and some on top of the fish, pressing it as close to the body as possible.

Prepare the sauce by mixing the butter, lemon juice, paprika, and eggs together in a saucepan and keep warm until serving.

Using the lowest rack of the broiler, about 8 inches from the source of heat, broil the fish for about 15 minutes on each side. The fennel will char and impart a special licoricelike taste. Make sure it is dampened by the contact of the fish so it will not cause a fire. This fish can also be made outdoors in a fish grilling basket lined with the fennel stalks on a grill.

Remove bed of fennel from fish before serving with the egg sauce.

Serves 6 to 8

Index